RICHARD MATHER
of Dorchester

B. R. Burg

RICHARD
MATHER
of Dorchester

The University Press
of Kentucky

ISBN: 0-8131-1343-1

Library of Congress Catalog Card Number: 75-41987

Copyright © 1976 by The University Press of Kentucky

A statewide cooperative scholarly publishing agency
serving Berea College, Centre College of Kentucky,
Eastern Kentucky University, Georgetown College,
Kentucky Historical Society, Kentucky State University,
Morehead State University, Murray State University,
Northern Kentucky State College, Transylvania University,
University of Kentucky, University of Louisville, and
Western Kentucky University.

Editorial and Sales Offices: Lexington, Kentucky 40506

For Thomas J. Harvey

Contents

Preface

Over the past fifty years, historians who have written of the first settlers of Massachusetts Bay have labored successfully to resurrect the early English immigrants from the depths to which they were consigned by writers in the early decades of the twentieth century. Kenneth Murdock, Samuel Eliot Morison, Edmund S. Morgan, and others have accepted Lytton Strachey's dictum that "human beings are too important to be treated as mere symptoms of the past," and in their biographical works they have turned colonial New Englanders from historical shadows into full-bodied human beings. They have often been able to do this by applying their consummate skill to a substantial corpus of written materials left by their subjects, but this has not always been true. In many cases, the records left by members of the first generation were few and not particularly helpful to biographers. Thus the task of making comprehensible the life and work of a man three hundred years dead was often complicated by the need to piece together events from inferences and deductions occasionally based on doubtful or uncertain premises.

The difficulty created by the lack of a certain type of documentation is particularly evident in the case of Richard Mather. For the most part, the written remnants that have preserved details of his existence were not structured in a way that divulged the innermost workings of the man. His manuscripts and published works deal entirely with theological topics or his involvement in ecclesiastical affairs, and he left almost nothing of the most valuable of all biographical sources, letters, diaries, or autobiographical writings. Neither was Mather's manner of expression particularly revealing. His prose, unlike that of William Bradford, revealed none of the strength that sustained him in his struggles nor did any of his writings exhibit the love and compassion found in the letters of John Winthrop. Neither did those who knew him either in England or America see fit to compose analytic assessments of his life or career. The men who wrote of him were too closely allied by ideological or consanguinary bonds to be concerned with his foibles. They wrote to magnify and polish his image, to make him larger and brighter than life and use him more effectively to their purposes.

The result is a Richard Mather who emerges from historical evidence only in brief flashes. Vast gaps remain in our knowledge of the cleric that are likely never to be filled. Nevertheless, when available information on Massachusetts Bay, the town of Dorchester, and on Mather himself is combined with material in his dry and highly technical treatises on various aspects of doctrine and polity, there is much to be learned of Richard Mather. Within the seemingly lifeless sum of his writings, there is revealed the heart of a man with a desperate need to verify his own personal worth and to make valid the way he had chosen to direct his life and to worship his God. Caught up by the demands of his class and driven by his own ambition, he discovered religion, and in it he found a means to gain his social, psychological, and spiritual ends.

Mather's ambition was modest. He strove in the sense that ordinary men strive for success, hoping to achieve not awesome heights of distinction and virtually unlimited power but only to gain acceptance, recognition by his peers, and a modicum of deference from those with whom he associated. Driven by his desire for these goals, he became a trimmer, ready to compromise his position first to gain approval from fellow nonconformists in his native Lancashire and later to gain acceptance from his clerical colleagues in Massachusetts Bay. This flexibility came easily to him. By the standards of his time he was not a man of unshakable faith. His commitment was not comparable to that of John Huss, Ulrich Zwingli, John Wycliff, Henry Barrow, or Henry Burton. He grew up in an atmosphere devoid of the extreme religious partisanship that was part of Tudor and Stuart England, and even his conversion experience at the age of eighteen was little more than normal adolescent trauma. Later, as the pressure for measurable success became intense, he responded by adopting nonconformity and becoming a minister, but his deviations from the practices of high Anglicanism were hardly profound, and even by 1633, when he ran afoul of the hierarchy, he found it exceedingly difficult to make the decision to emigrate.

After arriving in New England, Mather's adaptability became even more apparent. But despite his willingness to accommodate, he was to meet with continuing disappointment from the time he landed until his death almost forty years later. When he applied for membership in the Boston church during his first year in America, he was found wanting, and shortly thereafter, when he attempted to organize a church in Dorchester, his church was denied official approbation by the government and clergy of the colony. While his books, written to defend the Massachusetts Bay churches from attacks by English and Scottish clerics, were occasionally challenged, they were usually simply ignored. Even when he engaged in a small task, the translating of several psalms from Hebrew into English, his poetic ineptitude was made the butt of humor by at least one of his clerical colleagues. Though his outline of church polity was ultimately accepted as the definitive statement of the colony's religion in 1648, much of what he had suggested at the Cambridge synod was stricken from the final platform, and on the question of eligibility for baptism, he was repeatedly rebuffed not only by his church but by his own sons.

The failure of the settlers to establish a colony in harmony with God's commands deeply troubled Mather by the time of his death, and this only added to his disappointment. Other leaders of the first generation had been vaguely aware of a seeming decline in the Massachusetts Bay standard of piety and devotion to Holy Writ, but Mather, by 1669, experienced acute awareness of failure that was only sensed by Cotton, Winthrop, and others who had gone to their graves before the jeremiad had become a regular feature of New England life. Repeated failure embittered him. He became sharp with his critics and hostile even to those who sought to court his favor. Throughout his career in the Bay Colony, he participated actively in ecclesiastical affairs, but never gained the distinction he thought was his due. His career, while brightened by minor victories, was in his own estimation characterized by major defeats, and it was on those defeats, affronts, and rejections that Richard Mather built his life.

Unlike the men who regularly become the subjects of historical investigation, Richard Mather never influenced the destiny of nations or determined the fate of even a small portion of mankind. He spent his days in obscurity within the bounds of several tiny villages, all of which were removed from the political, cultural, and intellectual centers of Europe. Throughout his life of over seventy years, his words were read by a mere handful of men who were only occasionally persuaded by his logic or arguments. Yet it is this very obscurity that makes Mather's life valuable for the historian. The reconstruction of his experiences on both sides of the Atlantic reveal a man of the preindustrial world whose very ordinariness makes his life significant. His situation in Dorchester was similar in many respects to that of other clerics in the colony. Many of the forces that directed his actions were also at work on other ministers. The differences in doctrine and polity among the towns and churches throughout the Bay prevent any one divine from being identified as an "average" cleric, but the similarities between Mather, his village, his church, and the lives, towns, and churches of his many ministerial colleagues make him a model figure for the colony's first generation of clergymen. His life provides much that illuminates the careers and provides a broader understanding of the ordinary pastors and teachers in seventeenth-century Massachusetts Bay.

The capitalization, punctuation, and inconsistent orthography of quotations from seventeenth-century works are occasionally modified for clarity, but the modifications are kept to a minimum to preserve the meaning and flavor of the original writings.

A project of this nature requires the assistance of a large number of individuals and organizations. Because of the limitations of space, all those who aided me cannot be thanked individually, but there are a few persons who, because of the great amount of help they provided, must be acknowledged. Initially, I would like to make note of the debt owed to James G. Allen. It was he who first suggested Richard Mather as a possible subject for investigation. I am also deeply grateful to George W. Pilcher for examining my manuscript in its early stages. Another to whom I would like to express thanks is the Reverend Gordon L. Clarke of the Ancient Chapel at Toxteth Park, who graciously allowed me to visit the Chapel, photograph its interior, and aided me in examining the Chapel archives.

Organizations that have been extremely helpful in facilitating my research are the Alderman Library of the University of Virginia at Charlottesville, the American Antiquarian Society, The Borthwick Institute of Historical Research, the Boston Public Library, the British Museum, the Cheshire Record Office, the Congregational Library, the Genealogy Department of the Denver Public Library, The Historical Society of Chicago, the Historical Society of Pennsylvania, Henry E. Huntington Library and Art Gallery, Houghton Library of Harvard University, the Lambeth Palace Library, The Library of Congress, the Liverpool Athenaeum, The Massachusetts Archives, The Massachusetts Historical Society, The New York Public Library, Princeton University Library, Sion College Library, and the Yale University Library.

I would also like to express gratitude to the Faculty Grant-in-Aid Committee of Arizona State University, who provided funds for portions of my research, and to my wife, Kathleen, whose stern commentary on my logic and prose persuaded me to revise and rewrite portions of my work many many times.

RICHARD MATHER
of Dorchester

I.

In England

Over three hundred and fifty years ago, in the tiny Lancashire village of Warrington, an unusually conspicuous entry was made in the parish register for the day of September 30, 1591. Inscribed in a hand somewhat larger than the items that precede it and those following, it reads, "Thomas Mather and Margrett Abra[ms] the same."[1] This brief record of a marriage is one of the few remaining traces of the couple who, on a forgotten day in 1596, became the parents of Richard Mather. The Mather family was not new to Lancashire in the closing decade of the sixteenth century. They had been living in the area for at least one hundred years, for the name, spelled Madur, Madowr, and with several other variations, appears in documents dating from the reign of Henry VIII. During the time of their recorded residence, however, no member of the family ever prospered sufficiently to become a member of the squirarchy, nor had any Mathers attracted the attention of the heralds. Despite the lack of distinction, Richard's father was not one of the many landless agricultural laborers or unskilled workers found in the villages scattered about the countryside. He appears to have been a speculator or a member of the growing and acquisitive group of artisans, traders, and shopkeepers that had been developing in England since the latter years of the fifteenth century.[2]

Richard was born in the hamlet of Lowtown, only a short distance from Liverpool, but beyond the place and year of his birth, little is known of his early life. He was probably raised amid a welter of brothers, sisters, cousins, uncles, and aunts, for in each generation the Mather women regularly bore scores of children. The first evidence of Richard's youthful concerns dates from the time he began his academic training, but this record is only in the form of a recollection. Years later in New England, he once told his youngest son that he had never truly understood why his parents had chosen to send him to school rather than apprentice him to an artisan or tradesman. Actually, Mather need not have wondered why this decision had been made. Parents of Thomas Mather's aspiring class could easily provide their sons with at least a modicum of education in these years, for by the opening decades of the Stuart era, grammar schools were to be found everywhere in England. Many were located in London, every market town possessed at least one, and even the most remote sections of the land had their own academies to serve the rural children.

Winwick school, where Mather enrolled, probably between the years of six and eight, was largely devoted to training its students in classical languages, familiarizing the boys with Greek and making them proficient in Latin, but in some cases remedial work in reading and writing the English language may have been offered when deficiencies were discovered. The curriculum also included prayers, Bible reading, and probably catechism. Bishops of the diocese of Lancashire were insistent on the catechizing of children, and visitation records indicate that they made certain it was carried on properly. Mather appears to have been a good student, but his schoolmaster, William Horrock, was excessively harsh on his young charges. Just how brutally the master disciplined the boy is difficult to ascertain, but in describing the treatment his father received at grammar school, Increase Mather used the analogy of Junius whose education was almost ended because his master beat him eight times per day with or without cause. It is unlikely Richard was treated that badly, but excessive application of the rod tended to discourage him. At one point he asked his parents to allow him to terminate his education, but the elder Mather refused. Instead he told the boy he would speak with the master and ask him to be less severe in his application of punishment.[3] The outcome of that promise is not known, but Richard did continue his education. His only comment on the conclusion of the episode was the wistfully expressed hope "that all Schoolmasters would learn Wisdome, Moderation and Equity towards their Scholars, and seek rather to win the hearts of Children by righteous, loving, and courteous usage, then to alienate their mindes by partiality and undue severity, which had been my utter undoing, had not the good Providence of God, and the Wisdome and Authority of my Father prevented."[4]

While Richard was an able student, none of his actions indicated a deep concern for spiritual matters in these early years. He was exposed to Christian doctrine on a regular basis, as were all Englishmen in the seventeenth century, but the sermons of a Mr. Palin, the preacher at Legh, and the inculcation of the Holy Writ at school did nothing to stimulate any intense religious feeling. The young man's casual approach to Christianity was shared by members of his immediate jamily. The lack of spiritual commitment in the household was particularly apparent when Thomas Mather went through a period of severe financial distress while Richard was in his early teens. At that time, several Catholic merchants from Wales were passing through Warrington looking for youngsters to be apprenticed to them, and the elder Mather, fearing he could no longer afford the supplementary expense required for his son's education at the free school, decided to bind him to the tradesmen. It was only a last-minute intercession on the part of the local schoolmaster that changed the father's mind and enabled the youthful scholar to continue his academic career.[5]

Though the Mathers were not greatly concerned with ecclesiastical matters, they were undoubtedly aware of the basic theological disagreements that divided the country in the first years of the seventeenth century. The specific religious issues separating Englishmen were varied and complex, but one of the most serious was the question of Roman Catholic influence remaining in the national church. When Henry VIII broke with Rome, he decided to keep his country's religion much as it had been before the split. The only structural changes he effected were the substitution of himself for the pope as head of the church and the dissolution of the monasteries. After Henry's death, the regents who ruled in the name of the young king, Edward VI, were not willing to accept the church as Henry had left it. They were determined to follow the example of Protestant reformers on the Continent and cleanse their religion of all vestiges of its Catholic past. Unfortunately for the regents, Edward died before their plan could reach maturity, and his sister Mary, a devout Catholic, became queen. Under her direction, the momentum of the Protestant Reformation in England was halted, and she attempted to reverse the course of religious development and lead the nation back to the Roman fold. Intimidation, exile, and in some cases burning at the stake were the fate of those who opposed Mary. It was only her death in 1558, after a brief reign of five years, that brought the persecutions and the attempted Counter-Reformation to an end.

The efforts to purge English religion of Catholic practice, suspended since the death of Edward VI, were revived with the ascension of Elizabeth. Under the new queen, a reaction to Mary's ecclesiastical policies began, and it was augmented by the return of many extreme Protestants who had been forced to flee England between 1553 and 1558. While in exile they had imbibed the Calvinism of Geneva and other continental centers of Reformation and now were determined to model their national religion after these European examples. They demanded that the church eliminate all elements not specifically sanctioned by the Bible. They insisted on simplicity in worship and the abolition of every relic of the pre-Reformation past. The reformers hoped to end the practice of making the sign of the cross over children's heads in baptism, they raged against the kneeling for communion and the wearing of vestments, and they complained of an additional multitude of doctrinal and ceremonial procedures, all of which were nonbiblical in origin. Some of the more extreme reformers, while sharing the dissatisfactions of their more moderate associates, insisted reform must go further than simply a doctrinal cleansing; they demanded the elimination of the episcopal system with its hierarchy of archbishops, bishops, and lesser officials.

The returned exiles were not the only Englishmen who favored reform of the church in the years after 1558. There were large numbers in the land who were also dissatisfied with the national religion, but among them there was a wide divergence of opinion on the manner and extent to which it should be changed. Some of these nonconformists wanted only moderate ceremonial alteration, but others demanded, in varying degrees, a sweeping reconstitution of the church. Although presbyterian sentiment predominated among the extreme reformers who evangelized for far-ranging modifications in theology and structure, a great variety of views was to be found within their ranks.[6]

The Elizabethan Settlement diminished, to some extent, the movement for reform, and the queen's consummate political skill kept nonconformists from becoming a serious threat. It was not until the throne passed to James I in 1603 that the reformers again thought they had cause for optimism. Their new king was a Scotsman and presumably sympathetic with the Scottish Kirk where all ceremonies and doctrine that smacked of Rome were rigorously suppressed. Unfortunately for most nonconformists, moderates as well as extremists, their hopes were to be dashed. It was soon apparent that James was much more interested in preserving his temporal throne than in heeding the reformers' interpretations of God's word. He rejected their demands for purification, and instead of leading England along a new ecclesiastical course, he gave his full support to the Anglican establishment that had matured under Elizabeth.

One group of nonconformists, frustrated by the policies of their ruler and despairing of church reform, migrated to the Lowlands where they could be free to worship God without interference from the authorities, but the majority did not choose this extreme course. They elected instead to remain in England and work for ecclesiastical reorganization.

Like his predecessor, James was able to contain the threat from those who sought to modify the church even though their ranks continued to grow and the volume of their denunciations increased. Since the nonconformists were unable to institute change by official decree, they labored to encourage the adoption of their reforms on the parish level. Radical nonconformists were particularly successful in this activity, and many clerics who originally objected only to minor Roman ceremonial practices were urged to defy the hierarchy and adopt a whole range of reforms in their local churches. Large numbers of ministers were persuaded by the call for purification. They discarded their vestments, altered or refused to observe the requirements delineated in the Prayer Book, and conducted their services with an emphasis on preaching rather than on what they had come to consider hollow ritual. The reform sentiment grew so powerful in some localities that large numbers of ministers scattered throughout England managed to institute presbyterian forms of worship and polity, on an unofficial basis, within their parishes.

The king and his church did not entirely ignore the growth of dissent, and after 1620 those who refused to conform to established religious practice were persecuted, although with limited enthusiasm. They were denied the right to hold some public offices, they were harassed by officials of the hierarchy, and some clerics were removed from their pulpits, but at no time was the persecution vigorous, constant, or severe as it had been under Mary.

Nonconformity had grown strong in Lancashire during the first decade of the seventeenth century, but while reformed religion increased its influence in the county, young Mather was probably more concerned with his own misfortunes than with the growth of theological dissent. In 1611 he was forced to conclude his studies when the people of Toxteth Park, a village some twenty miles from his birthplace, asked the master of Winwick to suggest a young man to instruct at the school they had recently built. Mather was recommended for the post, and although he had hoped to go on to a university rather than a thinly populated area like Toxteth Park, his father accepted the offer on his behalf. The adolescent scholar, not yet sixteen years of age, began his first employment as a teacher of Latin and Greek.[7]

Throughout his tenure as a schoolmaster, Mather lived with the Edward Aspinwalls of Toxteth Park, and he later wrote that the strongly nonconformist family exerted a continuous influence on him. Over the months he resided in their house, he gradually became concerned with the difference between his mode of life and that of his deeply religious hosts. At the same time, he was subject to other religious stimulation. He attended church regularly, as was his custom, but this time he was moved by the pulpit oratory of a locally renowned minister, a Mr. Harrison, from the nearby town of Hyton.[8] The sermon that particularly affected Mather was on John 3:3 ("Jesus answered and said unto him, . . . Except a man be born again, he cannot see the kingdom of God") and used Christ's words to expound on the need for regeneration. No remnant of the sermon survives, but the emphasis on spiritual rebirth expressed in the biblical verse is a likely subject for a nonconforming cleric.

The first months as a teacher were difficult for Mather. His acceptance of the aspirations of his class coupled with the change in environment placed him under a particular strain, for at this point in his life he was, in his own estimation, a failure. He had been unable either to acquire the skills needed for mercantile activity or to learn a marketable trade or occupation. So at the age of sixteen he was unequipped to follow in the paths of any of the numerous male Mathers with whom he customarily associated. The social requirements of his class demanded more of him than the commonest unskilled activities or agricultural labor, but in the one area where he had striven for success, academics, he had also failed. Success, measured by his own standards and aspirations, was to go on either to Oxford or to Cambridge, but his dreams of a university education had been thwarted not by his own incompetence but by the impecuniousness of his father. Lack of family funds had forced him to be sent against his will to teach at the grammar school in Toxteth Park, a village that was remote even by the standards of seventeenth-century Lancashire. His dissatisfaction was probably made even more difficult to bear by the rapid transition from student to teacher and by the discomfort of adjusting to a strange household where an intense concern with spiritual affairs replaced the casual approach to religion taken by his own family.

The relocation at Toxteth Park not only placed considerable responsibility on him as the person charged with the task of educating a covey of rural and rustic children, but more disconcerting for an adolescent was the turmoil created by separation from the presence of those people—parents, siblings, uncles, cousins, and his schoolmaster—to whom he had looked when seeking models for emulation. The young man was suddenly forced to find a new set of exemplars. To make the problem of adjustment even more difficult, the deeply religious Aspinwalls and the clergymen who were the most convenient potential models could not be used as his new patterns, for they could not be imitated by simple acts of will. Merely learning a trade, laboring arduously, skillfully manipulating a tool or material, or living a life in harmony with God's commandments would not enable the schoolmaster to duplicate the features most worthy of imitation in these people.

These people could not be imitated by Mather because their chief claim to his admiration was that they had been selected by God as recipients of divine grace. They were set apart from ordinary men not because they had worldly successes or exemplary personal traits but because when they ended their earthly life they would join God and dwell with him in heaven for all eternity. This distinction could not be gained by the individual, as Mather discovered. It was conferred by God as an act of divine will rather than as a reward for human activity. In earlier years Mather had participated only in situations where reward was given in rough proportion to effort expended. This new arrangement was an entirely unexpected situation and at first he was unable to cope with it. It represented a substantial divergence from all previous circumstances, forcing him to seek out or develop some device to assure at least a minimum of continuity between his childhood experiences and his expectations for the future.

Depending on the degree of an individual's disorientation, common responses to similar situations can range from ordinary anxiety or neurotic behavior to outbursts of psychotic symptoms such as extreme antisocial behavior, complete rejection of society, or, less often, insanity. Fortunately, Mather's social discontinuity was not abnormally severe and he was able to discover a solution to his difficulty in harmony with normally acceptable behavioral modes of seventeenth-century England. He developed a passionate devotion to religion, and since his contacts were largely with nonconformists, it was to this style of religion that he was drawn. This meant that to participate fully in their faith he first had to receive assurance he was of the spiritual elect; such assurance was not easy to obtain.

Mather's initial reaction to the uncertainty was to exhibit a pattern of behavior that is easily recognizable as a normal adolescent response to a new and difficult situation. He first experienced a prolonged siege of uneasiness, followed by several periods of restlessness and anxiety. He tried to avoid contact with the Aspinwalls and their acquaintances whenever possible, and when alone, he subjected himself to ruthless self-examination and self-criticism. As he dissected his spiritual estate he searched always for something, no matter how slight, to indicate he was regenerate, a recipient of God's grace, and a future participant in the heavenly bounty. The manner of Mather's suffering was not new, nor did he discover the methods he used for self-torture by accident. He knew of others who had found they were among the elect by experiencing the same series of discomforts, and so as he passed through a time of wailing, missed meals, supplication, and prayer, he may have been able to take at least a measure of solace in knowing that others before him had found assurance of regeneration in similar fashion. In due course, his efforts bore fruit; amid tears and cries of joy he realized, as he knelt beside a Lancashire hedge on a day in 1614, that he was one of God's chosen.[9]

Mather's participation in a religious awakening sufficiently intense to confer assurance of election was crucial to him on the individual level, but it was also productive in another respect. It gained for him that which he had been seeking almost since his arrival in Toxteth Park: admission into the exclusive spiritual fold that included the Aspinwalls. Perhaps of equal importance to Mather, at least in practical terms, was the effect of his conversion experience on the Aspinwalls. His suffering not only provided him with assurance of sanctification but also gave the Aspinwalls and their fellow saints a validation of the order to which they had already made their own emotional commitment. The rural schoolmaster became for them another living witness to the spiritual coherence of their system. His suffering, he found, was as meaningful to the elect of Toxteth Park as it had been to him. It was a lesson Mather would carry with him in the years to come.[10]

After he had received assurance that he was a recipient of divine grace, a more comfortable Mather continued as master of the Toxteth Park school for four more years, at which time he entered Oxford to expand his religious and intellectual qualifications. His reasons for leaving the position of schoolmaster to enroll at the university are not known; however his previous desire to attend and the suspension of classes while a chapel was being built adjoining the school were probably responsible for the decision.[11] It is also possible that he or his family acquired means to provide for his university education. The fact that he entered Oxford with no financial aid suggests this might have been the case though there is no substantiating evidence.

Richard Mather matriculated at Brasenose College, Oxford, on May 11, 1618. The young scholar appreciated the new liberty he found to engage in scholarly activity, and he probably discovered that the academic atmosphere provided a welcome relief from the duties as a master at Toxteth Park. He was also pleased to meet again many of the students whose early education he had supervised when they were learning their basic Latin and Greek under his tutelage at grammar school. All was not perfect for the Lancashireman, however, and with the zeal of the newly saved, he complained loudly of his distress at the degree of profaneness and superstition he observed in many of the other students. Still, this was only a minor irritation when there was so much to be done. Prayers, Bible study, debates, lectures, and the writings of reformed clerics occupied the major portion of Mather's academic activities, and, as he read and studied, his commitment to nonconformity deepened as he fell more and more under the sway of John Calvin and the logician Peter Ramus.[12]

Scholars generally took seven years to complete their studies at Oxford, but Mather spent only a few months at Brasenose before the people of Toxteth Park asked him to return and serve as their minister. Still other factors influenced his decision to return to the village, but the only clue to their nature is the brief phrase in the biography written by his son stating, "After due Consideration, for weighty Reasons he accepted of."[13] With his departure from Oxford, Richard Mather entered the ministry of the God he was to serve for the next fifty-one years.

By accepting the offer to become minister of Toxteth Park, Mather became a participant in the raging conflict between nonconformists and the established church, but in 1618 his difficulties with doctrinal deviation were still in the future. His first experiences as a cleric were pleasant enough, hardly reflecting the intense religious dissatisfaction that was dividing England. When he returned to Toxteth Park, he found a new chapel ready for use. The man who preceded him, Richard Poile, had departed before the building was complete. Mather preached his maiden sermon on November 30, and, according to his son, Mather's initial attempt at doing the work of the Lord was well received—at least by the judicious members of the congregation.[14]

Evidently the clerical version of stage fright accompanied the new pastor during the preparation of his first exhortation, for anxiety at the thought of finishing too soon caused him to prepare sufficient material for several sermons. Although Mather's uneasiness in the pulpit lasted only a short time, he knew that he could not conduct the religious affairs of the village indefinitely without ordination.

The people of Toxteth Park urged him to take part in the ceremony that would officially confirm his position, and before a year was out he agreed. As one of a group of candidates for the ministry, he was ordained by Dr. Thomas Morton, the bishop of Chester, in March 1619. Afterward, Morton approached Mather for a private word. The newly ordained cleric was anxious over the request because he feared his tendencies toward nonconformity had come to the attention of the bishop, a man of reputed high-church principles. Mather's fears abated when the bishop said, "I have . . . an earnest Request unto you, and you must not deny me; It is that you would pray for me: for I know . . . the Prayers of men that fear God will avail much, and you I believe are such an one."[15]

Mather, now a cleric in the Church of England, continued to serve his congregation at Toxteth Park. The building used for worship had never been consecrated, but the hierarchy did not object to having an ordained minister officiating in it. The young man's pastoral rounds were not confined to Toxteth Park, but extended into the surrounding countryside. He delivered two sermons each Lord's day for his own flock, preached once each fortnight on Wednesday at the neighboring town of Prescot, exhorted at other locations on holy days, and preached at funerals. As was the case when Mather had been a schoolmaster, the duties of the occupation did not absorb all his time. After his installation as minister of the chapel, he became the suitor of Katharine Hoult, the daughter of Edmund Hoult of Bury. "She had (and that deservedly) the repute of a very godly and prudent Maid," but her father objected to the union because he was not enthusiastic about the prospect of gaining a nonconforming son-in-law. With encouragement from Katharine, Mather persisted in his suit. It took several years before the Squire was persuaded to give his daughter's hand, and it was not until September 29, 1624, that the long-sought marriage took place.[16] Shortly after the wedding, the couple purchased a house at Much-Woolton, some three miles from Toxteth Park where Mather continued to preach. On May 13 the pair were blessed with their first son, Samuel. Two more children followed shortly thereafter: Timothy was born in 1628 and Nathaniel in 1630.[17]

By all evidence, Mather's ministry was successful during his first years of marriage. When the Lord Mayor of Liverpool and several members of the town corporation requested two sermons per month to stem the tide of Roman Catholicism, he was one of those selected to participate. To insure sermons reflecting the doctrines of official Anglicanism, the bishop ordered the selected ministers to preach in a manner "conformeable to the Canons of the Church." Mather, by this time, had already developed the habit of nonconformity, but rather than jeopardize his chances to obtain further commissioned sermons, he took care to do or say nothing that might antagonize ecclesiastical officialdom. Though informers were present at the services to discover "whether any preacher there speake or doe any thinge to prejudice the doctrine or discipline of the Church of England," his sermons, delivered in April and August of 1630, contained only safe doctrine. They attracted no unfavorable attention from the authorities.[18]

Even though Mather's deviation from the Anglicanism of Canterbury and York was not extreme, it soon came into conflict with the rapidly changing religious climate in England. Charles I, having succeeded his father in 1625, was determined to be less lenient in religious matters than James, and the hierarchy began to reflect these feelings. Richard Neile, a cleric of high-church principles, was elevated to the archbishopric of York in 1631, and shortly thereafter William Laud was placed in the See of Canterbury. Both were determined to enforce rigid conformity to the canons of the Church of England. In an exchange of letters with the king during his first years as archbishop, Neile detailed his objections to conditions he found after conducting a series of inspections in his archdiocese, and he noted there was much to be censured. He pointed out that sermons were overemphasized to the neglect of the *Book of Common Prayer*, the practice of sitting rather than kneeling was widespread, religious buildings were used for secular as well as ecclesiastical functions, and some of the churches did not follow the required ceremonial plan.[19]

Neile's enforcement of conformity was not a gesture; it was efficient and rigorous. He sent investigators to rural areas to discover deviation and continued to press the bishops in his jurisdiction to adhere to the more rigid policies. In Chester, the diocese that included Toxteth Park, Bishop John Bridgeman received letters, orders, and commands from both London and York. The king gave him instructions on how to proceed and the archbishop reinforced the orders with his own directives. Bridgeman was happy enough to comply with the sovereign will. His program was similar in most respects to that being conducted by York. Investigators were sent into all parishes in his bishopric to search out nonconformist tendencies.

Bridgeman, on occasion, conducted his own visits and even wrote a book enumerating the practices the church wardens and swornemen throughout Chester were to notice and report to the proper authorities.[20] His prescriptions ran the gamut of deviation from established practice. Activities tainted by either Rome or Geneva were circumscribed. Clergy and laity were charged to report any type of nonconformity to the proper authorities, along with information about when and where it was carried on and the names of those engaged in the acts. Nontheological offenses were also mentioned in the book. Conduct on the part of ministers, such as frequenting alehouses and engaging in "Dice, Cards, Tables or any other unlawful games," was to be reported as well. Even the local schoolmasters were not free from scrutiny by the bishop's spies. They, too, were to be watched for signs of incipient "Poperie, Anabaptistrie or any other Schisme."[21]

In the general tightening of discipline that followed Neile's installation as archbishop, Mather came to the notice of the authorities, and the bishop of Chester ordered him removed from his pulpit in 1633. Fortunately for the cleric, he was not without friends in these difficult moments. He was championed by a group of persons, including Simon Byby, who had the ear of several members of the hierarchy. By November they were able to gain his reinstatement and Mather returned to his parish.[22]

If Mather had nurtured the hope that his persecution was at an end when he returned to his pulpit at Toxteth Park, he was mistaken. His encounter with the diocese was over, but he had yet to deal with the archbishop of York. It was only a short time after he had been restored to his church in the autumn of 1633 that his nonconformity carried him again into difficulty. Operating under the jurisdiction of Archbishop Neile, a board of investigators arrived in the village of Wigan near Toxteth Park in late November or early December 1633. Either because of his earlier record of suspension or because of new reports of nonconformity on his part, Mather was called before the conclave to answer for his religious conduct. Along with seventeen men and three women, he was charged by the authorities, but none of the specific accusations were recorded. Since the investigation was conducted as part of a metropolitical visitation, the offenses were probably all ecclesiastical, though the women could have been called before the court simply to show their licenses for midwifery.[23]

Mather was understandably distressed at being summoned before the synod, but his previous experience with removal and reinstatement gave him cause not to fear this latest attempt to silence him. He boldly "answered [the questions with] such words of truth and soberness as the Lord put into [his] mouth," but the investigators were not persuaded of his innocence.[24] Some idea of the mood and temper of the court on that day surfaced in a brief exchange that took place when one of the inquisitors asked Mather how long he had been a cleric. He replied that he had been occupied at the task for some fifteen years. He was next asked about the length of time he had worn a surplice. His reply that he had never worn one had an incendiary effect on the interrogator, and he roared to those present, "What . . . preach Fifteen years and never wear a Surpless? It had been better for him that he had gotten Seven Bastards."[25] The synod suspended Mather for the second time. If there were any more attempts to have him reinstated, they were ineffectual, and the suspension remained in force.[26] Having been removed from his position as minister of the chapel at Toxteth Park for the second time, and with almost no chance of being restored, Mather retired to private life.

By the time the deposed cleric had lost his pulpit, the Massachusetts Bay Colony was a flourishing enterprise. The increasingly rigid enforcement of Anglican discipline encouraged migration to the settlement, and its reputation as a refuge for persecuted nonconformists was greatly enhanced when John Cotton joined the New Englanders in 1633. Cotton, after his removal from Saint Botolph's Church in Lincolnshire, planned on traveling to the Lowlands, but a fortunate chain of circumstances carried him instead across the Atlantic with another dissenting cleric, Thomas Hooker. After their arrival in the colony, both Hooker and Cotton wrote letters to fellow nonconformists in England describing the wonders of Massachusetts Bay.

Hooker, without a trace of equivocation, stated his belief in the opportunities offered by the New World. In one of his letters he said that while there were many places where men could gain more riches, there was no place on earth where one could do more spiritual and temporal good to himself and others.[27] Cotton, too, made it known to those in England that the colony was much to his taste. In a letter addressed to "A Puritan Minister in England" written in late 1634, he gave the reasons for his and Hooker's move to North America. It was obvious, he wrote, that since the Lord had prevented nonconforming clerics from ministering to their flocks in England, he wanted them to serve elsewhere, and since they would have gone three hundred miles to obey the will of God, the three thousand miles across the Atlantic could not be allowed to impede the divine command. From this, it followed that he and Hooker could not remain in the homeland; they were forced to migrate. Several other reasons followed, then Cotton gave what was probably the most compelling motive for emigration. He stated that by coming to New England, he was able to practice all Christ's ordinances, not just those permitted by the authorities of the Church of England.[28]

Neither of the letters was in the nature of a personal communication to Mather. They were meant to be distributed throughout the nonconformist propaganda channels that had developed in England during the reigns of Elizabeth and James I, but the two epistles from Massachusetts Bay were more important than the ordinary tracts and manuscripts that circulated among the faithful. Cloaked in subdued language and cluttered with dialectic, they fairly begged the reader to come to Massachusetts Bay. Hidden within their prose was the message that the colony was more than a settlement, even more than the "city on a hill." It represented the truth of the Christian religion. Its failure would be the failure of the Reformation.

The reasons for moving to New England cited by Cotton and Hooker were not new to Mather or to the network of dissenting ministers spread across Stuart England. The subject had been extensively discussed by many nonconformist clerics, including those in Lancashire, and most saw the issues in much the same light. Cotton's

fears that he might be "choaked with such a perpetual Imprisonment, as had already murdered such Men as Bates and Udal"[29] were
echoed by dissidents in all areas where there was opposition to the
new ecclesiastical pressures. John Davenport, a leading opponent of
strict conformity to hierarchically determined practices, pronounced
himself willing "to lye and dye in prison, if the cause may be
aduantaged by it, but [he chose] rather to preserue the liberty of
[his] person and ministry for the seruice of the church elsewhere."[30]

Thomas Shepard, another dissenter, who admitted his motives in
opting for migration were mixed, agreed with Cotton and Hooker.
He expressed concern over his inability to practice God's ordinances
in England, mentioned his fear of incarceration, noted the likelihood
of further difficulties from Charles I, and then, unlike the two other
clerics, he added his concerns over the economic and spiritual
well-being of his family. "I saw," he wrote, "no call to any other
place in old England nor way of subsistence in peace and comfort to
me and my family. . . . I considered how sad a thing it would be for
me to leaue my wife and child, (if I should dy) in that rude place of
the North [Shepard was hiding with his family in Newcastle] where
was nothing but barbarous wickednes . . . . [and my wife] hauing
weaned her first son Thomas had conceiued agayne . . . and I knew
no place in England where shee could Ly in, without discouery of
my selfe, danger to my selfe and all my freends that should receiue
me; and where we could not but giue offense to many if I should
haue my child not baptized . . . I did therefore resolue to goe."[31]
Among those who set down their reasons for migration there was a
general discouragement with the course of events in England. The
feeling was well articulated not only by Cotton, Hooker, and
Shepard, but by another of the nonconforming brotherhood, John
Wilson. Writing to John Winthrop in 1628, he lamented, "But alas!
what times are these! No man knowes what is his owne, or whither
that he hath, be not kept for the enemies of god? and of our
peace."[32]

By the time of his most serious difficulties with the hierarchy,
Richard Mather had already acquired copies of the letters by Cotton
and Hooker, but while arguments advanced by the two clerics may
have been sufficient to induce some people to undertake the voyage
to the Bay Colony, Mather was not ready to abandon England.[33] He

was a careful man, and before he could make a decision of such magnitude, he first had to ponder the matter at great length. Clearly influenced by Cotton's reasoning, he weighed all the factors he could imagine which would favor migration. As was the case with other clerics who made the decision to leave the homeland for the wilderness of North America, Mather's motives were varied. The possibility of imprisonment, concern over actions that might be taken by the king, and the likelihood of God's wrath descending on England were vital considerations. Yet to men like Cotton, Hooker, Shepard, and Davenport, no one of these fears seemed to overwhelm all others in making the decision to migrate.

In Mather's case, considerations related to his own activities, to the preservation of true religion, and to the commands of God were submerged beneath an overriding sense of fear for the future. He was haunted by concern over a revival of persecution in the manner practiced in Mary's reign. No matter what question relating to migration he discussed, there was always an ominous note of foreboding about coming events in England. "To remove from a place where the Truth and the Professors of it are persecuted, unto a place of more quietness and safety, is necessary for them that are free," he said, and to illustrate his point he used the example of the revolutions in the Palatinate.[34] He continued in the same vein interspersing each of his reasons with some fear of physical persecution. Everywhere in his discussion of migration, concern over the renewal of the fires at Smithfield was apparent. "A voluntary staying in places of danger is a Tempting of God . . . .The sin of inhibiting the Lords Ministers, is a forerunner of some sudden and grievous Judgment. . . . it is the property of a wise man to foresee the plague, and to hide himself. . . . voluntary staying in places of danger [is] a degree of Self-murther."[35]

Mather's abiding concern over renewed persecution is easy enough to understand. Like most of his countrymen, he had been raised on the catalog of horror and agonizing death contained in Foxe's *Acts and Monuments*, and the tales of martyrdom had a greater effect on him than on others of the dissenting brethren. Perhaps part of the cause for its ghastly immediacy was his familiarity with many of the executions that had taken place near his village and his knowledge of local nonconformists who had suffered elsewhere. In his youth, the Marian persecutions were alive in the memories of the people. There were some in Winwick and the nearby towns who could describe events that had taken place in those terrible times. Mather knew of James Abbes who, in 1555, had been burned alive only a short distance away in Bury, and even more frightening to him was the tale of the two brothers John and Henry David, who were summarily burned in the same town when it became known that Mary was near death. Local officials feared that if they dallied, the men would be reprieved by the queen's successor.[36] The list of those who had died for their faith in Lancashire was long, and Mather knew it well. There were Jeffrey Hunt of Legh, the Midgeleys, father and son, Gosnall and Marck of Boulton, and Bourne and Bradford of Manchester.[37]

The account of the execution of John Bradford was especially important to Mather at this critical time. Bradford, whose letters from prison were contained in the *Acts and Monuments*, had been executed in London in 1555, but eighty years later, Mather carefully reread the letters and the detailed narration of how, after first kissing the stake, the heroic nonconformist turned to the man about to die alongside him and said, "Be of good comfort, brother; for we shall have a merry supper with the Lord this night."[38] Although the deposed minister of Toxteth Park only anticipated the possibility of a similar end, he could never, even in his writings, muster a comparable amount of bravado. He had no desire to prove his faith on the gibbet or at the stake. Neither did he feel compelled to suffer physically as an affirmation of his love of God. He saw clearly the possibility of the Divine Wrath being directed against an unrepentant England, and here, too, his concern seemed more intense than the fears of his persecuted colleagues. His writings from the period were filled with biblical examples of the suffering that had befallen God's servants. Christ's being stoned by the Jews, the Pharaoh's attempts to destroy Moses, and the fate of Sodom and Gomorrah all passed through his mind, and always, as he contemplated these and even greater horrors, the words of Proverbs 22:3 kept returning to him: "A prudent man forseeth the evil, and hideth himself: but the simple pass on, and are punished."[39]

The alternative courses of action for Mather were severely limited. Unskilled at any trade, a member of a class conditioned to regard upward mobility as normal, accustomed to the deference given men of his station, plagued by fears of a flaming death, saddled with the responsibility of providing for a family, ejected from his pulpit and his livelihood by a hierarchy that demanded strict adherence to its commands, and resident in a village that insisted on nonconformity, he saw migration to Massachusetts Bay as an escape rather than as a bold initiative for the perpetuation of true Christianity. Under these circumstances, he began preparing for the journey, getting his affairs in order, and making arrangements to take his family, now numbering a wife and four sons, to New England.[40]

The Mathers began their pilgrimage to North America on April 16, 1635. Leaving hurriedly to avoid pursuers sent to apprehend them, they traveled to Bristol, arriving on the twenty-third. Mather recorded that the first phase of the trip was "a very healthfull, safe and prosperous journey all the way ... taking but easy journeyes because of the children and footemen, dispatching 119 or 120 miles in seven dayes."[41] Despite Mather's insistence that it was an easy journey, seventeen miles per day was not a leisurely pace, and the party was able to travel that rapidly only because their fears of being captured had induced them to provide enough horses so all the children could ride and not impede the group's progress by their inability to keep the adults' pace.[42]

On arriving at the port town, they found that some of those who were going to accompany them across the sea had already assembled, but the remainder of the travelers did not arrive until early May. The tardiness of some members of the company did not delay sailing, however, for when they had all arrived, their ship, the *James*, was still not ready to put to sea. So while favorable winds blew almost daily, the Mathers were forced to wait three weeks while the vessel that had been promised for early May was loaded and made ready. Late in the month, the passengers were allowed to board, two officials checked the names of the travelers, administered the oath of allegiance to the adult members of the company, and examined certificates issued by ministers of their former parishes. They were given the necessary documents, and on May 25 they sailed.[43]

The weeks the Mathers spent at sea were largely uneventful, and by the standards of the seventeenth century, the journey was highly successful. The ship left England with one hundred passengers, twenty-three crewmen, twenty-three head of cattle, three small calves, and eight horses. Despite the length of time spent aboard, not one person or animal on the *James* died. A woman and her child came down with scurvy, and numerous others contracted an assortment of diseases, but none succumbed to their maladies. As for the Mathers, they, like the other passengers, were troubled with seasickness, but they experienced no serious illness during the crossing. The only difficulty the travelers encountered came in the last days of the voyage when the ship was caught in the fearful hurricane of 1635 described by John Winthrop in his *Journal*.[44] The storm caused the company aboard the *James* some hours of terror, but when it abated, they sailed on to Boston. Their voyage ended on the night of August 16, when their ship "came . . . to ancre . . . and so rested that night with glad and thankefull hearts that God had put an end to [the] long journey, being 1000 leagues, that is 3000 miles English, over one of the greatest seas in the world."[45]

On the seventeenth of August, the passengers disembarked, and although the trip across the ocean was over for the Mathers, their journey had not come to an end.[46]

II.
Settled

If Mather hoped to find peace and accord when he arrived in New England, he must have been sorely disappointed on landing at Boston, for he found there serious disagreement over matters of ecclesiastical doctrine and polity. The difficulties plaguing the colony were not new in 1635 when Mather disembarked from the *James*. They had begun almost as soon as the Winthrop fleet dropped anchor in Massachusetts Bay five years earlier. Basic to the unsettled state of the colony was the diametric reversal of position experienced by the nonconformists who had migrated from England. In the mother country they had functioned in opposition to the established order, and through the years they developed highly sophisticated techniques of dissent. To perpetuate their movement for reform, they had constructed effective systems for communicating among themselves, criticizing the church, evading the will of the hierarchy, and propagating their own particular version of the gospel. Their defiance of archbishop and king took many forms ranging from the persuasion and conspiracy common under Elizabeth and James I to more open defiance during the reign of Charles I. By the time of Mather's problems with the authorities they had achieved influence on some levels of the church far out of proportion to their positions as ordinary clerics. Their ability to gain Mather's reinstatement, at least the first time he was suspended, was only one example of their activities. John Cotton's reliance on the influence of religious sympathizers to protect him while he preached was so well known that one of his fellow ministers, Samuel Ward of Ipswich, was moved to remark, "Of all men in the world I envy Mr. Cotton . . . most; for he doth nothing in way of conformity, and yet hath his liberty, and I do everything that way, and cannot enjoy mine."[1]

By the time Charles I ascended the throne, the ranks of nonconformists had grown, and the new king, to insure the successes of his increasingly rigid ecclesiastical policies, was forced to adopt a program of repression. The wave of persecution that resulted from his directives was the immediate cause of many decisions to emigrate, and by 1630, it had contributed to the establishment of the Massachusetts Bay Colony by men for whom the burden of zealous archbishops and their horde of functionaries, when combined with other factors, had become too great. While those who crossed the sea were freed from English strictures on their consciences, they were confronted with challenges of equal magnitude. In America they were no longer dissenters. Instead, the leaders and clergymen found they had assumed the same position within their embryonic colonial society that was held by both church and state in England. In Massachusetts Bay the colonists were responsible for developing and maintaining the civil and ecclesiastical order, and the keen-edged weapons they had fashioned for aggressive opposition in England were no longer suited to their situation. They were automatically transformed to a defensive posture by virtue of their migration. From the moment of their landing, they could no longer enjoy the luxury of engaging in constant criticism; the settlers were forced to find solutions to the complexities of human organization and defend them rather than to criticize the works of others.

Complicating matters further for those charged with the responsibility of building a viable society from a group of immigrants was the mission some had chosen for themselves in America: to build a community in accordance with the will of God. Neither their civil government nor their churches could be imitations of those in England with their attendant corruptions; they had to reflect the prescriptions of the Lord. Yet in creating the secular government of this Christian order, the new arrivals were not free to erect any system they desired. They were restricted not only by the limited measure of control that could be exercised from the homeland but by the requirements of the local situation and the fact that those they were to rule were persons raised within the English pattern of government and law. This alone would have made the task difficult, but the realities of a new continent and a hostile environment created complications the leaders of the Massachusetts Bay Colony could never have imagined.

The complexity of organizing their churches and building a state while obeying the command of God was a difficult undertaking, but the settlers made rapid progress, and by the time Mather arrived, most of the problems of civil government had been met effectively, even though several serious ecclesiastical questions remained to be resolved. The specific nature of the religious discord was due, in large measure, to a theoretical rather than a functional bent that years of opposition from within the established church had given to segments of English nonconformity. Though earlier nonconformists had explored questions of doctrine and polity for decades, the discussions had been carried on within the organizational framework of the Elizabethan Settlement. Supported by this sturdy edifice, dissenters were able to study questions of the relationship between church and state; experiment informally, unofficially, and usually ineffectively with ecclesiastical organization; and discuss grace, faith, and salvation with the desire, but not the immediate need, to compromise their differences. With the migration to America, the settlers found almost unlimited independence in ecclesiastical matters, and they were free to build churches precisely as they desired.

While they had hoped for a situation where they could worship without interference from English officialdom, they were not ready in all respects to deal with it. There were, of course, many points of general agreement among the settlers of the Bay. All subscribed to the basic outlines of the Reformation and, more particularly, to a Calvinist view of it. There was some support for a congregational organization and this was reinforced by contact with the previously established churches at Salem and Plymouth. Numerous other points were widely approved by the colonists: the establishment of a hierarchy was rejected; the *Book of Common Prayer* would have no authority in Massachusetts Bay; vestments, kneeling for communion, and a host of Anglican ceremonial procedures were proscribed. Still, within this outline of agreement many matters needed to be resolved.

In Massachusetts Bay, failure to achieve accord on religious questions was not something that could be confined to the academic disputes of a handful of theologians. To many of the settlers, the omniscience of God was not a glib assertion to be mouthed as the occasion demanded. His knowledge was complete and his presence was all-pervasive. The divine hand guided every event from the greatest hurricane to the finding of a tiny scrap of cloth or a lost buckle. He wreaked swift and devastating punishment on those who deviated from his command, and he was mollified only when men lived according to his word. Ignoring, rejecting, or disobeying him was to invite retribution more terrible than any could imagine. It would be visited not only on the man who defied him, but on his family, his village, and, perhaps, his nation. Neither was this God a patient diety. He demanded from the new settlers immediate compliance with his decrees as the only way to avoid disaster. Unfortunately for the colonists, they would soon discover that those decrees were sometimes not entirely clear and that honest men of good intent often differed on their meaning. That obscurity, however, was not God's fault; it was the result of human failing. If men could not immediately discern what the Scriptures said, they must labor more diligently to understand them. God had prescribed only one way; that way had to be found before his limited patience was exhausted.

When Mather arrived in Massachusetts Bay, he soon found, to his discomfort, that the answers New Englanders discovered to ecclesiastical problems were often not the same as the solutions developed by nonconformists in the mother country. This was especially true on questions of eligibility for church membership. In his native Lancashire where a presbyterial style of polity was accepted by many nonconformists, membership was open to all who resided in the parish except for the openly scandalous or reprobate. This was not the case in Boston. The divergent practices were the result of differing nonconformist interpretations of predestination and the relationship of these interpretations to the visible church. Both groups of Calvinists held that all men were either saved or damned not as a result of any action on their own part but because God had chosen only some to be saved.

In the homeland, the distinction between the elect and the reprobate was clearly understood, but since there was little possibility of distinguishing accurately between the two, all who were not of scandalous demeanor were admitted to Anglican congregations, even those that were made up of dissenters from established practice. With the exception of those few nonconformists who had separated from the established church, this system presented no difficult problem. Saved and damned regularly shared fellowship and communion. Little could be done toward excluding persons of doubtful election in a land where a degree of conformity and attendance at religious services was a statutory requirement.

When the immigrants landed in New England, they offered fellowship to all professing Christians of good behavior. It was not until several years after the first settlement that the practice was altered. The change appears to have been brought about largely through the efforts of New England's paramount theologian, John Cotton. Even before he had been driven from his pulpit at Saint Botolph's Church in Boston, Lincolnshire, Cotton decided that God commanded the elect to be separated from the reprobate by some ecclesiastical distinction. While still in England, he devised a system to distinguish those who had received grace from those who had not. His plan was to allow members of his congregation who demonstrated certainty of their election to be set apart by subscribing to a special confession of faith. The other parishioners, although they remained members of the parish church, were excluded from the elite fraternity.[2] The plan was put into effect and remained a feature of religious life at Saint Botolph's until Cotton was forced to flee England.

Shortly after arriving in Massachusetts Bay, Cotton became teacher to the First Church in Boston. With the force of his reputation as a leading nonconformist preacher and scholar and with his considerable persuasive ability, he was able to determine the direction taken by his new church. A congregational polity was firmly established in the colony at his urging, and he was also able to induce the Bostonians to restrict church membership to those who could present sufficient evidence to signify they were of the elect.[3]

It was this restriction on membership that became important to Mather, for shortly after arriving in Massachusetts Bay he asked to be admitted to the First Church in Boston. To his surprise, the members refused his request, citing, as their reason, suspicion of at least one of his doctrines. The problem centered on the significance he accorded his ordination at the hands of Bishop Morton. Mather was not the only New England cleric who had been ordained by a member of the hierarchy. This was usual for most of the first generation of colonial ministers, and any objection on this ground would have been wholly fatuous. The hesitancy was not the result of the ordination, but the uncertainty he had exhibited about the widely accepted nonconformist interpretation of the laying on of hands in ordination and the meaning of the ceremony itself. If he held erroneous opinions on something of this sort, it was likely, the elders of the church maintained, that he lacked regeneration; it might be a sign to the church he was not one of God's elect.

Concern over the ordination issue was not new with Mather's application for admission; it had caused some uneasiness when the church was organized in 1630. At that time, John Wilson, the pastor, had held that he was a minister by virtue of his English ordination and that the laying on of hands in the colony was the church's ratification of his selection. In effect, Wilson believed that the essence of a minister's calling was communicated in ordination by the hierarchy and that election and the laying on of hands by a Massachusetts church was only a seal of his being chosen as their pastor. This was contrary to the view that ministerial authority was conferred by election of the church and that ordination conferred no powers but served only as an outward sign of a minister's appointment. Wilson eventually accepted the symbolic quality of the ordination ceremony, and when John Cotton became the church's second cleric three years later there was no problem. He accepted the doctrine that the authority of a minister was derived by election to the office by members of the church, not by the laying on of hands.[4]

Like Wilson five years earlier, Mather assumed his ordination in England was sufficient to insure clerical status for life, but in Massachusetts Bay he soon found that this was not the case and that his deviant opinions indicated the possibility of unregeneracy, thus providing cause for exclusion from the Boston church. Mather could not permanently endure such a situation. He had been a cleric for nearly fifteen years; religion had formed an integral part of his life; he had fled England to seek a safe haven in America; and after his arrival it seemed inconceivable that he would be unable to participate fully in the colony's religious life. But there was little he could do to alleviate his difficulties. He examined the problem, prayed, discussed the matter with the church elders, and after three months capitulated to the New England view of ordination. Even then, some of the elders were not sure of the sincerity of his conversion or his complete understanding of the doctrine. They asked that he write down his opinions for further examination before voting to admit him. Mather was unhappy with the request, but acceded to it, producing a hastily penned justification of his newly acquired belief.

In the tract Mather made it clear that he now understood the function of laying on hands as a seal of election by a church. The purpose of the ceremony, he said, was "to set a man apart, and to dedicate him unto God in an holy calling. . . . to impose the burden and chardge of the people upon the person ordeyned . . . to bee as a seale to approve and confirme the ministeriall gifts of the persons ordeyned."[5] The explanation was sufficient to allay the fears of a recurrence of John Wilson's earlier errors. On October 24, 1635, Mather was admitted to the church.[6]

The resolution of his difficulties with the Boston church did not conclude Mather's differences with the Bay Colony authorities. His next encounter began shortly after his admission to membership when he received invitations to serve churches at Plymouth, Dorchester, and Roxbury. Being unfamiliar with Massachusetts, the immigrant found it difficult to choose, and once more he sought the guidance of those whose advice he had followed in making his decision to emigrate, John Cotton and Thomas Hooker. Both ministers suggested he accept the Dorchester offer. Mather heeded their words for the second time, and he and his family made preparations to move. It was this decision that prompted his next series of confrontations.[7]

Mather's difficulties in Dorchester had their roots in the history of the town's church, a religious body that was characterized by controversy almost from its founding. Much different in origin than the other churches in the colony, it was founded in 1630 by John White, the rector of Trinity Parish in Dorchester, England. It had been gathered on English soil at the New Hospital in Plymouth, and at that time John Warham and John Maverick were chosen ministers. On March 20 the members of the newly organized fellowship sailed for New England aboard the *Mary and John*. Arriving about a week before the flotilla carrying John Winthrop and his group, the travelers anchored at Nantasket on May 30. From the beginning, the church members, or at least a sizable portion of them led by Warham, continued to favor the practice of open church membership.

One month later, Samuel Fuller wrote to Governor William Bradford of Plymouth, informing him that Warham and many of his parishioners rejected the idea of a church composed only of those who could demonstrate they were saved. At first this created no difficulty. In the years before Cotton's arrival, the churches in Massachusetts Bay were flexible, and divergent opinions concerning church membership had been no real problem. But as the trend toward membership restrictions gained adherents after 1633, those who opposed it were moved into an increasingly difficult position. God had prescribed only one system for operating a church, and if Cotton, his flock in Boston, and a growing number of churches in surrounding villages were correct to exclude all who were not assured of salvation, then Warham was wrong to allow sanctified but possibly unregenerate persons into his church. Once it was agreed that eligibility requirements for church membership were divinely specified, it was evident that deviations of this nature could not be tolerated indefinitely. In a society that believed God would destroy those who did not heed his command, the presence of dissenters endangered the well-being of the whole colony.

Warham's church was divided when a faction led by his co-minister, John Maverick, approved the practice being followed at Boston. At this juncture, Warham's only solace was the knowledge that Thomas Hooker, the minister at Cambridge, shared his opinions.[8]

Warham's disagreement with Cotton was only a single phase of his tribulation. Another difficulty began when Israel Stoughton, one of the village's representatives to the General Court, challenged the interpretation given to certain unnamed provisions of the Massachusetts Bay charter by Governor Winthrop and his supporters. The dispute was largely political, but in a colony where religion and government were closely intertwined despite their organizational separation, problems of one inevitably involved the other. Warham, hoping to extricate Stoughton from the difficulty, asked him to put his complaints in writing so that he could better explain his parishioner's position to several members of the clergy. This was done, and most of the ministers approved of Stoughton's action, but John Cotton added fuel to the controversy by sending a copy of the objections to the governor. Stoughton soon found that objections could not be made against the government without serious consequences. He was called before the governor and members of the General Court where, after heated debate, he was deprived of the right to hold public office in Massachusetts Bay for three years.[9] Although Cotton later explained to Stoughton that he had given the objections to Winthrop only to have the governor resolve some questions they raised in his own mind, the effect of the episode was to increase the isolation of Warham and his faction.

As the situation of those who dissented from Cotton's doctrines grew more uncomfortable, residents in both Dorchester and Cambridge began to consider moving from Massachusetts Bay. Though the importance of religion to the colonists may have been sufficient to induce some to depart, there was more than ecclesiastical disagreement behind the sentiment to leave the Bay. In 1634 and 1635 large numbers of emigrants had already left the colony, attracted, as John Winthrop explained in his *Journal*, by the more fertile land to the west.

Many persons, traveling as individuals, journeyed to the Connecticut Valley, and in 1636, Thomas Hooker, having gained permission from the General Court to emigrate, led his Cambridge flock to the present location of Hartford. At the same time, the Dorchester church led by Warham moved to Windsor, Connecticut, where a group from their village had already settled.[10] Between two-thirds and three-fourths of the membership made the trek, and though the governor insisted that the reason for the emigration was a shortage of good land, this was only one of the causes. If any doubt remained that ecclesiastical disagreement had some bearing on the decisions to leave the colony, it must have been dispelled early in 1636 when another church, led by Thomas Shepard, was gathered at Cambridge to replace the one taken by Hooker to Connecticut. A crowd had assembled on the day the new church was to be organized. After opening prayers, an elder of the newly constituted church asked a group of clerics their opinion on membership qualifications. The answer was that only those who could testify that they had good assurance of salvation should be allowed to join. This was accepted by the leaders of the new church, and when the visiting ministers were asked to approve the organization by extending the right hand of fellowship, "Mr. Cotton . . . in the name of their churches, gave his hand . . . and desired the peace of the Lord Jesus to be with them."[11]

Shortly after Warham and his fellow townsmen traveled westward, John Maverick, the other Dorchester cleric, died. The departure of the church and the death of the minister who remained in the village were the reasons that Mather received the invitation. It meant that when he arrived in March 1636, he had not been invited by a settled church but by those who had remained in the hamlet. A new covenant had to be drawn up for the remaining members and another church organized. While this was a difficult situation for a new minister, it would have been worse if Mather had been required to organize a church from the beginning. Many of those who had chosen not to migrate were members of the old religious body, and divine worship had not been suspended in the town even though there was no church. Religious services were held regularly; the only difference may have been that the sacraments were not administered.[12] In effect, Mather had to organize a new church.

By the time Mather arrived at Dorchester, the gathering of a Massachusetts community of saints had become a matter of concern to many outside the village. On March 3, 1636, the General Court restricted the organization of new religious bodies. This made it necessary for a group to obtain official permission to gather into a church. The approval was to be given by a council composed of magistrates and elders from the neighboring towns within the colony. The General Court proclaimed that any person who was a member of a church gathered without the permission of the government could not be admitted to freemanship in the Massachusetts Bay Colony.[13] This statute effectively deprived members of unrecognized churches of any political rights.

The original impetus for this restrictive legislation had been the disruptions occasioned by Roger Williams, an engaging but literal-minded cleric who had arrived in the colony in 1631. He had raised objections to the relationship between colonial churches and the

Church of England and the close cooperation between churches and the state in Massachusetts Bay. The seriousness of his complaints and the tenacity with which he pressed them almost created a schism in the colony. But while the furor Williams produced before his banishment may have led the General Court to pass the March legislation restricting the formation of new churches, qualifications for membership in the colony's ecclesiastical bodies was the primary force causing them to move as they did.

The magistrates understood well the dangers presented by the doctrines of Hooker and Warham. The desire of the ministers from Cambridge and Dorchester to open their churches to all professing Christians was not only contrary to God's word, as Cotton had shown, but it created serious organizational problems for the colonists. Since the founding of the settlement, migration from England had been steady and the policies of Charles I seemed to augur a continuing increase as larger numbers were driven from the homeland by the royal demands for conformity. As more persons arrived, it became clear that while most were professing Christians who dissented in some respect from the Anglican Church, many were not as devoted to the deeply religious purpose of the colony or at least to the Massachusetts Bay version of a Christian society, as were the original settlers. If the trend were allowed to continue, and the colony's churches retained open membership, they would soon be dominated by men whose salvation was unlikely and whose devotion to a community based on God's command was not complete. When this happened, Massachusetts Bay, if it were not destroyed by a wrathful God, would become another one of the world's nominally Protestant lands, and the true word of the Lord would perish.

The danger from Hooker and Warham's advocacy of open membership was minimized when they moved their churches to Connecticut, but the General Court's uneasiness over Dorchester was not ended by the move. Many who had been members of the church, including Israel Stoughton, remained in the village, and though Stoughton was under legal disability, he was still the town's most prosperous and respected citizen. His presence was a danger sign. The colony's officials knew, moreover, that many who stayed behind retained sympathy for Warham's doctrines. These old residents, many who had been members of the now departed church, were being joined by new arrivals from England, and it was feared that the two groups might unite in opposition to locally accepted polity and theology. The General Court took steps to prevent this situation, approving the law making official sanction mandatory for new churches. This was done, however, only after the legislators were moved to action by the fear of a union between Warham's sympathizers, recently arrived immigrants, and a minister whose earlier schismatic views on ordination suggested the possibility of a second Roger Williams among them. This much was indicated not only by the court's timing—passing the ordinance in the very month Mather was preparing to bind his townsmen in covenant—but also by the testimony of Thomas Shepard, pastor of the church that had been organized at Cambridge only weeks before. Commenting on the earlier practice of allowing the random gathering of churches, he admitted that errors had been made. "We have been generally mistaken in most men," he wrote, "these times have lately shown and this place hath discovered more false hearts than ever we saw before."[14]

In obedience to the new regulation, Mather began preparing to meet the legal as well as the spiritual requirements for the organization of a church. For several weeks, he held religious services with his parishioners, and in early spring of 1636, he and his following sought to gain ministerial and official approbation for their religious body. By the time the Dorchestermen were ready to gather their church, the ceremonial aspects of the procedure, like the colony's theology, had become less flexible and more complicated than in the past. Five years earlier, John Winthrop, Thomas Dudley, Isaac Johnson, and John Wilson had met under an oak tree to organize their church. Their brief meeting was a simple matter and, excluding the time they spent in prayer, it could not have taken more than a few minutes. A brief written covenant of slightly over one hundred words was adopted, and then some sixty persons were admitted to fellowship.

Mather was forced to undergo a more lengthy process. In addition to the legal requirements, the minimum number needed to form a church had been established, after a study of biblical precedent, as seven, but this was not the only facet of gathering that had become more complicated. The written covenant had been extended in the intervening time. While a 113-word declaration of purpose was a sufficient statement of faith to form Winthrop's church, the document required for Mather's church was almost four times as long.[15] Before the appointed day, the prospective members observed a period of fasting and prayer to insure success, and on the morning of the interrogation four or five more hours were devoted to prayer. On April 1 they assembled before the magistrates and representatives of the neighboring churches. The examination followed a regular procedure with each individual going before the examiners, making personal profession of his faith, and testifying how God's grace was manifested in him. If the officials had any questions about the doctrinal position of the individual, they were free to question him on any specific matter. Normally, when the officials were satisfied that all of those who were to belong to the church were reasonably sure of regeneration, they would approve the church. The examiners then would congratulate the members and, as they had done at Cambridge, extend their right hands in Christian fellowship indicating they approved of the presence of another "candle" in their midst.[16]

This was not the sequence used with Mather's church, for after extensive questioning the Dorchestermen were denied permission to gather their church.[17] The questioners found that a number of Mather's company had based their ideas of salvation on theologically unsound tenets. The questioning revealed that most of the applicants had not experienced a genuine religious awakening, as had Mather in 1614. They had erroneously based their notions of personal salvation "upon dreams and ravishes of spirit by fits; others upon the reformation of their lives; others upon duties and performances, etc.,"[18] and some of the applicants had confused the relationship between sanctification and justification, thereby denying the validity of free grace. These doctrinal deviations would have been sufficient in themselves to bring about rejection of the application, but the investigators discovered numerous other errors among Mather's flock. The examination revealed that a few in the group had come to hate sin not because it was evil incarnate but because its practice was hurtful rather than beneficial. From this, the investigators deduced that these individuals had committed one of the most grievous of Calvinistic heresies—that their belief came from within themselves, not that it was derived wholly from Christ. With doctrinal errors of this magnitude circulating among members of a group who aspired to be a church, the investigators could only refuse the application. The board suggested they apply again at some time in the future.[19]

The deep humiliation felt by Mather as a result of the rejection can only be imagined. But the rebuffs he received did not seem entirely out of line with his recent experience. Everywhere he could see the traditional concepts of reality giving way before an onslaught of grasping and covetous men who refused to recognize their stations and remain satisfied with them. The tendency could be observed on all levels. England was ruled by a king who dismissed Parliament and collected illegal revenues. Control of the nation's religion had fallen to a band of papistic benifice-seekers who reveled in the doctrines of the Romish "Whore of Babylon" and harried godly ministers from their pulpits only to replace them with a horde of sycophants. It was an age when servants ignored the commands of their masters, masters connived to extract the last measure of effort from their servants, and schoolmasters needed to administer large doses of terror to subdue their scholars. Everywhere the ordered nature of society seemed to be crumbling as traditional concepts were measured against perceptions of the present.

The changed situation probably appeared more evident to Mather after immigration, for surely, following his initial experience with the Boston church, he was inclined to see degeneration in New England both in the abandonment of what were to him traditionally hallowed patterns and in the substitution of an altered ecclesiastical system at the behest of an aspiring would-be Calvin from Lincoln-shire. The doctrine and polity of Boston and its environs in 1635 and early 1636 represented a substantial departure from familiar Lancashire patterns, and as the bearer of these patterns, Mather found himself conspicuously out of joint with the times when he landed in the New World. He was a man of the past standing in the American present, a carrier of a set of traditional values in a society consciously striving to abandon tradition with its attendant corruptions and build a society according to the will of God. His first impulse on encountering this situation had been limited resistance and a petulant refusal to abandon previous tenets on ordination, but realizing after a short time that he had no viable alternative to submission, he bent to the antitraditional doctrinal pressures and accepted the Bostonian pattern.

In March 1636 he was again a victim of the countervailing tendencies of traditional nonconformity and Massachusetts Bay's strictly defined divergence. He had organized his church hastily, without due regard for the official insistence on regeneracy, and had presented his group for approval, only to be rejected. In Mather's apprehension of the circumstances of the refusal, he was dimly aware of his position at the center of two antithetical tendencies: the pressures from the General Court and the influence of Cotton's doctrines on one hand, and the tradition-bound Dorchester villagers on the other. The difference in direction between these two poles of colonial opinion was not obvious to him in 1636, but the variation between Boston and Dorchester was clearly apparent.

Boston, by 1636, had already grown from a village to a small city, and its size alone worked against the retention of traditional practices. Its population was drawn from widely separated areas of England and this diversity also hastened the erosion of traditional behavioral norms. The town's preoccupation with commercial activities, even as early as 1635, created occupational diversity, whetted the desire for personal gain, and increased the number of residents whose primary attraction to the colony was commercial rather than theological.[20] Bostonians had earlier exhibited their divisive tendencies in the dispute over the doctrines of Roger Williams, and by 1636 they were hotly engaged in another controversy: discussing the divine authority for Anne Hutchinson's variety of Antinomianism.

In Dorchester, the situation was different. Men there held to the traditional framework of ideas brought with them from the homeland. The original settlers of the village were drawn largely from Dorsetshire, and later immigrants, those who arrived after Warham and the church had departed, were unfamiliar with the innovations emanating from the First Church in Boston. They preferred to retain the nonconformist patterns of religion with which they were familiar. There was neither the diversity of population nor the commercial distractions to weaken attachment to their perception of God's way.

In trying to discern the operation of these forces and adjudge the reasons for failure, Mather was unable to recognize differing responses as manifestations of town and village. He did realize that he had been caught between the desire of the General Court and its Boston leadership who were anxious to prohibit the gathering of deviant churches and his villagers who were apprehensive lest the new doctrinal dispensation rapidly taking shape coalesce and become operative before they had their church functioning.

Mather first accepted part of the blame for the rejection. He was proud, vainglorious, and lacking in the requisite humility to be a minister, he wrote.[21] But this was hardly convincing. While Mather may have been learning still another lesson in the uses of humility, he was not a humble man, and when the ritual self-deprecations were over, he placed the blame where he thought it lay—with the government and clerical leadership of Massachusetts Bay and with his parishioners. Though he did not accuse the General Court of harboring nontheological motives for its refusal to recognize his church—this was already obvious from the passage of the law that had occasioned the Dorchestermen so much difficulty—he did accuse the court of haste in passing the legislation, thereby allowing him insufficient time to prepare his villagers for the interrogation. The other portion of opprobrium for the failure, he then noted, was with his flock, for it was their urgings that forced him to appear before the examining board before they were ready. "They pressed mee into it," he explained, "with much importunity, and so did others also, till I was ashamed to deny any longer, and laid it on me as a thing to which I was bound in conscience to assent, because if I yielded not to joyne, there would be (said they) no church at all in this place, and so a tribe as it were should perish out of Israel, and all through my default."[22]

Despite his frustration at this second rebuff since his arrival in the Bay Colony, Mather must have realized, after his mental flagellations, that only one course was open to him. Returning to England with a wife and four sons was at best an impractical alternative, especially since he faced the possibility of incarceration. Furthermore, having been a cleric for over a dozen years, he was unable to pursue any other trade or occupation in a fashion commensurate with his Oxford training, class expectations, and individual aspirations. He had no choice but to bury his outrage and try once more to gain approval for his church. This was made easier for him by the encouragement given by several clerics, including Thomas Shepard, and as Mather explained to himself, since the Bible provided numerous examples such as David and Ruth who had sought success and found it only after repeated failures, he must try again.[23]

Actually, the situation of the aborted Dorchester church was not as desperate as it first appeared. Not all the members of his group were stigmatized as unfit for membership in the church. Mather and one other person were found to have theologically sound opinions and to have demonstrated that they had received divine grace. It was only five of the seven applicants who were deemed deficient in some qualification.

During the months after the rejection, as Mather conducted religious exercises with his parishioners, he labored to correct the errors of belief. Hours of patient explanation were spent setting them right on individual points of doctrine and trying to make them understand why a life in harmony with biblical prescription was not sufficient evidence of justification. Remembering how he had been rushed to gather the church in the spring, Mather took his time for the second attempt. Almost half a year passed before he sensed the group was ready to make another application for official sanction. The second interrogation revealed the prospective church members had been well taught by their master. When questioned, their answers contained no doctrinal errors or misconceptions. On August 23, 1636, the clerics and magistrates were at last satisfied that the group could be allowed to covenant together.[24] Mather, triumphant at last, was then officially elected teacher of the church, but while his earlier recalcitrance and hostility may have been forgotten by some, submerged as they were beneath a freshly acquired veneer of submissiveness, the humiliations he had experienced continued to smolder within him.

III.

Defense of the New England Way

In September and October, as Mather preached and lectured to his new church, a threat to the local religious order was developing which was far more serious than any the colony's ecclesiastical leaders had yet faced, namely, the crisis over Antinomianism. In brief, the difficulty in Massachusetts Bay had its beginnings when Anne Hutchinson and her family arrived in Boston from their Lincolnshire home in 1634. Exceptionally headstrong and assertive, Hutchinson had brought her family to the Bay Colony so that she could continue to hear the word of God preached by John Cotton, whose church she had attended on several occasions in old Boston. Soon after she settled in the town, the colonists began to recognize Hutchinson's considerable abilities as a nurse, and even John Winthrop, who later became her most persistent and effective adversary, was forced to concede her virtues as a helper of the sick.[1] But she was not the sort of woman who could be characterized as an unassuming angel of mercy. "She belonged to a type of her sex for the production of which New England has since achieved a considerable notoriety .... She knew much; but she talked out of all proportion to her knowledge."[2] In her mid-thirties when she moved to New England, she immediately applied for membership in the Boston church. After some initial apprehension about her spiritual condition, she was admitted.[3]

Some time after her arrival, Hutchinson began holding weekly meetings in her home to explicate the sermons preached by Cotton on the previous Lord's day. Gradually the sessions grew in size until as many as eighty persons attended. As the audience increased, the format of the meetings underwent a perceptible alteration. Instead of repeating only the substance of the sermons, she began to edit and comment on their theological content. At this time, Cotton was occupied with the task of vindicating the concept of free grace, and the woman, in an excess of enthusiasm for his doctrines, apparently adopted an extreme extension of his theological stand. As her fame continued to grow, those who accepted her views increased in number, and by June 1636, her weekly lectures were firmly established in Boston.

The problem began for the colony when Hutchinson, faithful to what she understood to be the teachings of John Cotton, denounced the Boston church's pastor, John Wilson, as unregenerate, lacking in God's grace, and damned. A large part of the church shared her opinion, thereby creating a schism. Although ninety-one separate counts of heresy were ascribed later to the prophetic Hutchinson, John Winthrop noted that her errors revolved around only two incorrect beliefs. The first of these was that the Holy Spirit resided within every justified individual. The second was that sanctification was not reliable evidence of justification. These heresies, generally falling within the compass of Antinomianism, spread from their point of origin in Boston to many surrounding towns. The Opinionists, as the Hutchinsonians were called, worked actively at proselytization, visiting neighboring churches and denouncing the teachings of their ministers.[4]

If the followers of Anne Hutchinson ever invaded Mather's meetinghouse while he spoke, the teacher did not note it, but he was, nevertheless, deeply interested in the controversy. By this time he was regarded with less suspicion by the colony's religious leaders. His decision to submit first to the Boston church in the dispute over ordination and later to the General Court's demand on the gathering of churches made him appear a reliable member of the clerical community and so, when heresy threatened, he was invited to participate in a conference of ministers who met with Hutchinson to discuss her theology. No record of the discussion survives, but the limited information available on Mather's performance indicates he pleased his clerical colleagues. At one point in the deliberations he was able to cast a question so ably that it drew from the defendant an admission that Christ dwelled within her, a reply that provided positive proof of her Antinomianism.[5]

By January 1637 the conflict over Anne Hutchinson's doctrines had grown so severe that a fast day was declared. It did not aid in solving the problem, and in March a member of Hutchinson's family, the Reverend John Wheelwright, was formally accused of sedition for some of his public utterances. The summer saw the controversy grow to such intensity that a synod was summoned to resolve the matter before the colony was split beyond hope of reconciliation. Thomas Hooker, now of Connecticut, and Peter Bulkeley were chosen as moderators, and clergy, magistrates, and the curious public were on hand for the opening sessions. The investigation of the synod was well ordered and advanced along systematic lines similar to those used by Puritans in written disputation. In the first week, the errors of the Antinomians were attacked by the colony's clergy, with the exception of Cotton whose position in the controversy—dangerously close to that of Hutchinson—had placed him in conflict with most of his colleagues. The two weeks following were spent in debate. Even though great effort was expended in argument and reply, the synod failed to persuade the Antinomians of their errors. The heresy continued to spread so rapidly that by November the General Court was forced to take action. The severity of its measures indicated the seriousness of the problem and the depth of the chasm separating the two segments of the community. Early in the month, the civil authorities banished Anne Hutchinson, and several weeks later her followers were ordered disarmed to forestall insurrection.[6]

After her sentence of banishment had been pronounced, Hutchinson was allowed to remain in Massachusetts Bay throughout the winter—not in Boston, but with the Joseph Weld family of Roxbury.[7] In the spring, before her scheduled departure, she was brought to trial before her own church. The question at issue was not whether the banishment levied by the General Court should be rescinded, but whether Hutchinson should be excommunicated from her church before her expulsion from the Bay Colony. At the proceeding, leading members of the community, both secular and ecclesiastical, questioned her again on doctrine and assisted in deciding her fate. Painstakingly each of the points at issue was once more discussed. The interrogators asked question after question, and despite her weakened physical condition, she answered with spirit, affirming the tenets that had so agitated clergy, magistrates, and a large segment of the population.

Throughout the months of conflict that finally led to the excommunication proceeding against Anne Hutchinson, Mather had been deeply concerned with the effect Antinomian tenets could have on the colony. He understood well the destructive result of carrying the Opinionist beliefs to their logical ends, and he was also fully cognizant of the problems generated in his own colony by the basic Antinomian belief in a divine presence lodged within each justified individual. If most of those who suspected they were of the elect claimed to harbor a Holy Spirit, there could be no guarantee of civil or ecclesiastical order, and the institutions of the Bay Colony would collapse amid the chaos of toleration and an inability to secure domestic peace. To the best of his ability, Mather had labored to insure this would not happen. In his sermons and lectures he strongly condemned the notion of an in-dwelling Holy Spirit and was so successful in keeping ideological contamination away from his church that when the General Court issued the order disarming the Opinionists, Dorchester was one of the few towns where no citizen was deprived of weapons because of deviant theological views.[8]

Mather's hostility to Opinionist doctrine was nowhere more in evidence than when he participated in the excommunication of Anne Hutchinson. Although Mather was only one of a score of clerics who took turns in the questioning, he made it amply clear why he had not experienced any serious Antinomian disruption in his church. Whenever he spoke, he revealed himself to be an uncompromising foe of the heretical opinions. When the defendant's brother-in-law suggested more time be given the accused woman to consider repentance, Mather not only objected strenuously to the extension but railed against the plea for mercy, demanding instead that she be cast out of the Boston church. When the moment came for a final decision, he proved his dependability. He voted with the colony's leading clerics, Cotton, Wilson, and Shepard (Cotton, by this time, opposed Hutchinson), for her excommunication. The combined will of the clergymen carried the day, the woman was cast out of the Boston church, and shortly thereafter she left the colony with a small entourage composed mostly of family members.[9]

Mather was a minor participant in the Antinomian crisis. His efforts had consisted primarily of aiding in the prosecution and working to keep his own church free from contamination. Yet by siding with the majority, he showed the clergy of Massachusetts Bay that he was no longer a cleric of uncertain reliability who presided over a troublesome church. His vigorous opposition to Anne Hutchinson, when taken with his apparent humility in agreeing to regather the church and his careful shepherding of the Dorchester flock, marked him as a man of constancy and devotion to the colony's predominant ecclesiastical pattern.

Having proved his reliability, Mather was soon asked to participate in another investigation, this time involving doctrine on church membership—one of the very difficulties that had led to the emigration of Warham's church from Dorchester to Connecticut less than five years earlier. The trouble had been brewing for some time. It began in the town of Weymouth, a short distance from Boston, where religious disagreement had grown so serious that in 1637 the General Court decided to send the governor, the deputy governor, and several of the magistrates to investigate. The root of the problem was that the town's minister, Benjamin Hull, had differing ideas on church polity from those of the colony's clerical leaders. Hull and his villagers were opposed to the Massachusetts Bay practice of gathering a church around a covenant and restricting membership to those who could offer sufficient proof of spiritual regeneration. They preferred the practice of English parish churches which admitted all who were not of scandalous character.

Some residents of Weymouth, dissatisfied with Hull's deviation, called another minister, Thomas Jenner, to organize a second church. He accepted the call but the stratagem was not successful. Though he labored mightily, he was unable to gain the allegiance of enough villagers to provide his maintenance. Jenner's failure meant that pressure had to be exerted from another direction to insure conformity. The General Court entered the case and, after a period of intimidation, Hull was forced to notify his parishioners sometime in 1637 or 1638 that he intended to leave. The villagers were not as easily cowed by the magistrates as was their minister, and to make sure their next spiritual leader had views conformable to those of his predecessor and contrary to those of Jenner and the General Court, they called Robert Lenthall to take charge of their church. Many in the town had been residents of his parish in England and he seemed a suitable replacement for Hull. Lenthall accepted the call and moved to Massachusetts Bay, probably arriving late in 1638.[10]

As had been the case with his predecessor, there was much about Lenthall's doctrines and polity that did not please the clergy and civil administrators of Massachusetts Bay. Once his views became known, he was summoned to appear before a meeting of the colony's elders at Dorchester on February 10, 1639. From the beginning, the proceeding did not go smoothly. Lenthall, piqued at having to defend his opinions, was far from humble in the opening debates. He was also an astute observer of the colony's workings and its power relationships. He suspected that his interrogators questioned his beliefs not to help him avoid the pitfalls of error but only to find fault and eventually to bring him before the General Court. The conclave lasted two days, and in that time both Lenthall and the elders found that their suspicions had been well grounded. The minister saw that the elders were indeed trying to have him disciplined by the magistrates, and the elders were confirmed in their opinion that the cleric actually harbored several unacceptable beliefs. Throughout the intemperate exchanges between participants in the affair, the investigators discovered that Lenthall not only had Antinomian tendencies but, like Wilson and Mather in earlier years, he was confused on the Bay Colony's manner of ordination. He held that a minister's calling came from the bishop's hand rather than from the call of the church.

Lenthall was finally disabused of his erroneous views on the inner light, on ordination, and on several minor points, but both he and his supporters from Weymouth made it clear that they were still not in harmony with the Bay Colony's pattern of formally gathered churches composed only of the elect. Instead, they intended to allow all who resided in the parish to join the church. This was evident when one of Lenthall's parishioners denounced the colony's manner of forming churches and attacked a manuscript defense of the covenant written by Richard Mather. Another Weymouth resident, who was particularly disturbed by the deviation of Bay Colony churches from the Church of England, accused the ministers of favoring the precepts of Robert Browne, an advocate of complete separation from the national church. It was clear from the tone of the discussion that on the issue of church membership there was to

be no mutual accord, and after applying their best persuasive techniques, the elders turned the case over to the civil authorities.

In the weeks between the adjournment of the Dorchester meeting
and the session of the General Court on March 13, Lenthall, for
reasons unknown, changed his position and when he appeared before
the government interrogators he informed them that he was now in
agreement with the majority of the colony's clerics. Some of the
magistrates were not satisfied with his recantation or his expressed
contrition and demanded he be fined. This was rejected, and instead
a written declaration of his new views was accepted on the condition
he make a public recantation in Weymouth.[11] Two of Lenthall's
followers who had helped him organize the church were fined, as
was another of his parishioners. A fourth, James Brittane, who had
no estate, was whipped for "grosse lying, dissimulation, and contempt of ministers, churches, and covenant."[12] Lenthall was also
ordered to appear before the next session of the General Court to
insure his compliance. The colony was evidently convinced of his
reformation, however, for he did not appear at the specified time
and no action was taken.

As was the case in the Antinomian controversy, Mather was again
an active but not a leading participant in the investigation of
Lenthall. More revealing than his participation at the hearing was the
selection of the Dorchester meetinghouse as the place where the
inquiry was to be held. The choice of Dorchester was probably
dictated as much for convenience as by the knowledge of the
minister's correctness, since the town was located between Boston
and Weymouth. But it is apparent that if any doubts remained about
the doctrine or polity favored by Mather and his church, the investigation would have been held at another convenient town where the
church and minister could be counted upon to oppose Lenthall's
brand of deviation.

Some time after the inquiry at Weymouth, John Winthrop noted
in his *Journal*, "About two years since one Mr. Bernard, a minister at
Batcomb in Somersetshire in England, sent over two books in
writing, one to the magistrates, and the other to the elders, wherein
he laid down arguments against the manner of our gathering our
churches, etc., which the elders could not answer till this time, by
reason of the many troubles about Mrs. Hutchinson's opinions,

etc."[13] With the conclusion of the Antinomian affair, however, the way was clear for a written reply to Bernard, and Mather was chosen to write it. At the same time, he was given the task of penning the colony's response to another set of questions about New England's religion sent from England by a group of nonconforming clerics. Mather's selection for this work was not due entirely to his reliability. He was known to have some ability in theological writing, having compiled an answer to thirty-six questions about Bay Colony church practice for a friend in England three years earlier. Moreover, Bernard was not a leading cleric and therefore did not demand attention from a theologian of the stature of John Cotton or John Wilson.[14]

As Winthrop had written, the need to provide replies about religion in Massachusetts Bay to questions from the homeland was sufficient reason to answer Bernard and the group of clerics. But in a decade of rapidly evolving ecclesiastical institutions, the need for a statement of faith was apparent not only to keep nonconformists in the mother country informed about developments but also to provide a declaration of principle and practice to insure the unity demanded by God. This latter purpose was particularly important at this juncture in the Bay Colony's development. Although John Cotton had written "Questions and Answers upon Church Government" in an attempt to provide a frame of reference for resolving fundamental disagreements that seriously threatened the establishment of an acceptable degree of uniformity within the colony, it was by this time over five years old. To be sure, Roger Williams was gone, the Antinomian disruption had passed, the colony's churches were functioning, and there was widespread agreement among the clergy about many features of God's will, but even with these victories over divisive persons and their doctrines, there remained a tremendous potential for ecclesiastical disruption within the accepted outlines of the colony's religion.

Previous disagreements had illustrated how the basic Protestant reliance on the doctrine of election and free grace created a fundamentally anti-institutional theology where ministers, churches, covenants, sacraments, and other features of religion were subordinated to the selection of the individual as a recipient of salvation. This reliance had been carried further than the local clergy would allow by Williams's insistence on separation and the Antinomian doctrine of an "inner light" or an "in-dwelling Christ." The colony's ministers had answered both of these serious challenges by disposing of the challengers, but the potential threat in 1639 was centered not around those who held radical doctrines but around those whose views were much closer to the locally accepted truth and therefore more difficult to combat.

Again, the congregational polity adopted by the churches of New England—a system whereby each church was an autonomous unit, responsible to no one but God—did not mean that all were free to worship in any manner they saw fit. God had prescribed only one way, and though deviation was permissible in minor matters, it could not be tolerated in more important aspects of religious procedure. The system of autonomous clerics and churches carried within it the seeds of division, and these were encouraged to germinate by the comparative isolation of some of the churches around the Bay. The colony's clerics were not ignorant of the tendency toward fragmentation. In addition to the more serious confrontations, they had witnessed it in the cases of Warham and Hooker and on other occasions in the first years of settlement when discussions of religion were held to explore questions of doctrine and polity. They had seen how men who had gone through much the same experiences and training in England harbored honest and often irreconcilable differences, even though communication had been maintained among them and great efforts expended in attempts to secure agreement.

To mitigate this situation and produce a system that would maintain ecclesiastical cohesion for the colony's churches, ministers moved in two directions. The clerics enlisted the civil government to serve as a hierarchy, and they continued to meet informally to discuss deviation and to find an acceptable compromise. Another factor tending to give a measure of unity to the autonomous churches was the practice common among both clerics and laymen of traveling to hear the lectures of other ministers and of regularly having ministers visit and preach to their own churches. In this way, variations beyond accepted norms would be revealed and could be contained before they had grown to dangerous proportions.

Even if the Massachusetts Bay Colony had remained a small and isolated enclave on the North American shore, it is unlikely these precautions would have been sufficient to insure unanimity, but the rapid development of the colony made them totally inadequate. The closing of the first decade in the history of the settlement was a time that saw thousands of immigrants crossing the Atlantic, and although the great majority of them were nonconformists, they presented enough shades of deviation from practices in the colony to create administrative difficulties and, more seriously, they could even enrage the Creator and turn him against Massachusetts Bay. The new immigrants had come from many parts of England, and many of them, both clerics and laymen, were unfamiliar with local practices. Some means had to be found to assimilate these new arrivals into the community, and one step toward achieving this goal was to provide an accurate statement of faith that would set forth and substantiate the colony's doctrine and polity.

The English requests for information and justification of the Bay Colony practices were the stated reasons for Mather's undertaking the task, but they were not the most compelling factor. The works that ensued were not doctrinal polemics; rather, they reflected the ecclesiastical problems that existed in Massachusetts Bay. This was nowhere more evident than in *An Apologie for Church Covenant*, Mather's answer to Richard Bernard. This work was the much-needed justification for the colonists' use of covenanting in organizing their churches.[15] By 1639 the practice of covenanting had created considerable local opposition, but since one of the main purposes of the work was to heal internal division in the settlement, the author did not indicate anywhere in his defense the depth of dissension the covenant had aroused between one segment in the colony who had accepted it as part of a divine order and another group that had rejected it entirely. Mather was fully aware of the role played by the covenant in Massachusetts Bay, and like most of the early immigrants, he was emotionally committed to it as a God-given ordinance. But to a man who had joined in covenant first at Boston and then at Dorchester, the device used by the colonists to hold their churches together was much more than this.

Another significant quality of the covenant, he realized, was its functional position as a unifying force. It bound together those who were certain enough of their election to become members of a Bay Colony church. It served as a visible symbol to Mather of his acceptance and worth and was a further evidence of his wisdom in choosing to emigrate. In the uprooting from Toxteth Park and in the passage across the Atlantic, Mather had lost contact with the reference points necessary to maintain his social orientation, and the secure position he and his family had occupied in their English village no longer had meaning. His lifetime accumulation of prestige had remained behind in England. In Boston and Dorchester his reputation as a leading local cleric was not secure as it had been in Toxteth Park. His defiance of the hierarchy, his refusal to wear the surplice, and his marriage to Squire Hoult's daughter conferred on him no special distinction in the New World. His sense of isolation and disorientation in America were compounded when he suddenly found himself immersed in a community similar in many respects to the one he had left, where the similarities made it seem natural for him to receive his accustomed measure of deference, but the security acquired in England as a result of birth, family, and life-long involvements was entirely absent. The only way he could gain immediate acceptance in the community was by joining one of the colony's covenanted churches. By the ensuing recognition of the new member as a recipient of divine grace and an initiate into the fellowship of the elect, church membership provided a most expeditious way to regain the security that had been the natural product of familiar surroundings in the village societies of the homeland.

Tangential to the function of the covenant in establishing Mather's identity in a new community was its role in affirming his decision to leave England for the New World. This was particularly important to Mather who seemed to lack the deep commitment that had brought others to America. While Cotton, Hooker, Davenport, and Shepard apparently saw it as their spiritual duty to leave the homeland—though their exodus was speeded by agents of Charles I—Mather seemed uneasy about his decision. After his arrival, this feeling was magnified when he was questioned by the Boston church about his spiritual condition. But upon his admission to membership, the exclusive character and close-knit quality of the covenanted group were sufficient to overcome his doubts. The sense of mutual obligation among the members and their combined awareness of purpose restored much of his departed self-esteem and intensified his feelings of belonging not only to the church but to the larger community.[16] The intensity of devotion on the part of many New Englanders was well illustrated by Mather's colleague John Wilson, who once stated, "The want of a holy Covenant in England is the root of all corruption there; and God forbid that any should come hither to bring over and set up such practices and corruptions! It were better they were buried in the bottom of the sea."[17]

While the covenant mitigated many of the adjustment difficulties for thousands of immigrants like Mather, the facets of the covenant that made it so effective in aiding some to assimilate—its exclusive character and the bond of solidarity it created—were the very things that made it the object of suspicion to large numbers of immigrants who were unable or unwilling to adjust their beliefs as Mather had done to gain membership. Mather's depth of devotion to the covenant was matched by its opponents' hatred. Even before the assembly of elders was convened to deal with the open-admission policy of the Weymouth church, Mather knew that feelings in the village had become so agitated at one point that swords were drawn against the magistrates. There were many in the town, and in other towns as well, who, like Weymouth's Ambrose Martyn, considered the covenant "stinking carryon and a humane invention" but were deterred from saying it publicly, as he had done, by the fear of receiving a similar £10 fine.[18] It was primarily to these men who questioned the validity of the covenant that Mather's arguments in *An Apologie* were directed. Cotton confirmed this when, after hearing Robert Lenthall defend the Anglican-style parish church, he cited the scriptural justification for the covenant and instructed him to read Mather's explanation "sent to Mr. Barnad [Bernard] ... [and] you will see the most of these things."[19]

Knowing from his own experience that those who had never met or joined in covenant in England would be suspicious of its validity, Mather opened *An Apologie* by carefully defining the covenant as "A solemne and publick promise before the Lord, whereby a company of Christians, called by the power and mercy of God to fellowship with Christ, and by his providence to live together, and by his grace to cleave together in the unitie of faith, and brotherly love, and ... binde themselves to the Lord, and one to another ... as the Gospel of Christ requireth of every Christian Church, and the members thereof."[20]

After he had done this, he began to justify the use of the covenant with scripture. He was aware that covenanting was an innovation peculiar to the colony, but he could hardly admit this was the case. God did not innovate and restructure his churches periodically on the basis of whim. The covenant could not be given validity as a recent revelation without creating insurmountable theological problems and denying much of what the Bay Colony ministers endorsed. But its presence spoke of novelty and this had to be explained. Diffidently, Mather admitted that many changes had been made from the polity followed by parish churches in England, but he justified them by asserting that what seemed to be innovation was actually only the rediscovery of ancient practices that had long been abandoned.[21] Referring to Cotton's discernment of the correct method for gathering churches and the failure of most New England ministers to use the covenant while in the mother country, Mather said, "Some of us when we were in England, through the mercie of God, did see the necessitie of Church-Covenant; and did also preach it to the people amongst whom we ministered, though neither so soone nor so fully as were meete, for which we have cause to be humbled, and to judge our selves before the Lord."[22] Scores of scriptural citations and Old Testament precedents were employed to prove to the most skeptical that the covenant had always been one of God's ordinances and that the colonists who espoused it should be praised rather than damned for recognizing their earlier sins of omission and then for bringing their practices into harmony with a rediscovered law of God.

Since his discussion was directed toward the increasing number of new arrivals, one of Mather's most difficult tasks was to prove that the churches in England were not reprobate institutions. Over the years, nonconforming clerics had railed at Anglican abuses and denounced them in language that admitted no qualification. Yet three thousand miles away with no bishop at hand to admonish him and no ecclesiastical court to remove him from a pulpit, Mather could not deny the validity of religion in England. Many of the immigrants at this time had not renounced their parish churches but had moved only for the greater opportunities, spiritual as well as temporal, that Massachusetts Bay seemed to promise. Denial would imply also a rejection of all those nonconformists who remained in

the mother country, a course taken only by the separatists. The Bay
Colony churches had to be depicted as walking a middle path
between rejection of English religion and complete endorsement of
it.

This ambiguous position created logical difficulties, since the
refusal to deny categorically the correctness of churches in England
meant that within the homeland true churches existed. These true
churches, however, did not use the covenant in their procedures;
hence, if they could observe God's commands without the covenant,
there would seem to be little need for it in New England. Mather's
effort was to demonstrate that churches in the mother country used
an implicit covenant which was as genuine as those used in the Bay.
The reasoning to reach such a conclusion was complicated as that of
a schoolman and comprised the longest discussion of any single topic
in *An Apologie*. He did not want to give anyone in the Bay Colony
the opportunity to create disruption by leveling charges of separation against the colony's churches. The colonists also felt a concern
for the spiritual estate of those who remained behind. Denying the
validity of all churches in England meant that Bay Colony religion
was separate from English churches and also implied that the godly
nonconformists who had not emigrated were placed among those
who did not live according to the word of God. Mather had to devise
a means for assuring the colonists that their friends and relatives had
not been abandoned. The implicit covenant, which Mather asserted
was present in some English parish churches, was designed to placate
this segment of potentially dissident people. As was the case with
the whole of *An Apologie*, this reasoning was calculated to serve a
dual purpose: to provide a defense and justification of Massachusetts
Bay's religion for those in the homeland and to deal with present
and potential difficulties in the colony.

Throughout the discussion, while Mather sought a viable compromise that would bring together divergent views on ecclesiastical
polity, he took care not to undermine the value of the covenant by
softening its harsh exclusiveness or by implying that somehow it
could mitigate the uncomfortable reality of predestined salvation.
He explained to those immigrants who assumed their English baptism would entitle them to fellowship in New England that "Baptisme is a seale of the Covenant betweene God and the Church, but

neither makes . . . members of the Church, nor alwayes so much as proves men to be members."[23] Any new arrival who was accustomed to the English church as it was under Laud and Charles I and who thought that he could earn membership by careful observation of God's law was similarly corrected. "If men in entering into this Covenant looke for acceptance, through any worth of their owne," he wrote, "or promise dutie in their own strength, they shew themselves like to the Pharisees . . . and turne the Church-Covenant into a Covenant of workes."[24] He informed those who remained in doubt about the right of some to enter into fellowship and the right of the churches to exclude others, "Those that . . . joyned were beleevers before they joyned. . . . for Gods converting grace depends not upon mans daring, or not daring to receive it. If to be joyned be no more but to be converted. . . . nor suffer Faith to be wrought in them; which is grosse Arminianisme, suspending the converting grace of God upon the free will of the creature."[25]

During the time that he wrote *An Apologie*, Mather labored on his answers to the questions sent to Massachusetts Bay by the group of English clerics. Since the reasons for the composition of both pieces were identical, there was little difference in substance between the two works. *The Answer to Two and Thirty Questions* was somewhat more diverse in its subject matter and answered several questions that were untouched in the other effort, but like *An Apologie* the discussion was executed to insure stability in Massachusetts Bay. It presented an authoritative statement on the colony's procedures for admitting members to the church, the organization of congregations and their relationship to one another, the ceremonial and operational aspects of the ministry, and the colonial assessment of churches in England.[26]

Although the essential purpose of Mather's two writings was to maintain cohesion within the colony by providing a model and a justification for church order, the stated purpose of the effort—the desire to explain the faith of Massachusetts Bay to dissenters in the homeland—was an important feature of the work. The New England clerics did not assume that their observance of God's laws alone could bring England to the true religion. They knew they needed an active and devoted cadre in the homeland to continue to press for reform while they worked out God's plan in America. The procedures and practices of dissenting churches had to be explained to clerics in the mother country to expedite change in England. It was not through intuition but by example that men would know how to build true churches.

The separatists in England had operated churches long before 1630, but their methods were inadequate and their theology faulty. Separation from the established church was not a valid way to effect reform. Moreover, the separatist experiment had been confined to a small number of men, not large enough to modify a church or government on a national level. The only nonconformists who had met the problems of organizing and operating their churches on a scale of any magnitude were the settlers of Massachusetts Bay. They had experimented, debated, struggled, and ultimately discerned the will of God. The next step was to communicate the results to sympathetic readers in England so that when the time was ready to reestablish true Christianity in the mother country, those to whom the task fell would not be found wanting in the ecclesiastical technology.

The Bay colonists were not in a position where they could foist their information on an unwilling group of recipients. Those nonconformists who remained in England were vitally interested in all aspects of the Massachusetts Bay Colony, and they realized, as did the colonists, that effective coordination between England and America was essential for the aims of both groups. It was this interest in colonial affairs that was largely responsible for inducing nonconformists in the mother country to make inquiries about religious practices in New England. Those clerics who questioned the colonists were not, for the most part, eminent men or officers of a hierarchy who had to be persuaded of the error of their way. They were, in 1639, ordinary nonconformists, village clerics as were the colonists, whose interest and support were necessary if an alliance were to be successful. The New Englanders knew that their audience in the homeland would be large. Their tracts would be copied and recopied by scores or even hundreds of hands and circulated widely among nonconformist clerics and educated dissenting brethren, many of whom would make their own copies to retain for reference and inspiration. The exchange of questions and answers was designed by the dissenters to maintain unity within their movement and prevent dissipation of its strength by geographical separation across the ocean.

How successful this effort at cooperation might have been is impossible to ascertain. Had the situation in England remained static, perhaps colonial and English nonconformists could have achieved their reforms by working from within the established church; but this was not to be, for Charles I was an ambitious monarch. While England seemed well on its way toward over-whelming the nonconformists by 1639, this was not true in the kingdom north of the Tweed, and it was apparent that if the established church was to be supreme in Britain, Scotland must be forced to conform. This was not an easy undertaking. Unlike his father whose years of experience had taught him much about the unbending northerners, Charles was more English in his outlook, and he reflected, to some extent, the traditional English view of Scots-men, a curious mixture of distaste and outright contempt. He thought that a few swords north of the border would be sufficient to end the infatuation with John Knox and the Kirk. Events were to demonstrate that the Stuart king had underestimated the abilities of his adversaries, and after an unsuccessful campaign against the Scots, Charles found his army defeated and his treasury empty. The easiest recourse was to summon Parliament. In 1640, after an absence of eleven years, Parliament was assembled, and the king found, much to his displeasure, that he could not obtain funds until he made concessions to the powerful nonconformist leadership of the body.

Unwilling to bend to the demands for ecclesiastical reforms, Charles dissolved Parliament, borrowed money from private sources, and in the summer of 1640 set out once again to chastise the insolent northerners. The second attempt, however, was even less successful than the first, and as the summer came to a close, Scottish forces, driving the defeated enemy before them, advanced southward into England. The victors were halted in their advance only when the king negotiated an agreement in which he made numerous conces-sions, including the promise to pay the Scots a large indemnity. With his army defeated, the royal coffers wanting, and new and arduous financial obligations, Charles had no alternative. Parliament was again called into session.

The nonconformists now had the upper hand, and church reform seemed imminent. The tide of optimism was immediately reflected by a drop in the number who emigrated to Massachusetts Bay. Whereas over 20,000 had moved to the colony in 1640, representing approximately three or four thousand families, the rate of immigration dropped to a trickle the next year, and many residents of the colony, certain they were now safe to follow the commands of God in the homeland, returned to England.

With the shift in power and direction in the mother country, there was a corresponding readjustment in the colony. The pressures of an expanding population were removed as were many of the distant but nevertheless worrisome problems created by the established church and crown. But while the triumph of true religion seemed to be approaching, much remained to be done to assure its safe arrival. The exuberance found among many nonconformists was not unanimous among the New England clergy. The calling of a Parliament with deep-seated hostility to the prevailing ecclesiastical order did not change the opinions of the king, remove the archbishops from the sees of Canterbury and York, or expunge all traces of Rome from the land. The elimination of ecclesiastical abuses was only half of the task of the Reformation. Once England was purged of corruption, a new religious order had to be built.

After a decade of experimentation, the colonists were sure that they had discerned the prescribed way, but were far from certain that their way would be accepted in the mother country. It appeared from events in the homeland that the most popular style of nonconformity was not that advocated by Massachusetts Bay but the system used by the Scots. Unlike the colonists, the proponents of the Scottish or presbyterian form of church organization hoped to establish a system of church government as strictly ordered as the Anglicanism they proposed to dismantle. If this were to be done it would be necessary to reject the Bay Colony's insistence on church purity and to open membership to any professing Christian. To exclude large numbers from a comprehensive and nationally organized church, especially when many of those excluded had been members of the Anglican body, both as conformists and nonconformists, was quite impossible. The presbyterian nonconformists knew it would be politically disastrous, but more important, their interpretation of God's will prohibited it.

By allowing all but those of openly scandalous behavior to become members of their churches, those favoring a presbyterian system were automatically placed at odds with the New Englanders in another area, that of intrachurch government. The colonists regularly allowed the brethren to participate with the elders in governing their own churches. With tight restrictions on membership this was possible, but under the presbyterian system of open admission, control had to be lodged with the elders rather than risk decisions made with the participation of a relatively undifferentiated congregation.

A further difficulty that set presbyterians against the New England way was their suspicion of congregational independence. Being aware of the problems that would be created by allowing each church to be an autonomous unit and being unaware of the ecclesiastical role played by the civil government in Massachusetts Bay, the supporters of the Scottish polity insisted on a hierarchy of synods and assemblies to adjudge religious disputes and make authoritative pronouncements on matters of doctrine and ecclesiastical government.

By 1642 ministers in the Bay became more uneasy as they watched the course taken by nonconformity in England. They carefully listened to accounts of the Root and Branch Bill in Parliament and heard reports of debates on episcopacy and ecclesiastical courts, and as they did, they became aware of the lack of influence exerted by the New England example. Nowhere was this more evident than in the reaction to an invitation that arrived from England in the autumn of 1642. John Cotton, Thomas Hooker, and John Davenport were asked to participate in an assembly of divines to be convened in London to chart the ecclesiastical course for all England.[27] Though Cotton and Davenport expressed some interest in participating in the conclave, they were dissuaded from making the journey by the outbreak of the Civil War. Hooker, who had no intention of returning, judged the situation more accurately than his two colleagues when he said that the extent of power they would wield at Westminster would be so small that there was no "sufficient call for them to go 3,000 miles to agree with three men."[28]

The absence from the Westminster Assembly of any representative from the churches of New England did not imply automatic condemnation of the American experiment. There was, instead, a great curiosity among those present about the forms, methods, procedures, doctrine, and polity used by the colonists. The representatives were aware of the colony's success with church and government, and while the Assembly was dominated by the advocates of the Scottish mode of church organization, the members who favored the New England system were heard with interest and their ideas accorded respect. There was a need, however, on the part of those favoring the New England pattern to persuade rather than simply to be heard, and it was at this juncture that Mather's writings on Massachusetts Bay's ecclesiastical settlement were, much to his surprise, pressed into service. The reason for their employment was the initial strength that English interest in colonial practices had created for the supporters of the doctrine and polity advocated by the Bay's clerical leaders.

Hugh Peter, having returned from America only a short time before, was particularly conscious of both the need and the opportunity to popularize further Massachusetts congregationalism, and he quickly obtained manuscripts of several New England works. Adding his own introduction and using two sets of printers to speed the work, Peter assembled a curious tome. Published by Benjamin Allen and placed on sale in his shop at Popeshead-Alley, it was not one book but three consolidated into a single volume. The published tracts were Mather's *An Apologie*, and his *Answer to Two and Thirty Questions*, along with John Davenport's *Answer to Nine Positions*. Each of the works had been written four years earlier and since the time of their composition they had been circulating in manuscript among Americans and nonconformists in England. Although the domestic difficulties in the colony which Mather's works had been written to mitigate no longer plagued the settlement as severely as they had done in earlier years, his polemics were pressed into service once more, this time to explain and justify the congregational system against the style of polity advocated by the presbyterians.

The effort by Peter to have the works of Mather and Davenport influence the English was not particularly effective. By 1643 congregationalists in the Westminster Assembly needed not a set of anonymous descriptions designed to effect uniformity among a group of squabbling colonial churches but an authoritative description of New England's predominant religious pattern.[29] This was a crucial consideration at this point because it was only through persuasion that the colonists could hope to influence the course of events in England. While the choice of Mather to compose the first major statement of religion in the Bay Colony was planned to be an effective way to still dissent on the local level, it would hardly do for the present undertaking. The need was for a work by a cleric whose stature was widely recognized in England. The only colonial minister who fit this description was John Cotton. He had already composed a lengthy description and justification of colonial church practice that had circulated widely in manuscript but had not been printed. Recognizing by 1643 that much of it was inadequate, Cotton decided to write a new and definitive treatise. It would be published later as his *Keys to the Kingdom of Heaven.*[30]

Meanwhile, as Cotton labored over the book that would replace Mather's work as the most widely available and generally definitive statement of Bay Colony practices yet produced, Mather did not retire from religious disputation. Although his limited reputation precluded his taking a substantial role in the defense of Massachusetts Bay religion, he was determined to continue the work which fate had briefly assigned him: leading the defense of colonial congregationalism. It was only a short time after *An Answer to Two and Thirty Questions* was printed that he had his chance, when a minor presbyterian polemic arrived in the colony. Awkwardly titled *The Independency on Scriptures of the Independency of Churches*, the slim volume was written by "Master Herle, a Lancashire Minister."[31] Charles Herle, the author, was an ardent champion of the Scottish form of church government. After preaching on several occasions before the Long Parliament, he had become a member of the Westminster Assembly. His attack was not a sweeping indictment of congregationalism but was limited to the doctrine of the independence of individual churches. Since he believed that all who wrote in defense of the congregational pattern said essentially the same thing, he did not direct his work to any specific colonial cleric or to any single New England treatise. Beginning with objections to the assertion that there was no power in a synod to compel the obedience of churches, he maintained that such church assemblies had, by the command of God, the authority to compel obedience, hear appeals, make decrees, ordain clerics, and excommunicate.

Herle's work, coming as it did from the pen of an obscure cleric who possessed limited competence in theological dispute, was not a serious challenge to the New Englanders, not serious enough at any rate for attention by ministerial leaders such as Cotton, Hooker, Shepard, or Davenport. Quite possibly it could have been ignored by the colonists, and probably would have been, had not Richard Mather and William Tompson, the pastor at Braintree, both harbored a personal interest in answering Herle. Beyond Mather's determination to remain an active polemicist, the two Bay Colony ministers had been acquainted with the English divine for many years before their emigration. Herle and Mather had attended Oxford together, and their friendship developed either at the university or shortly afterward when Herle became rector of Winwick, the village where Mather had attended grammar school. Mather's church at Toxteth Park was only a short distance away and the two men had many contacts during the early years of the reign of Charles I. William Tompson, Mather's collaborator, had been Herle's predecessor as rector of Winwick.[32] With these close connections, the New Englanders took it upon themselves to correct the errors committed by their friend and fellow Lancashireman, even though the book was no genuine threat to the colony.

In *A Modest and Brotherly Answer to Mr. Charles Herle*, Tompson and Mather had little difficulty in replying to the presbyterian. The Englishman's effort was an unsophisticated endeavor and the colonists were able to reduce it to shreds not with complex argument or extensive scriptural refutation but simply by demonstrating its inconsistencies, contradictions, and poor structure. If Herle ever chanced to read a copy of the New England demolition of his work, he must have surely regretted his encounter with the two expatriate Lancashiremen.[33]

After his rebuttal of Herle's work, Mather authored two more polemics against advocates of the presbyterian method of church organization. The first was *A Reply to Mr. Rutherford*, written in response to Scottish divine Samuel Rutherford's monumental *Due Right of Presbyteries*. The second was a detailed refutation of a pamphlet written by William Rathband, a minor presbyterian cleric.

Neither of these works was a significant statement of religious practices in New England. Each was written in response to a threat posed directly to Mather rather than to any of the colony's churches. To be sure, Samuel Rutherford was a leader in the movement to establish the Scottish polity in England and his stature meant the work could not be ignored in the colony. A presbyterian of considerable reputation, he had been educated at the University of Edinburgh, had built a name as a theologian, and had become a leader in the Westminster Assembly. He had written extensively on church government, but differed from many participants in the debate over ecclesiastical order in that he sought to minimize the distinctions between the congregational and presbyterian systems. *Due Right of Presbyteries*, his major work, was important enough to be answered by a leading New England cleric, and Thomas Hooker was selected to write a reply. Mather's rebuttal to Rutherford was not a complete rejoinder to his book; it answered only those portions of *Due Right of Presbyteries* that were critical of the answer he and William Tompson had written to Herle. The complete New England reply to the Scotsman's book was Hooker's *Survey of the Summe of Church Discipline*.[34]

The responses to Herle and Rutherford were not Mather's most ambitious attempts to establish himself as a leading spokesman for the religious order in the Bay Colony. What he planned as his greatest contribution was a work written in reply to William Rathband. The selection of Rathband's book, *A Brief Narration of Church Courses in New England*, as a vehicle to carry his response was unfortunate, for Rathband was an obscure figure, having little or no following on either side of the Atlantic.[35] His *Brief Narration* was another presbyterian polemic of insufficient quality to cause consternation among the Massachusetts Bay ministers, but it was, nevertheless, a set of arguments that Mather felt compelled to answer, since Rathband, in building his case, had relied almost entirely on information garnered from Mather's *Answer to Two and Thirty Questions* and from a letter he had written to a friend in 1636 describing local church practice in the colony shortly after he had arrived. Though Rathband had made a feeble attempt to keep the author of his sources anonymous, it was widely known in the colony that Mather, more than any single man, had been responsible for the answer to the thirty-two questions and that the initials R.M. used by Rathband to hide the identity of the writer of the 1636 letter stood for none other than the teacher of the church at Dorchester.

To counter this embarrassing attack, Mather composed "A Plea for the Churches of Christ in New England." The scope of this work indicated its author intended it to do more than repel a personal affront. The book was a lengthy tract which contained not only the rejoinder to William Rathband but an expansive statement of congregational doctrine and polity, with considerable justification, sufficient in volume and detail, Mather hoped, to supersede John Cotton's labor in authoritativeness and persuasive power and to establish its author as the foremost defender of colonial religious practices.

Mather spent approximately two years preparing and writing the four sections of the 600-page manuscript for the press. Unfortunately, he was to be frustrated in his attempt to vindicate his earlier writings and achieve a measure of preeminence. His careful efforts were to be for naught, for while he wrote in America, William Rathband died in England, Thomas Weld published a shorter but nevertheless adequate rebuttal of Rathband's *Brief Narration*, and the political situation in England had changed enough to make the expenditures required to publish the "Plea" hardly worth the result it might achieve.[36]

The replies to Herle and Rutherford and his combined answer to Rathband and statement of Massachusetts Bay church practice were examples of Mather's quixotic determination to be a leader among his ministerial colleagues. Even while he penned his "Plea," he knew that Cotton and Hooker were at various stages of completion on their own great expositions of faith, and although he had little to add, he continued his work, hoping perhaps to present his case more effectively than his fellow theologians. At the same time, Mather was also laboring on several other projects that he hoped would promote his reputation. It was well known in New England that the Westminster Assembly was engaged in composing catechisms of varying lengths and though Thomas Hooker had dutifully responded with two pieces, Mather was not deterred. He, too, set to work to try to influence the Assembly and produced a pair of catechisms he thought were adequate.[37]

In the same flurry of polemical activity that produced the replies to Herle and Rutherford, the catechisms, and probably consumed sufficient time to prevent him from making two separate works out of the attack on Rathband and his extensive statement of faith, Mather also wrote *An Heart-Melting Exhortation*, another work designed to influence events in England. Written as an admonition to his fellow Lancashiremen, begging them to reform their ways or face terrible consequences, Mather clearly aimed the book at a wider audience. Again, as had been the case with the "Plea," this work, and the catechisms as well, brought disappointment rather than esteem to their author. By the time the catechisms were ready for publication the opportunity to influence the Westminster Assembly had passed, and when the manuscript of *An Heart-Melting Exhortation* arrived in London, the city's printers, Mather lamented, were so occupied with other more important works that it required a five-year wait before it reached the presses.[38]

Between the years 1639, when Mather authored his first important theological works, and 1646, when he completed his answer to William Rathband, a radical change had taken place in the circumstances that motivated New England polemical writing. Although *An Apologie* and *An Answer to Two and Thirty Questions* were addressed to inquiries and minor challenges from England and ostensibly composed only to satisfy the queries and repel attacks from the mother country, almost every portion of them was a response to the internal requirements of the colony. Both works were part of an attempt to provide a doctrinal and political framework for a system of church polity that was a fertile breeding ground for disagreement, dissension, heresy, and ultimate dissolution. Mather, with the counsel and probably the occasional participation of members of the ministerial fraternity, worked to fashion an outline of church practice that would explain, justify, and persuade all colonials, clergy as well as laymen, of the divine sanctions embodied in Massachusetts Bay's developing religious practices. For a brief time, perhaps, in 1640 or in early 1641, it may have seemed that Mather and the clerical brotherhood were nearing success. With the departure of Warham and Hooker for Connecticut and the banishment of Roger Williams and Anne Hutchinson, it appeared that harmony might be achieved. No difficulties had yet surfaced from Quakers or Baptists, dissent in Newbury and Hingham was not as severe as it would become, several minor disputes had been settled easily, and the agonizing problems surrounding baptism were in the future. There were some minor questions still unanswered among the clergy, but these were trivial compared to the past disruptions.

Yet there remained England, and by the time the members of the Westminster Assembly took their seats it was evident the only method for impressing a congregational pattern on the mother country was through effective argument. With this great task at hand, the techniques of persuasion had to be altered substantially. No longer could a locally accepted, moderately competent, but otherwise obscure, cleric carry the burden of defending New England religious practices. The requirements to exert meaningful influence in England were different from those needed to insure uniformity at home. The Bay Colony needed authoritative writings produced not by an unknown minister but by men whose words would be heard and respected in London. The only way this could be done was to press John Cotton and Thomas Hooker into service and ignore Mather.

Hooker and Cotton were well suited to the changed demands of 1643. They were widely known and their opinions counted for much among nonconformists in the homeland. Only men whose prestige and demonstrated ability could sway the presbyterian majority at the Westminster Assembly would be able to answer Samuel Rutherford. Neither Hooker nor Cotton could have written the earlier tracts composed by Mather to insure constancy of doctrine and polity. Hooker had earlier left the Bay Colony in part as the result of a dispute over membership in the churches, and Cotton had taken an active and partisan role in the disagreements that had led to the first emigrations from Dorchester and Cambridge and he had been identified to some extent with the discredited Anne Hutchinson. Clearly he could not speak for unity in 1639. A noncontroversial cleric—or at least a cleric who was no longer controversial—was needed. Mather was selected, the work was written, and then, carrying a nominal attribution to the "Elders of New England," it was circulated in manuscript among the colonial clergy.

Mather, of course, never truly understood this. He assumed, as did his son and grandson, that his selection was made on the basis of merit, and when his works were printed at the instigation of Hugh Peter in 1643, he was only more convinced of his abilities as a theologian. The publication of *An Apologie* and *An Answer to Two and Thirty Questions* was to him the result of their singular merit or irrefutable arguments and not because they were the only works available that would fill an immediate need. The failure of his clerical colleagues to select him to answer English criticism or his inability to publish the monumental "Plea for the Churches of Christ in New England" discouraged Mather, but it did not dissuade him from further efforts with his pen. Though the political situation after the defeat of Charles I in the second civil war and the actions ultimately taken by the Westminster Assembly and Parliament meant there was little point in engaging English clerics in debate, he continued to write, although the type of work he produced was far different than that of the 1640s.

IV.
The New England Preacher

While Mather wrote in defense of Bay Colony churches, not all his time was taken by the demands of ecclesiastical polemics; many hours were spent with his growing family. In the spring of 1637, a fifth son was born to the Mathers, and the father's pride in the child was surely compounded when the baptism of tiny Eleazer took place in his own church.[1] Within two years a sixth son was born to the minister and his wife. The most recent Mather was also baptized in the father's church and given the ungainly name of Increase because "of the never-to-be-forgotten Increase, of every sort, wherewith GOD favoured the Country, about the time of his Nativity."[2] The joy occasioned by the birth of two sons was not without a measure of sorrow. A short time after the family's arrival in New England, Joseph, the last to be born in England, died, but in spite of this, when given the high incidence of infant mortality, the parents of such a brood must have considered themselves fortunate to have lost only one of their children.[3]

In the same years that he watched his family grow in number and trained his sons for manhood, Mather continued to attend the manifold tasks of a Massachusetts Bay cleric. Of those many duties, one which may have caused his thoughts to return to his student days at Oxford, or even Winwick, was the translation of several of the psalms from Hebrew into metrical English. The occasion for the translation came in 1636 or 1637 when the settlers of the Bay Colony first recognized the need for a Psalter that was uniquely their own. Until that time they had been using the Psalm book composed by Thomas Sternhold and John Hopkins in the middle of the sixteenth century, but the colonists had never been entirely comfortable with it. Like other nonconformists, they were very dissatisfied with the volume's many deviations from the original Hebrew text.

An attempt to render a closer translation had been made years before by Henry Ainsworth, the pastor of the English separatist congregation in Amsterdam. An accomplished Hebraist, he corrected most of the errors made by Sternhold and Hopkins, neither of whom were students of the ancient language. His new and annotated translation was adopted by his own congregation and by that of John Robinson in Leyden, and in 1620, the Ainsworth version was carried across the Atlantic to be used by the churches at Plymouth. The most convenient course for the settlers of Massachusetts Bay would have been to abandon Sternhold and Hopkins and adopt the 1612 Ainsworth psalms, but they were adverse to using the same translation favored in the Lowlands and at Plymouth.[4] They hoped to emphasize their connection with the Church of England and to set their colony apart from the separatists. This alone was sufficient for rejecting Ainsworth, but there was another reason: his metrical constructions were exceedingly difficult to sing.[5] The only solution was to prepare a new Psalter, and portions of the 150 psalms were assigned to selected Bay colony ministers for translation.

When the work of setting the psalms into English poetry was completed, it was printed at the new press in Cambridge and then distributed throughout the colony. It was adopted by almost every congregation; only the churches of Ipswich and Salem declined to use it. Almost immediately, however, its defects were discovered. Not only was the book lacking in artistic merit, but many of the verses were hideously contorted to preserve the Hebrew meaning in its entirety and yet jam the contents into an English metrical construction.[6] Although the specific psalms assigned to Mather are not known, those he prepared were done with observable lack of artistic skill. This much was indicated by Thomas Shepard who could not resist the opportunity to poke fun at the lack of literary ability exhibited not only by Mather but also by Thomas Weld and John Eliot of Roxbury. In a short piece of doggrel he wrote:

You Roxburough poets take this in Time
See that you make very good Rythme
And eeke of Dorchester when you the verses lengthen
See that you them with the words of the text doe strengthen.[7]

The translation of the psalms was an important project for the colony, but it was only one of Mather's activities during his first hectic years in New England. Though there were many such demands on his time, his most important task was preaching. By 1643 his abilities in the pulpit had become so widely known and admired that he was asked by the General Court to prepare and deliver the annual election sermon the next spring. His selection for the honor was an indication not only of the esteem he had gained from the colony's leaders but also of his reputation for doctrinal correctness. Mather did not disappoint those who had chosen him, and the General Court was so well pleased with his oration that they ordered the printer "shall have leave to print the election sermon, with Mr. Mathers consent."[8] But the pleasure of the governing body was not without bounds. No provision was made to pay for the printing out of the public treasury, and for that reason there is little likelihood the sermon was ever put to press.[9]

The election sermon, though an honor of some magnitude for Mather, represented only a tiny segment of his preaching burden. More than any other single activity, the preparation and delivery of sermons occupied the greatest portion of his life, and it was through the preached word week-by-week that he had his greatest impact. Since he was unassisted in the early portion of his Dorchester ministry, the authority of his words was undiluted by any differing opinions, criticisms, or challenges from a colleague as well educated and knowledgeable in scripture as was he. The orations he presented thus became an important element in the spiritual life of the village, for it was Mather's preaching rather than the theological writings or the pulpit presentations of the Massachusetts Bay Colony clergy as a whole that formed the conceptions of Christianity shared by the villagers.[10]

In preparing and delivering his sermons, Mather used William Perkins's *The Art of Prophecying*, the preachers' standard handbook for nonconforming clerics in both England and the colonies. As Perkins prescribed, Mather divided his exhortations into four sections. He began with the text, then "opened" the passage, gave a statement of doctrine, and listed the numerous uses of the scripture. After the roster of uses, he rhetorically added objections, answered them, and concluded with a repetition of his earlier statement of doctrine. Morning worship on the Lord's day began with a prayer and an exposition of a biblical passage. The congregation next sang psalms, followed by the cleric's sermon which lasted three to four hours. Prayer and a blessing concluded the morning service. After intermission for a noon meal, the afternoon service began. It differed little in format from that offered in the morning. In churches where there were both pastor and teacher, the duties in the morning and afternoon were usually alternated, meaning each man had to prepare a single long sermon. Since there was only one cleric in Dorchester, Mather was forced to compose and present two lengthy sermons for each Lord's day.

Preaching was not a one-day-a-week activity in Massachusetts Bay. It was the custom in Dorchester, as it was in many churches, to offer a weekly lecture for the parishioners in addition to the sermons. The lecture differed from the Lord's day exhortations only in that it was not accompanied by the full complement of prayers, psalms, and other activities. At his afternoon or evening lectures, Mather preached the gospel just as he did on the Lord's day, and the regular attendance of many of Dorchester's people not only at the local lectures but also at the midweek orations held in neighboring villages emphasized their importance. Mather often attended the lectures of other clerics. A surviving portion of his notes for the year 1639 contains information on lectures by Samuel Newman, Henry Flint, John Allin, Hugh Peter, Thomas Weld, John Cotton, Jonathan Burr, William Tompson, John Knowles, and others. In all, the handwritten fragment includes information on sixty-two sermons preached within a period of only a few months.[11]

Actually, the voracious appetite of Dorchestermen for pulpit oratory was not something peculiar to the village or to New England. It was one of those many features of nonconformity that had been carried across the Atlantic along with the bulk of the colonists' religious practices. Since the time of Elizabeth, preaching had been increasing in popularity throughout England, and in some cases it was actually encouraged by officials who hoped it would improve the educational qualifications of ministers and assure that some measure of doctrine was being presented to the people. As larger numbers became interested in pulpit oratory, the need for clergymen increased. In 1584 Emmanuel College was established to help in their training and a dozen years later, Sidney Sussex was founded for the same purpose. As the fortunes of dissent rose in the latter years of the sixteenth century and on into the reigns of the Stuarts, the demand for preaching continued to grow. Sermons became so popular by the reign of James I that even conforming clerics began to depend on them to a great degree, but for the nonconformists they were most important. In Massachusetts Bay, in fact, the desire to hear more sermons seemed almost insatiable. At one point "there were so many lectures . . . in the country, and many poor persons would usually resort to two and three in the week, to the great neglect of their affairs, and the damage of the public. The assemblies also were (in divers churches) held till night, and sometimes within the night, so as such as dwelt far off could not get home in due season, and many weak bodies could not endure so long, in the extremity of the heat or cold, without great trouble, and hazard of their health."[12] Ultimately, the problem became so serious the General Court was forced to regulate the amount of preaching, and the days and hours when sermons and lectures could be delivered were restricted by statute.[13]

It is often difficult to comprehend the intense devotion the colony's pulpit orators inspired from those who heard them preach, and although the imagery in sermons of consummately able ministers like Shepard or Cotton still reveals sufficient passion to convey at least an intimation of what it must have meant to hear them from a meetinghouse pulpit, this is not true for the extant sermons of most New England ministers. In the case of Richard Mather, especially, it is exceedingly difficult to discern the attraction his exhortations had for the Dorchester folk who heard him preach over a period of decades. It is apparent from his existing sermons that the attachment was not the result of his literary virtuosity. Though a portion of the power normally accompanying a work designed for oral presentation is lost in a written text, any examination of Mather's sermons indicates a lack of sufficient artistry to inspire or enchant no matter how mightily they may have been delivered. Mather's sermons bore no similarity to the metaphysical masterpieces of John Donne, Jeremy Taylor, Lancelot Andrewes, or any of the Anglican stylists of the century. He used little imagery or charm to hold his listeners, and on the few occasions when he attempted to add a touch of color or emphasize a point by using a keenly descriptive passage or one of the simple but powerful analogies for which nonconforming clerics were known, his efforts were wooden and unimaginative without exception. The best he could produce in years of oratory was a brief description of a monster birth in punishment for sexual misconduct and, somewhat later, he concocted the image of a riotous fellow condemned to the flames of hell who suffered exceedingly because he "could not have so much as a drop of water to coole his tongue." Obviously neither these descriptions nor any of Mather's other artistic devices were of a quality that would place a congregation in his thrall. To be sure, there were legal requirements for attendance at religious exercises, and this accounted for the presence of some of his listeners, but neither compulsion nor the traditional dependence of nonconformists on the spoken word explains the Dorchestermen's devotion to pulpit oratory.

Beyond the force of tradition and the statutory requirements, there were a number of minor factors that contributed to the regular attendance of many at Mather's services. One of these was the common human desire to observe and participate in ceremony or ritual. Though the Massachusetts Bay clerics had categorically rejected religious exercise as a form of entertainment, the lack of ornament in Mather's stark unliturgical sermons was not as simple and uncontrived as it might have seemed. In his church, as in others in the colony, the studied and careful rejection of ceremony became a ritual of its own, and the structured progression of a Dorchester Lord's day, with its regular ordering of events, the standard sermon form, the set procedure for administering the Lord's supper on a monthly basis, and the stylized pattern for admission to the fellowship, provided a liturgy that appealed to men who sought to deny the value of nonessential ceremony. It was, without doubt, a ritual even though it was born not of pomp and ornament but of regular progression and serried structure.

The attraction of the ritual was reinforced by a genuine mystical quality in New England religion that had a great appeal to some who listened for hours while Mather spoke. Like the fascination with preaching, mysticism had long been part of nonconformist practice, though it was often submerged beneath a thick overlay of intellectualism. But despite the moral and legalistic direction taken by nonconformity, the emphasis on direct communication with God (i.e., the conversion experience and the Lord's supper) indicated a faith with genuine mystical properties. In England the mystical element was most prominent during the Protectorate when Cromwell surrounded himself with mystics such as Henry Vane and Francis Rouse, who exerted considerable influence as did similarly inclined preachers John Saltmarsh and William Dell. In New England the manifestations of mysticism had come much earlier with the Antinomian controversy, and while the banishment of Anne Hutchinson by Mather and his fellow ministers was sufficient to discourage another such outbreak, the Quaker movement some years later indicated mysticism had not been destroyed by the victory over colonial dissent in 1637.[14]

The intense attachment to preaching that existed in Mather's Dorchester was the result of these and other more general considerations—those determinants of human conduct that are usually lumped together under the catchall terms of society, culture, and personality. Although these terms often lack precise meanings, it is within their compass, with a fuller understanding of their overlapping and sometimes contrary impulses, that the Dorchestermen's devotion to the preached word is, in part, explainable. In Mather's village, the familiar nonconformist sermon represented a significant change from the Anglican and Roman Catholic religious observances. The growth of the sermon as a motivating force in sixteenth-century English life reflects, in many respects, the interests and ambitions of the nonconformist element. In the homeland, nonconformists drew much of their support from the new commercial and ecclesiastical classes who were yet unsure of their position in a rapidly changing society, for although members of these classes sought security within the national structure, and strove for advancement within it, they experienced most hostility from the established church and the aristocracy.

Though Theodore Beza had taught nonconformists the evils of episcopacy, it was not only polity that soured them on the bishops and their host of retainers. The upper reaches of the ecclesiastical hierarchy, at least after Edmund Grindal was replaced by John Whitgift as archbishop of Canterbury, were well secured from penetration by reformers. This was also true of the upper levels of English society where position was guaranteed by wealth, family, power, and tradition. For the nonconformists, the sermon was useful in combating this exclusiveness.

Unlike the mass or the services from the *Book of Common Prayer*, the authority of the sermon did not reside in a specified sequence of mystical acts performed by members of a divinely designated elite. It was the word of God sent directly to man. The agent of transmittal, the preacher in the pulpit, was the possessor of no transcendent powers nor was he the appointee of a distant, aloof, and occasionally hostile hierarchy. He spoke from the pulpit not at the behest of king or bishop, but of his own church. He was chosen by its members and served at their pleasure. He stood apart from ordinary men not because he was a member of a priesthood, endowed with magical powers, but because he had acquired considerable theological knowledge through years of study. The effect of this, combined with the sermon that carried with it the implication that God spoke directly to man, offered an element of social security to classes singularly deficient in that quality. When Mather preached, he was more than a theological exegete intent on explaining God's will. He spoke the undisputed word of Christ. In his sermons there was no attempt to duplicate the precision of ecclesiastical debate. His oratory contained no hint of the theological disagreements that had almost created schism in the colony and had fueled civil war in England. They were direct, plain, and contained no latitude for doubt or disagreement. This was what his listeners wanted to hear: God's commands received directly, not through the representatives of the upper class who labored assiduously to thwart their aspirations. This direct relationship was confirmed and strengthened by the common nonconformist acceptance of predetermined salvation, which implied the devaluation of the rites of high-church Anglicanism (with its sacramental, magical, and institutional distribution of grace), and the corresponding elevation of the preacher and his upwardly mobile, socially insecure parishioners.[15]

The aggregate force of all these considerations, tradition, law, and the attraction of ritual and mysticism, especially when combined with the social imperatives of seventeenth-century village life, go far toward explaining the devotion to preaching found among Mather's flock. But it is equally apparent that there were other factors that brought his congregants to the meetinghouse for the regular Lord's day activities and for the weekly lecture. Perhaps the most essential single force in assuring a deep and abiding devotion to Mather's preaching was the content of his sermons. Mather left no explicit evidence indicating he ever pondered the reasons for the fascination of his congregation with the preached word or that he ever wondered at the motives of those who regularly filled the meetinghouse to hear him expound, but his sermons indicate a careful concern for cultivating his audience.

Mather was fully aware of the distinction between the two parts of his congregation, the members of the church to whom God had given grace and the remainder who, though excluded from salvation, regularly attended worship. Many of the Bay Colony ministers saw in the two strata of worshipers the truth of the parable of the wheat and the tares, and on at least one occasion Mather expressed the same idea describing the situation with the analogy of the people at the Temple who were welcomed into the inner court and the remainder who observed the divine commandments but who could enter only the outer court (Rev. 11:1-2). To Mather, this dichotomy explained the devotion of the saints to the thousands of sermons they heard preached by God's ministers. The grace within them kindled an irresistible desire to hear God's word. As for those who had not been elected, Mather's sermons reveal that he spent considerable thought and effort inducing the hearers' devotion to the faith, and the Dorchestermen listened to him year after year not because they were devoted to tradition, or held mystical longings, or exhibited a desire to gain status but because he offered the most coveted commodity for a seventeenth-century New Englander: he told them of a method to gain salvation.

Mather's preaching of a way to be saved would seem to suggest that the common assertion that most Massachusetts Bay clerics were "Calvinists in the closet and Arminians in the pulpit" was true in Mather's case, but in fact it was not. Mather was a Calvinist throughout, at least in that he accepted the soteriological teachings of John Calvin, but within the broad framework of the Genevan theology he offered something more. In his sermons he offered the hope for salvation most often associated with the doctrines of Arminius. But at the same time he built an elaborate casuistical pattern to imbue his hearers with a need and a desire for justification by works that did not explicitly reject basic tenets of the New England style of nonconformity. For a man who counted himself a believer in predetermined salvation, it was difficult to suggest a way in which men could be saved, but it was, nonetheless, a requirement of Mather's Dorchester ministry. He, like other nonconformist clerics, knew that few persons could accept a clear and strict division between the saved and the damned, and that the human needs and desires of his congregants who were not recognized as within the visible church required more than mere acquiescence in a predetermination that would consign them to hell for eternity.

It was an involved task to weave a complete net of teleological thought aimed at providing an acceptable psychospiritual mooring for ordinary men and women and at the same time not violate the doctrines laid down by Calvin. It required years of carefully organized oratory, each segment building on its predecessors and at the same time offering new premises, deductions, and conclusions. The sequential pattern was not a new form of procedure for seventeenth-century nonconforming clerics. Long before the first colonists arrived in New England a plan of conversion had become part of English nonconforming pulpit oratory. First came election, the bestowal of grace on those to be saved. The elect then received their vocation. As the result of these two manifestations the individuals were then aware of their justification and knew that their sins had been remitted by Christ. The acquisition of purity through grace carried them to the next plateau of salvation: sanctification, or the living of a life in accord with divinely prescribed teachings. This led to the final stage: glorification by God. Fatalism and Antinomianism were the theological dangers created by either extreme. If God chose men for salvation and then ignored them, it could be inferred on one hand that man could do nothing about his spiritual condition. On the other hand, the assurance of election could create a sense of superiority to law and traditional conceptions of morality. Nonconformist preachers, in most cases, avoided these extremes by insisting that the elect must not only be prepared to meet God but they must continually seek assurance of their condition. They preached that the avoidance of preparation was a fair indication of the reprobate while easy assurance of salvation was the mark of the hypocrite.[16]

In some respects the plan of conversion followed by Mather was similar to this widely used pattern, but it differed in that while the most commonly employed sequence was constructed in a direct and easily comprehensible fashion primarily to explain to the elect the mechanism for salvation and to guide them against heresies, the oratory in Dorchester was, of necessity, more complicated and circuitous, since it was aimed at an audience whose needs were deeper but whose faith was not as firm as was the faith of those who had been accepted as members of God's elite. For the elect, Mather's preaching made clear, there was need only for preparation. Grace, vocation, and justification were theirs, and this produced sanctification without the danger of Fatalism, Antinomianism, Socinianism, or any other belief displeasing to God. The elect could gain great gifts from hearing sermons, but since their need to be guided by the preached word was not pressing, Mather was free to direct his sermons toward those who most needed the Word, the men and women who failed to offer sufficient evidence of regeneration to be admitted to the church. It was for them that his particular system was constructed. It was designed to explain how in a universe where salvation was predetermined and where some were already justified and sanctified, each of those who had not received grace might still gain salvation by preparation and sanctification. As Mather knew, logic was not sufficient to resolve the conflict between salvation through grace and salvation through works. But this did not make his task unnecessarily difficult, for in the end it was by means other than logic that he was able to convince his fellow townsmen that the gates of heaven might well be open to them.

Mather was not the only New England cleric who walked a path between the grim finality of absolute belief in predestination and the Arminian heresy that each man could determine his own fate. It was not merely the desire for congregational unity or a wish to spare parishioners a life of spiritual and psychological torment that drove Mather to find a solution to these logically irreconcilable premises. Like other English nonconformists, he had a certain inherent revulsion to a doctrine that regarded the majority of men as reprobate even though they attempted, to the limits of their capacities, to live according to the commands of God.

In an earlier day, this doctrine had presented no difficulty for William Perkins who had provided the model on which nonconformists patterned their sermons. He admitted no vacillation on the question of election to intrude into his works. Perkins and most of his associates at Christ's College accepted the doctrine that mankind had been damned as a result of Adam's fall. From that event on, humanity was forever debased, and God could in no way be faulted if he had chosen to allow man to continue eternally in perdition. Though he might have chosen to do this, God was merciful. Some men would be saved, he decreed, on condition that they scrupulously observe his laws for human conduct. Unfortunately, at least for those who lived between the time of the expulsion from the Garden of Eden and the coming of Christ and who set out to try to obtain eternal life through this covenant of works, the restrictions imposed were so rigid that fallible man could not observe them with sufficient fidelity to insure salvation. God knew this and offered a new way to acquire eternal life through a covenant of grace. Under this covenant, man was obliged to do nothing. Those who were selected for salvation were saved by God's gift of grace alone while the remainder of humanity was cast down to dwell with Satan for eternity. Nothing could alter what God had decreed.

The doctrine of predestination adopted by Perkins from the writings of Calvin admitted no qualification. Those who insisted the damned would go to hell because God had foreseen they would be evil were denounced for trying to distort the divine will. God's reasons for choosing some men and rejecting others, said Perkins, could not be fathomed by mortal man.

Most of the Bay Colony clerics had agonized over their own elections at one time or another, doubting and questioning their salvation. Even John Cotton, while a student at Cambridge, found the advocacy of free grace and human helplessness so disconcerting that after hearing a number of Perkins's sermons, he deliberately absented himself when Perkins spoke. He later revealed how he had secretly rejoiced at the sound of the bells tolling Perkins's death because he felt he would then be troubled no more by the man or his teachings. Cotton was wrong in his assumptions. The ideology Perkins had planted grew within him, and after a lengthy period of uncertainty he accepted the doctrines that had previously caused him such discomfort. He was converted and the doubts in his mind concerning salvation were erased.

Cotton was not the only nonconforming cleric who had gone through this experience. John Norton, Thomas Shepard, and many others who later emigrated to New England had endured similar times of anguish. Mather, too, had shared the same doubts not only in his youth but on at least one occasion after his arrival in America. For these men, fears of damnation were later replaced by confidence in their own election, but for those who were unable to discern sufficient signs of their being chosen to keep them operating within their social group, something had to be done to mitigate the harshness of the doctrine of predetermined election without driving them into Fatalism or an abandonment of Christianity. Cotton, while still in England, accomplished this by giving his sermons a liberal infusion of the doctrines of Richard Sibbes, a fellow of Saint John's College and a widely known nonconformist cleric. Sibbes was not a powerful theologian in the manner of William Ames, Paul Baynes, or Perkins. He was what his colleagues called a physician for the soul. His purpose in the pulpit was to bring to the saved a knowledge of their condition and to ease the pangs of periodic doubt. In doing this, he disregarded the uncomfortable subject of reprobation that formed a vital part of Perkins's theology. By implication he preached what Perkins had condemned, a doctrine of universal calling.

Cotton, like Sibbes, was caught in the logical trap inherent in the acceptance of an omnipotent and omniscient god, but while influenced by Sibbes, he ultimately arrived at a slightly different solution. Avoiding a doctrine of universal calling and facing directly the issue of the damned, Cotton preached a more complete brand of theology which included both segments of the Christian's dichotomy, salvation as well as reprobation. Though he was completely attuned to the concepts of free grace and predestination and avoided the slightest suggestion that faith and works could bring salvation, Cotton argued that grace was given absolutely to the elect—not the result of faith or works—while those who were damned were damned only conditionally upon the willful rejection of God's word either by refusing the means of grace or by ignoring the knowledge of God. Men were condemned to perdition, Cotton taught, not by Adam's fall alone, but by their own sins, their abandonment of God, and their disobedience.[17]

Mather did not accept either Sibbes's doctrine of universal salvation or Cotton's attempts to extend the compass of predestined salvation. Unlike Sibbes who labored to plant assurance in the minds of a universal elect or Cotton who tried to inculcate the desire to strive for salvation among those who had not been elected by God's free grace, Mather based his appeal on the value of insecurity, the inability of anyone to discern with absolute certainty whether he was of the elect or the condemned. This line of reason was directed not to those who were reasonably sure they were of the saints and had been joined to the Dorchester church but to those who were looking for assurance—the men and women who filled his meetinghouse but were excluded from the Lord's table because they could not convince themselves, the church, or both that they were likely to be numbered among the elect. It was to these individuals that Mather most often spoke from his pulpit.

Richard Mather's sermons held his congregation because he was able to implant in the hearts of his flock the idea that every man among them might well be among the elect. What had been rejected by Perkins, assumed by Sibbes, and avoided by Cotton was made by Mather to be the reasonable hope of almost every individual who heard his sermons. Some knew of their salvation, he said, but most could only wonder. It was for the latter group that he produced an elaborate casuistical web of circular reasoning.

Mather had to begin his teleological sojourn at the center of the problem, the very nature of grace, but before he could do that, he had to persuade his hearers that there was the possibility of election for each of them. The apostles provided Mather with a perfect example of the potential of every man for election and he explained that among them there were "men of no great eminency nor excellency in their beginnings [who were] fitted and called of god." He supported his point often using the examples of Simon Peter, a fisherman; Matthew, a publican; and Paul, a tent-maker. The Old Testament provided even more material for Mather to illustrate the humbleness of those chosen by God; he could cite the example of the prophet Amos who was a herdsman of Tekoa, David who was a simple shepherd, and several others whose origins were less than exalted.[18] This point was essential, for if Mather's listeners doubted its substance, the remainder of his message would be ineffective. He drove it home again and again: neither poverty nor worldly condition were prohibitions against receiving grace; "there is none but god that knoweth who they are that are predestinated."[19]

After this had been established by regular example and repetition, Mather then proceeded to his major line of argument: an exposition on the nature of grace or, more precisely, on the manner in which it came to man. He explained, in a way entirely conformable with Perkins's doctrines, that grace was given freely by God without condition. After Mather had stated this, his explanation was amplified, altered, and extended beyond the terminus established in Geneva for divine grace. "The word of god," he added, after delineating the immutable nature of grace, "is very plaine . . . [God] will give grace to whosoever will receive it and come for it. . . . it is a great encouragement and comfort that the righteousnesse of our god will move him and prevaile with him, to performe what he hath promised, and so to give unto his the grace of faith."[20] This kind of statement provided the breach that gave Mather his first opportunity to storm the citadel of predetermined salvation.

Mather continued his seemingly heretical line by adding, "God will give grace to whosoever will receive it and come for it." This was surely a sentiment that would have been anathema to Baynes and William Perkins. At this point it might have seemed that Mather was succumbing to the heresies of Arminius or Aquinas, but this was hardly the case. He knew that such a pronouncement could not be made categorically in seventeenth-century Massachusetts Bay. The problem, as Mather explained to his congregants, was more complicated than simply appealing to God in prayer and requesting grace. Man could not approach God directly, but only through his son, Jesus Christ. The essential element in election, according to Mather's explanation, was faith in Christ.

At this point the needed qualifications appeared. In explaining the functioning of this relationship, Mather noted, "The grace of faith as well as any other part or point of happinesse is the effect and fruit of Christ's passion; for he being lifted up (both upon the crosse in his suffering of death and in his ascension into heaven, and in the ministry of the gospell wherein these things are preached to all nations, being thus lifted up) he drawes all [men] to him . . . which is by this grace of faith there being no other way whereby we can come to Christ."[21] This, then, did not yet show men the way to salvation. Mather had first assured his hearers that any of them might be a recipient of grace, the essential element in salvation, but then, adhering more closely to the tenets of Calvin and Perkins, he preached that while all might be saved, the only ones who were actually numbered among the elect were those who had been given God's grace.

Mather's problem, at this juncture, was the same that had been solved by Sibbes with his assumption of universal salvation and by Cotton with his advocacy of conditional reprobation. Mather sought to instill spiritual uncertainty among his congregants. According to him, faith was the link that followed grace in the chain of anticipation. If the attribution of grace to some and not to others seemed arbitrary, perhaps a rational God could be fathomed more easily if Dorchestermen understood the integral part played by faith in the divine ordering of things. According to Mather's schema, faith was the ingredient that made predestination more comprehensible. "That none can be justified before they have faith or without faith is evident, because justification is after vocation or calling . . . and consequently it is after faith, because faith is wrought in calling, as the answer of the soule to the calling of god calling to come to Christ and to god by him. The answer of the soule to this call is nothing else but faith . . . . so that justification beeing after calling, and faith comprehended and wrought in calling, it must needs bee that justification is not afore faith nor without it, but followeth afterward."[22] There remained, however, one condition: faith, like grace, was not a quality inherent in man. If Mather were to concede that saving faith was innate in some individuals, he would be forced to deny the whole nonconformist position on salvation. Faith, then, like grace, came from God. To let matters rest there, however, meant that little progress had been made communicating spiritual uncertainty and its complement, the hope for salvation, to the Dorchester congregation.

To explain how justification was possible for man to attain, Mather added Christian knowledge to his logical structure.

Knowledge was more immediately comprehensible than grace, faith, or calling and was to be the key to his explanation. Knowledge of God and Christ, obtained from the dual purveyors of the Word—Bible and sermon—"begetts holy longing desires after grace and the things of heaven . . . . As it was said of virtue that if it were seene it would stirre up wonderfull desires upon it self, so it may be truly sayd that the bewty, the fullnesse, the allsufficiency that is in god and Christ is such, that if it bee but knowne the heart must needs go out in longing desyres after the same. And if so, then that must needs follow abundance of grace, for when the heart is [illeg.] in grace desyres after these things, these desyres shall undoubtedly be satisfyed; for so is the promise." "This holy knowledge is not without faith but is the begetter and bringer of it . . . . and if faith and humility, which are the means of all grace, if these be by means of this knowledge it may well be sayd that all things, pertaining to life and godlinesse are given by means of this holy knowledge." The implication of these passages was clear enough to Mather's hearers: knowledge preceded both grace and faith. Knowledge is the first thing given to the soul; it is the beginning of all other gifts. Knowledge, when joined with faith, justification, and suitable actions, brings salvation.[23]

Mather's manner of presenting holy knowledge to his hearers was similar, at least in several key aspects, to the pattern he had used to describe faith, but while he was forced to equate the origins of grace, faith, and calling as gifts of God, he indicated that knowledge could be apprehended by man. Holy knowledge (available by man's own effort) was primary; then came grace, faith, justification, and suitable actions to produce eternal life. Here again, the insertion of suitable actions provided a catch, but it was not as formidable as a God who dispensed salvation seemingly at random. It meant that after gaining holy knowledge, grace, faith or calling, and justification, only suitable actions (i.e., sanctification) were required. These, then, were the ends of Mather's string of logic, one end tied securely to holy knowledge and the other neatly wrapped and knotted around sanctification—two qualities at least partially obtainable by understandable human actions.

Holy knowledge and sanctification not only were the attainable qualities that contained the unachievable gifts between them but also were the doctrinal guards against the threats of Fatalism and Antinomianism. Even more important, however, sanctification as a sign of justification in a community accustomed to legalism and piety was a measure with enough familiarity to persuade almost every individual that he could be one of the elect. The next step was to find enough sanctification to make it seem more certain, and here Mather provided a detailed set of guidelines.

According to some of the acceptable signs described in the Dorchester meetinghouse, those who might assume themselves sanctified in some degree avoided conspicuous vices like "bravery in apparell above [their] estates" and instead were comely, frugal, and honest in adornment. They eschewed "excessive drinking, excessive taking of tobacco," gluttony, sexual excess in marriage, fornication, sodomy, and nonattendance at worship. Even too much relaxation indicated a lack of sanctification. This vice particularly disturbed Mather who noted, "The holy ghost speakes so much against excessive sleeping and lying in bed that wee may see here is also temperance to be used in Respect of sleepe," and he added, revealing the cause of his perturbation over immoderate snoozing, that "It is therefore no small fault to sleepe unseasonably as in tyme of sermon or prayer."[24] Such declamations against sin, though not central in his theology of salvation, were used to illustrate his sermon and to permit the lengthy digressions that made it impossible for any listener to follow his logic. Once this was done, the sequence could easily be altered, and by rearranging relationships Mather was able to insinuate his message that man could be saved. He explained: "Now sanctification is the means . . . of entering into the Kingdome of grace, and the kingdom of glory, and an abundant degree thereof, oh then let us strive after an abundant measure of all the graces of sanctification and holynesse, which wilbe followed with such an abundant measure, and degree of everlasting glory and happinesse."[25]

The point of Mather's method was to establish without explicit advocacy that grace could be obtained in a manner other than the random action of God, a clear softening of rigid insistence on absolute predestined salvation. This was heresy if stated categorically, but lest he be challenged on this point by a visiting cleric or a layman skilled in the intricacies of logic and theology, he was careful to cover his doctrinal flank by assuring the audience that through "Perfection of grace and glory is through the knowledge of the son of god. . . . This knowledge is it selfe the gift of god."[26] This last statement represented a hasty retreat to the acceptable doctrines on predestination. But to assume that Mather believed that sanctification could be had without justification or that "sanctification is the blessed will of God" and that all his previous reasoning was designed only for rhetorical effect or to complete a circle of logic is to misunderstand his purpose.

In discerning what Mather was actually saying in the years between 1646 and 1650, when he preached this particular set of sermons, one must note the factors of repetition, elaboration, and emphasis, rather than make a strict examination of his sometimes confused and often misleading logic. His sermons and lectures must be read in context and with the understanding that this large corpus of logically inconsistent material was presented orally in small cohesive segments over an extended time period. Moreover, the sermons Mather preached to his Dorchester congregation differed from his closely reasoned theological polemics. When he wrote to defend the New England way, he had time to revise, reconsider, rethink, and redraft countless times. His arguments were carefully constructed after lengthy deliberation. They were examined in their entirety, criticized by his colleagues, and before they were put to press the inconsistencies and incongruities of argument were removed or corrected. When his works were read they would be examined minutely for defects in reason or biblical interpretation that could be used to detract from God's churches in North America. This was not the case with his sermons. None of his listeners had time to weigh and evaluate accurately the significance of each sentence, analogy, or citation without missing his next words. There was no way for his audience to evaluate those points emphasized by oratorical technique against those pressed with minimal vigor by the pitch, intonation, and the gestures of the man in the pulpit, and, most important, no man could follow his preaching over an extended period of time and examine and analyze the sermons as a unified and consistent body of thought or doctrine. And even if this could have been done, no examiner would fault Mather. If his sermons sometimes seemed to be leading toward heresy, he always retreated to safe doctrine. If dubious points were made with great elaboration and meticulous attention to detail, he always clarified them or brought them in line with accepted ideology by a concluding sentence or phrase. Who, then, could know or prove the understanding that remained with the hearers was not that produced from a single sentence but the more extensive and elaborate depiction of the path to salvation and glory.

Unfortunately, it is impossible to recover the manner and method to which Mather's oratorical techniques were applied to arguments, doctrines, and ideas. But it would be wrong to assume, in Mather's case, that one cannot differentiate between those ideas driven home by his unadorned preaching and those that were passed over lightly. It is here that emphasis due to repetition becomes an important tool in evaluating meaning, for it is by doing this that Mather's pulpit techniques become understandable and a reader of his sermons can see the totality of meaning in his preaching and the effect of that meaning on those who heard his words.

In this manner, Mather's deviation from the convictions on predestination held by Calvin and Perkins becomes apparent. Mather insisted that divine grace was bestowed freely, but the involved, convoluted, and contradictory nature of his logic, when compared to his carefully reasoned polemics, indicates Mather's casuistry was designed to confuse rather than to explain. Mather was not trying to clarify Calvin; he hoped to insert serious modifications in his doctrines without actually appearing to do so. Thus he was forced into his elaborate casuistical pattern, for it was only through extensive and complicated elaboration and obfuscation that oratorical emphasis could convey knowledge of the individual's possible salvation, avoid an explicit and coherent statement of content, and at the same time affirm the widely accepted nonconformist principle of predetermined salvation.

Beginning with proof that earthly condition was no bar to election, Mather proceeded to the divine grace given by God, moved on to faith or vocation, and here, while noting occasionally that faith like grace was of divine origin, he portrayed faith as something that was, in some mysterious way, imbued with the breath of human origin. He then denied this was the case and moved on to the acquisition of holy knowledge, the initial or penultimate step in the progress toward salvation depending on which sermon one reads.

This was the first break with the Genevan tradition. Holy knowl-edge, according to the cleric, was derived in two ways: from the study of the Bible and by "attending upon the publicke ministry of them that are sent of God to enterprett and open the scriptures, and the milk of God contayned therein."[27] Through these twin instru-mentalities, man could obtain the prerequisites for salvation. Knowl-edge, according to Mather's interpretation, begat faith, faith begat vocation, and, although Mather never stated this explicitly, vocation begat grace. Holy knowledge, the basic quality, was acquired through sanctification, and thus, as man strove to increase his degree of sanctification, by reading and hearing the Word and by cultivating all other aspects of piety, he was moving toward justification. The sequence and causal relationships of faith, grace, vocation, sanctifi-cation, and holy knowledge varied from sermon to sermon, but one factor remained constant—the implication that any man could par-take of glory by acquiring first either holy knowledge or sanctifica-tion.

With this revelation, the wall surrounding Geneva seemed to have been cracked by the Dorchester Joshua. This, however, was not so. Mather was aware of the ramifications of his sequences and when-ever he verged on abandoning predestination he carefully inserted disclaimers such as "This knowledge is it selfe the gift of god."[28] Always he returned to locally acceptable doctrine and safety. Again and again he brought his congregation to the brink of Arminianism and then turned them aside with a quiet, inconspicuous, and low-keyed word of equivocation. Mather's sermons followed a similar course to his reading of parables. During the first reading members of his flock learned the outcome of the story; during the second reading it was the message contained in the story that became significant; in subsequent readings the significance of the story increased along with increased understanding. The end product of Mather's logic was always known, but with each retelling of the progress from holy knowledge to grace, to faith, to justification, to sanctification, to glory, the process grew in importance and the disclaimers, appended here and there, faded from the minds of the audience, remaining only to protect the minister from accusations of heresy. Repeatedly the Dorchester villagers heard at length and in detail how they could ultimately gain grace by reading the Bible, hearing the Word, and practicing holiness. This was what they hoped most devoutly to hear and Mather provided it for them. He showed them the way to eternal life. If Mather's occasional equivocations disturbed some, this was minor. They were small, infrequent, and buried amid the mass of his rhetoric. Mather's implicit message overwhelmed its qualifications. When his congregation entered the village meetinghouse, they came to be assured there was a place for them in heaven and to hear again an answer to the question posed long ago to Paul and Silas by a trembling jailer who asked, "What must I do to be saved?"

V.

The Cambridge Platform

Of all the difficulties and disappointments Richard Mather faced throughout his years in New England, those of the 1640s were, perhaps, some of the most difficult to bear. In this decade he came to understand that he had not gained the reputation he sought as a leading theological polemicist, and amid his realization of personal failure, the colony's predominant congregational system, which he had labored assiduously to defend, came under severe attack from local dissenters who received considerable encouragement from Massachusetts Bay's enemies in England. Mather, as he had done in previous years, defended the colony's churches against the newest series of dissenters, but while he worked unremittingly at this task, the rewards of victory were again neither ecclesiastical harmony nor the personal recognition he had anticipated.

The two aspects of Bay Colony doctrine and polity that created a veritable crisis in the churches were the system of ecclesiastical control that had no means within itself to enforce doctrinal homogeneity and the restriction of baptism to the children of church members. On the surface, these complaints seemed to have little in common, but in the Bay Colony's tightly composed theological organization few issues or controversies stood independent of one another. The first of these difficulties, the inability of the churches to insure an acceptable degree of uniformity, was the result of a reaction by English nonconformists to the civil domination of ecclesiastical institutions that was the accepted pattern in the homeland. The relationship between secular and church authorities in England had its ideological beginnings long before the first settlements in Massachusetts Bay. With the coming of the Reformation and the subsequent development of national religions in many parts of

Europe, secular rulers soon discovered the manifold advantages of achieving domination over newly created churches. In many cases, however, some doctrinal justification was required to make this control complete, and to this end, the writings of Thomas Erastus, a Swiss physician and theologian, were pressed into service. Although Erastus was primarily concerned with problems of excommunication rather than with the relationship between civil and ecclesiastical authorities, it was discovered that his doctrines, when properly amplified, could be used to justify the extension of secular power over religious matters.

The idea of civil supremacy over religious affairs was not new with Erastus. Some of its theological underpinnings dated back to the Apostolic church, it had been examined occasionally by medieval ecclesiastics, and in the sixteenth century the idea of secular dominance of the church had been central to the policies of Henry VIII. By the time of Elizabeth, Erastianism was a widely accepted concept, and its validity was confirmed by a host of commentators, including John Whitgift, Richard Hooker, and somewhat later by the great Dutch theologian and philosopher Hugo Grotius. Nevertheless, despite the general acceptance of the legitimacy of the secular domination of the church, there were some in England who would have preferred the elimination of the ecclesiastical hierarchy and the substitution of a reformed system of polity similar to that used in Scotland or Geneva.

By the early years of the seventeenth century, even this measure of reform seemed insufficient to some individuals who, under the influence of William Ames, rejected both episcopal and presbyterian systems of church government and demanded an end to secular control of ecclesiastical affairs. The number of Ames's supporters was not large, but they hoped that with perseverance and the aid of God they might exert sufficient influence to have their doctrines eventually incorporated into the teaching and practice of the Church of England. With the death of James I and the institution of a series of reactionary ecclesiastical policies by his successor, any such illusions were destroyed. A group of these dissidents, angered and disheartened by what they considered to be the beginnings of a counterreformation and plagued by social and economic difficulties, elected to leave England and journey to North America. One of the features they hoped to build into their new society was a church organization free from the corruptions of the homeland. Among those corruptions, of course, was the ecclesiastical hierarchy and its domination by civil authority.

The Massachusetts Bay Colony was founded by these men in 1630, and as Ames had prescribed, they gathered churches in their settlement that were free from civil domination. To insure some measure of coordination and uniformity in the absence of secular and hierarchical supervision, the churches were banded together in a loose synodical relationship. This arrangement continued until the arrival of John Cotton three years later. It took the persuasive Lincolnshire cleric only a short time to convince the colonists that even this casual system of cooperation was contrary to scriptural warrant. He explained that the churches could be united by no institutional bond. They were to be congregational, each standing independent and equal before God, unseparated from him by king or bishop. Their only connection with one another would be a sharing of mutual love, respect, and a common devotion to the true religion.

It was not long before this uncoordinated system had proved itself entirely unworkable, and an Erastian pattern of civil intervention in ecclesiastical matters began to develop.[1] This might have been avoided and the congregational system preserved in the purity that Ames had envisioned if it had not been for the tendency of each man to interpret divine writ in line with his own experience and predispositions. But divergent views created problems in the colony as men heard God instruct them in different ways. This was a serious threat, for almost everyone in Massachusetts Bay agreed that ecclesiastical anarchy could not be tolerated. The colonists knew that whatever God commanded, he commanded for all. He did not prescribe one ecclesiastical order for Boston, another for Salem, and still another for Cambridge. Yet as more independent churches were gathered in Massachusetts Bay, it became apparent that no spontaneous identity of doctrine and practice would emerge and even the common bond of the same Scriptures was inadequate to insure sufficient homogeneity among the churches.

Actually, the first steps toward Erastianism were taken even before Cotton's arrival when, only a short time after settlement began, the inherent weakness of church independence became obvious to the magistrates, who, in the new colony, were required to assume many of the tasks usually done by the clergy in England. Matters that had been part of the parish administrative machinery such as recording births, deaths, and marriages, supervising the support of paupers, conducting marriage ceremonies, and a number of duties usually handled by ecclesiastical courts all became the work of secular authorities. The clerics, for doctrinal reasons, regarded such labors as the work of the state not the church. The shifting of the burdens was done with acquiescence on both sides, and this mutual consent was to be fairly typical of the way state power would expand in the early years of the colony's history.

By 1633 the colony moved closer toward an Erastian relationship when the General Court encouraged the colony's clergy to meet together regularly and discuss their disagreements. But the success of the tactic was limited by the reluctance of at least two clerics to embark on any program of association that could develop into a coercive body. The following year the General Court took another step in the same direction when it ordered the churches to draw up a uniform code of discipline.[2] These feeble measures of officially encouraged cooperation were wholly inadequate to deal with the civil and ecclesiastical problems. Their failure was well illustrated in the conflict with Roger Williams. After his arrival in the colony in 1631, Williams engaged in a series of confrontations with the colony's leaders. He quarreled with the church at Boston and then with the magistrates over his election as a teaching elder at Salem, but throughout the disagreements, the Bay Colony clerics ignored the magistrates' request for a general conference to deal with the recalcitrant cleric. It was not until after the matter had festered for three years that the civil government moved to find its own solution. The request of Salem for a grant of land on Marblehead Neck was denied because the town had rejected the advice of the magistrates and had chosen Williams as its minister.[3] Williams was not intimidated by the court, which was then forced to take stronger action. After the pleas of an aggregation of clerics failed to sway Williams, the General Court of September 3, 1635, convicted him of having "broached and dyvulged dyvers newe and dangerous opinions, against the authoritie of magistrates, as also writt letters of defamation, both of the magistrates and churches here."[4]

The Massachusetts Bay clergy, with all their arguments and admonitions, had failed to cope with Williams, and the colony was obliged to find an alternate method to restrict him. The pattern of church independence provided no ecclesiastical method to do this. The clergy had no power of enforcement, and therefore they turned to the only available source of power to solve their problem, the civil government. Thus Williams was banished from the Colony by secular authority. The expedient worked well, and the colony's leaders, having set a precedent, turned again to the civil government when difficulties with the churches in Dorchester and Cambridge made it prudent to restrict the formation of new churches. Meeting in March, the General Court decreed,

> Forasmuch as it hath bene found by sad experience, that much trouble and disturbance hath happened both to the church and civill state by the officers and members of some churches, which have bene gathered within the limitts of this jurisdiction in a vndue manner, and not with such publique approbation as were meete, it is therefore ordered that all persons are to take notice that this Court doeth not, nor will hereafter, approue of any such companyes of men as shall henceforthe joyne in any pretended way of church fellowshipp, without they shall first acquainte the magistrates, and the elders of the greater parte of the churches in this jurisdiction, with their intentions, and have their approbation herein.[5]

It was this decree forbidding the formation of new churches without official approval that had brought Mather to grief when he first tried to gather a church at Dorchester. More important, however, was the fact that its enactment was a giant step in the direction of extending secular domination over the colony's ecclesiastical affairs. The failure of the clergy to find a common ground on various doctrinal and political disagreements meant that the secular government had to be used further to assure at least a semblance of ecclesiastical uniformity. This was nowhere more evident than in the Antinomian controversy where even before it was apparent that the persuasive powers of the clergy were insufficient to insure a united front and to squelch heresy in the churches, the civil government stepped into the fray. At first, the magistrates were hesitant and attempted to justify their intervention to the clerics who felt "saddled" by their interference.[6] They explained to the skeptical ministers that civil authority was necessary to disarm the heretics and preserve the peace. Later, when they had become more secure in their position, the magistrates acted boldly to finish what the churches were unable to accomplish, the expulsion from the colony of Anne Hutchinson and a band of her most devoted followers.

In the Antinomian crisis, Mather understood that the problem had been widespread, and he justified the interference of the civil government as a measure to prevent the dissolution of the Massachusetts Bay settlement. But while he undoubtedly regarded Hutchinson as sufficiently dangerous to the community to assuage any misgivings he had about the participation of civil authorities in church affairs, these reasons may have seemed less convincing after he had participated in the heavy-handed solution to the doctrinal problems created by Robert Lenthall, the minister at Weymouth. Here Mather had a firsthand view of the way that civil authorities stepped into a dispute when the clerical leaders failed to gain their objectives, and he could observe closely how the General Court forced Lenthall to recant and punished several of his supporters for their doctrinal deviation.

It was only two years after the investigation of Lenthall was held in the Dorchester meetinghouse that Mather had still another opportunity to observe the peculiar relationship between the churches of Massachusetts Bay and the civil magistrates. The Antinomian controversy and the confrontation over the church in Weymouth had involved him on the side of the ecclesiastical and governmental powers, but in the dispute that developed in 1641, he found himself no longer sitting as a prosecutor or judge. He was once more a defendant just as he had been when he had applied for church membership at Boston in 1635 and when he had attempted to gather his own church in the early months of 1636.

The immediate cause of the crisis in Dorchester was the growing amount of time and labor required by his duties. Although his wife had assumed a great proportion of his "secular tasks" to free him for the work of the Lord, it was apparent that Mather needed an assistant. With hopes of procuring aid for their teacher, the Dorchester church invited Jonathan Burr to join their covenant with the intention of raising him to office after he had become a church member. Burr was eight years younger than Mather, having been born at Redgrave, Suffolk, in 1604. Well educated and with some ability, he was admitted according to plan, but when he was offered a teaching eldership, he refused it. He explained to the puzzled church that Mather had accused him of Familism, and in 1641, this was an allegation serious enough to prevent his becoming a teaching elder.

The Familists, or the Family of Love, as they were sometimes called, had been founded by a Hollander named Henry Nicholas and had gained a foothold in England by 1570. They maintained that the love of God, mystically experienced by the soul, was the same as love of man. Loving God and themselves, men should live together as one great family. Nicholas and his followers scorned those who considered themselves any manner of spiritual elect and instead insisted that all were eligible for divine favor. Only a few years earlier, the colony had been on the verge of armed conflict over Antinomianism and, though Anne Hutchinson's doctrines and those of the Familists were distinctly different, there was a tendency on the part of the Bay Colonists to lump them together. Indeed, a common epithet hurled at the Opinionists was that of "Familist." While the colony's theologians were easily able to distinguish between the Antinomian inner light and the Familists' attachment to a spirit of divine love, this was probably not the case for most members of the Dorchester church.

Mather's accusation meant that a serious impediment had been placed in Burr's way, and it had to be removed before he could become a pastor to the church. Mather and Burr had to find some ground for mutual understanding so that Dorchester would not fall into error and the clerics could work harmoniously in the same church. To aid in reconciliation, Burr wrote out his differences with Mather and presented the teacher with a copy. The younger man's objections have not survived, and though Mather countered by charging there were numerous errors in the manifesto, there is no way of ascertaining their precise nature. The teacher only denounced Burr's doctrines as incorrect and insisted that Burr had placed so many qualifications upon his statements they were made to pass for the word of God. The controversy, already heated by Mather's emotional characterization of Burr as a Familist, grew intense when the teacher received the written set of differences that Burr had composed. Finding a chance to embarrass his opponent, Mather reported Burr's objections to the church, denounced the errors, but deliberately failed to speak of the qualifications the younger man had included with his statement of belief.

With this act, the rumblings in the church erupted into full schism, and a Burr faction formed in opposition to Mather's defenders. Unlike the Antinomian controversy, none of the documentation, if it ever existed, has survived from the Familist confrontation in Dorchester. The outlines of the disagreement probably centered on the relationship between the Holy Spirit, man, and the visible church. Familism embodied certain antinomian qualities that had been articulated by the Opinionists some years earlier, and so Burr and Mather probably differed on the nature of God's gift of justification—the two men contending over whether the elect consisted of a small segment of humanity who had received divine grace or whether much if not all of mankind was saved and that within each of those who had received salvation there dwelled the spirit of the true love of Jesus Christ. The accusations traded by both sides were surely exaggerated but, in all likelihood, the core of the difficulty was that Burr ascribed more of the spirit of divine love and inspiration to regenerates than Mather was willing to accept. Although the division in the church grew deeper as the days passed, the will to compromise did not vanish on the part of all concerned. Some elders and members spent many days trying to effect a reconciliation, but the opponents remained too far apart to worship the Lord together. It was apparent the matter would not be resolved in Dorchester. The members were forced to turn to the larger community for aid, and realizing the churches of the Bay Colony alone would be insufficient for the task, the civil authorities were called in to settle the dispute.[7]

A summons was sent, and in the winter chill of 1641, the arbitrators assembled in the divided village. The presence of Governor Winthrop emphasized the importance of the issues at stake and the widespread concern of the colonists over questions concerning Antinomianism, Familism, and any other doctrines that asserted divine inspiration or the indwelling of Holy Love or the Holy Spirit.

The proceeding droned on through four grim days, with the dozen participants hearing argument after argument and one lengthy rebuttal after another. Prayers and errors interspersed with reason and dialectics were presented, evaluated, and accepted or rejected.

In its conclusions, the conference endeavored to steer a middle course and condemned both parties. Burr's errors were denounced and Mather was censured by the colony's clergy and magistrates for making them public without their qualifications. The solution meant that the real or imagined threat of Familism was decisively rejected, and a possible danger to the colony's doctrines was curbed. Yet the censure pronounced on Mather enabled the Burr faction to retreat with little loss of face, while Mather, the senior in years, experience, and prestige, was compelled to submit humbly before the combined weight of the magistracy and the ministerial fellowship. Burr joined the chastened Mather and the two men confessed their mistakes while "the rest of the church yielded a silent assent, and God was much glorified in the close."[8] With the doctrinal impediments removed, the way was clear for the forging of a productive ecclesiastical partnership. If the vision of cooperative achievement was ever shared by the two clerics, that desire was not to reach fruition, for within the year Burr lay beneath the New England soil.[9]

The difficulties with Roger Williams, Anne Hutchinson, Robert Lenthall, and his own dispute with Burr were sufficient to make Mather realize, if he had not perceived it soon after landing in Massachusetts Bay, that the secular authorities were a basic part of church affairs even if congregational theory demanded organizational separation of the two. Yet these instances of interference were not the only examples of secular domination of the churches that he had witnessed. He had seen the magistrates dominate clerical officials either directly or indirectly in Salem, Piscataqua, Plymouth, and New Taunton, and he had even joined his fellow ecclesiastics in an unsuccessful protest against the General Court's attempt to restrict the number of lectures delivered each week in the colony.[10] The Erastian pattern that had developed was obvious not only to Mather but to at least one other contemporary observer of New England ways who remarked, "Every Church hath power of government in, and by it self; and no Church, or Officers, have power over one another but by way of advice or counsaile, voluntarily given or besought, saving that the generall Court, now and then, over-rule some Church matters."[11] The statement is accurate enough, except the assertion that the Court intervened "now and then" could be rendered more correctly by the phrase "when needed."

The court's interference was particularly noticeable to Mather in disputes over the correct form of church government. This had presented no problem of adjustment when Mather was newly arrived from England. Although a presbyterian-style ecclesiastical organization had been accepted by him and his fellow nonconformists in Lancashire, he had adapted to Cotton's congregationalism with no apparent difficulty. Other clerics, however, had not been so flexible. For a number of years, Thomas Parker and James Noyes, the clergymen at Newbury, had been expressing the opinion that the congregational form of church government needed a synodical authority with some power of enforcement, but their advocacy of a presbyterial-type superintending body did not become a threat until the successes of the presbyterians in the English civil wars. With the growing popularity of the rigid and highly structured Scottish form of control in the homeland, it was possible that those in the colony who favored a synod with power to make binding pronouncements in matters of doctrine would gain substantial support. Yet even the possibility of support from England was not enough to induce all the Newbury church members to agree with Parker and Noyes.

The conflict between the two groups progressively worsened as the strength of the colonists who favored presbyterian style modifications grew. When it became clear the rift was too deep to be mended by the church itself, representatives from several of the Massachusetts Bay churches were summoned to examine the problem and recommend a solution. In September 1643 the ruling elders of nearby churches, some fifty in all, assembled at Cambridge. Mather's attendance at the meeting was particularly crucial, for it was probably during this time, while the Newbury church members were divided over the proper form of church government, that Dorchester was experiencing a similar disruption as dissenters from the congregational pattern attempted to persuade their fellow townsmen to follow the lead of Parker and Noyes.[12]

The conclusions reached by the conference reflected a triumph for congregational polity. The assembled elders rejected the form of church government advocated by Parker and Noyes, deciding, among other things, "That Consociation of churches, in way of more general meetings . . . as Consultative Synods [only] are . . . necessary for the peace and good of the churches."[13] Clearly, there was to be no softening of congregational principles. The Newbury ministers and their supporters were not persuaded by the recommendations of the meeting, and they remained convinced of the divine prescription for synods with enforceable authority.[14]

The Newbury church's opposition to the congregational polity, strengthened as it was by events in England and by local dissatisfaction over restrictions on church membership, created an ominous situation in the colony; when combined with events in Hingham, the situation became dangerous. The Hinghamites, who also expressed presbyterian sympathies, were the first to attempt to gain concessions from the Bay Colony magistrates by threatening to carry their religious disagreement to England for resolution. A struggle over the command of the town's militia troop was the immediate occasion for the unrest in Hingham, and a faction that found itself in conflict with the magistrates over the selection of a commander challenged the charter powers of the colony's government. Their petition carried with it the implication of an appeal to England if they did not receive satisfaction. Given the differences between Massachusetts Bay's ecclesiastical polity and that of the presbyterians on the other side of the Atlantic, this would have been perilous for the colony. If the presbyterian-dominated government in the mother country could be persuaded to take the part of the Hingham dissenters, then the precedent would be set for continued involvement in colonial affairs.

The threatened appeal was never carried out. The General Court intervened at this juncture, imposed a settlement in the militia dispute, and dampened the enthusiasm of the Hingham minister for an appeal to England with the levy of a £20 fine. For a short while, the leaders of Massachusetts Bay thought the danger had been turned aside, but in this they were mistaken, for it was only a matter of time before presbyterians more determined than the Hinghamites sought to use their tactic to gain parliamentary support against the colony's magistrates. The attempt was made by William Vassall, one of the assistants named in the 1629 charter. Vassall and a group of supporters objected to several facets of colonial government, and they saw in a presbyterian appeal a way to gain support in London. The presbyterian threat from within and from across the ocean created a twofold problem for the clergy and magistrates of the Bay. They were determined to reject a Scottish-style polity and preserve their congregational organization, but they feared they could not do it if they were to antagonize the presbyterian Parliament. Alienating the home government and inviting intervention were unwise, but to create dissention among nonconformists when they were on the verge of triumph over episcopacy was unthinkable. Again the General Court would be forced to act, but by 1646 the courses of action open to them were not easily apparent.

The difficulties over questions of church polity and the danger of interference in colonial matters by the mother country were further complicated by severe local disagreement on questions of baptism and church membership. Baptism had presented no particular difficulty for the Bay Colonists before they left England. Most had received the sacrament as infants, and they, in turn, had their own newborn children baptized. When their doctrine changed after coming to America, the method used in the homeland was no longer satisfactory. In the process of adjusting their churches to the isolation of a new continent, the colonists discovered that God had commanded Christians to gather churches composed only of those who had received grace and thus were assured of salvation. To insure that their religious bodies included only these saints, the churches developed a complex system of examination, requiring applicants for membership to answer questions about their theological opinions and to relate publicly the reasons why they thought they were selected by God for salvation. This limited the number of those who were eligible for fellowship, but initially there seemed to be no danger in the practice, for the continuance of the colonial churches was assured not only by admitting new adult members but by joining the children of members to each church and confirming the association by the seal of baptism. According to the sequence of events envisioned by the colonial leaders, these children linked to the church by their parents' covenant would grow to adolescence, undergo a religious experience indicating that they were one of God's elect, communicate their assurance of salvation to the church, and be admitted to full membership with the right to vote and partake in the Lord's supper. The colonists were worldly enough to know that not all children of members would be saved, but their plan was predicated on the assumption that a sufficient number would receive grace so that the life of the churches would not be endangered.

The system would have worked well enough if events had followed the prescribed sequence, but this was often not the case. Many members' children grew to adulthood, married, and had children long before they underwent the requisite conversion experience. Others never received assurance of salvation. Though persons who were connected with a church solely by their parents' membership regularly failed to receive assurance of their own election, this failure did not mean they denied the veracity of the Christian religion. They remained believers; and as believers who had been joined to a church by birth, they naturally desired to extend this relationship to their own offspring. Any other course would mean that they, as followers of Christ, were the parents of children unconnected with any church; in effect, they would be raising families of heathen.

Yet it was dangerous for the churches of Massachusetts Bay to give the first sacrament to the children of baptized men and women who were not church members. By placing the seal on these infants, the church would be accepting persons whose spiritual condition was uncertain. To some, such an act was a violation of Christ's command that the church be pure. Thus, in most churches the sacrament was administered only to the infants of church members even though some residents of the colony had argued that when persons were baptized, the ceremony confirmed their association with the church, and if they had never been ejected or excommunicated they retained this association and their children were entitled to baptism.[15]

At the same time, while the churches had grown more restrictive, the number of baptized nonmembers who wanted the restrictions lifted was increasing. Their ranks were being swelled by many new immigrants who had been church members in England but found—as had the residents of Weymouth after 1638—that in Massachusetts Bay their newly born children were ineligible for baptism because the parents had been judged unfit for membership in the colony's churches. It was this dissatisfaction over baptism that brought the dissidents into a natural alliance with colonists who favored a presbyterian style of church government. The immigrants who were unhappy with Bay Colony practice on admission and baptism knew that those who favored presbyterian-type synods would be sympathetic to them, for if the two groups combined forces and obtained support from England, Massachusetts Bay might be forced to adopt a church polity similar in some respects to that in Scotland. If this were done, and the colony instituted authoritative synods and parishes where each resident was expected to be a church member and receive sacraments, all their common problems would be solved. This was a great deal to be hoped for—more, in fact, than many of the dissenters wanted—but to some it seemed not only desirable but possible.

By the time the interrelated difficulties of admission to the churches, eligibility for baptism, and the threat of English interference in colonial affairs arose in conjunction with the practices advocated in the towns of Newbury and Hingham, the efforts to reach a solution were made more difficult by the growth of a feeling of uneasiness among members of the colonial clergy in regard to the exercise of secular power. By 1646 de facto Erastianism had become the pattern in Massachusetts Bay, and the ministers had never seriously resisted its development, but even while the churches increasingly came under civil domination, there had always been a residue of suspicion among some over the growth of secular power in ecclesiastical affairs.

John Warham, Mather's predecessor, was one of the first to have misgivings about the expansion of secular power. From 1630 onward, Dorchester had used a system of parish membership following the English pattern, and this had created no problem while the Bay's churches were in a flexible state. But four years later, when church doctrine had been made more uniform by John Cotton and exclusive membership became the rule, Warham's position became uncomfortable. It was partially in response to disagreement over qualifications for church membership that he and Hooker ended their dispute with the civil government in the Bay by emigrating to Connecticut with many members of their churches. But this was not the end of clerical uneasiness. Again in 1639 several ministers, agitated over the increasing strength of the civil government, objected to the reelection of John Winthrop on the grounds that he might become governor for life. At the same time others complained about the projected reduction of the number of deputies in the General Court. The dissatisfied clerics were not successful in either of their protests. Winthrop was elected and the number of deputies was limited by law. Two years later some of the clerics opposed enactment of the *Body of Liberties*, but others favored the measure and again the objections were overridden and the code was adopted. The same pattern was apparent when those clerics who had misgivings about expanding secular power were ignored in their opposition to the standing council and to Winthrop's election in 1643.[16]

It was not until 1644 that the erratic and limited clerical opposition began to coalesce into discernible resistance to the civil government. One of the incidents that brought home to the ministerial community the defects in relying on continued support from the General Court was the dispute between Goodwife Sherman and Captain Robert Keayne over the ownership of a sow. By the time of this clash there had already been several disagreements between the deputies of the General Court and the assistants, but none had been as serious as this and none involved the ministerial brotherhood as deeply. To be sure, the case of the sow and the subsequent rearrangement of the colonial government into a bicameral legislature did not bring a dramatic reaction from the ministers. The hope of the majority was surely to preserve the association between church and state that had developed in the colony, but their perceptions of the courses of action best befitting a Christian commonwealth were often more in harmony with the assistants than with the deputies. After 1644 this meant there was one powerful segment of the Bay Colony government whose views were often out of kilter with those of the clergy, a clear sign that the civil authorities would not be nearly as reliable as allies as they had been in the past. Not that the views of the deputies were necessarily antiministerial; often they simply reflected legitimate differences of opinion. But while the ministers occasionally took the part of the deputies, they were usually counted on the side of the assistants against the representatives of the towns.[17]

Perhaps as important as the sow case in persuading clerics to reevaluate their dependence on the General Court were the petitions drawn by Vassall and others who hoped to get redress for their grievances. Behind the complaints of these men were diverse mixtures of religious and political motives, but their strategy of protest was the same, and at least from the Bay Colony clerics' point of view it held promise of being disturbingly successful. All the petitioners understood the nature of the institutional relationships in the colony. They saw clearly that the ecclesiastical settlement was superintended by the secular authorities and that their religious complaints could not be adjusted by appealing to their local churches. The only way to gain redress in Massachusetts Bay for religious grievances was by appeal to secular authority.[18]

Another factor directly related to the petitioners' challenge was their knowledge that the proportion of the Bay Colony's population that belonged to the churches was diminishing as the years passed. While this might have moved ministers closer to the magistrates as they attempted to induce the legislators to enact more laws to insure a godly climate in the colony, it also made them very uneasy. The ministers' years in England as members of an outgroup taught them the lesson of how power in the hands of the worldly constrained the freedom of the saints.[19] It did not take a great deal of reflection on their part to see that as the portion of the population that belonged to the churches diminished, the magistrates, under pressure from the petitioners, fearing English intervention, and alarmed at a growing segment of colonists who were profoundly dissatisfied, might take action to insure a broadening of church membership just as they had extended the franchise under pressure during the first years of settlement.

The specter of regulation of colonial religion by England frightened the clergy, but so also did the prospect of the petitioners' receiving a successful hearing from local authorities. If those among them who objected to church practices on admission and baptism were to exploit successfully the split between deputies and assistants and gain relief from the General Court, then much of Massachusetts congregationalism would be severely compromised. In retrospect it seems quite unlikely that this could have happened, but in 1646, it was not entirely beyond the bounds of possibility. With civil authority exerting power over the churches, this could occur if the General

Court did not continue its steadfast support of the churches. With the growth of presbyterial sentiment in the colony and the ever-widening schism in the General Court, this was eminently more possible than it had been in 1640. The very nature of congregationalism as well as reformed church doctrine prohibited a complete repudiation of secular involvement in religion. These years, in fact, saw the passage of a spate of laws designed to aid the church. But despite these efforts by the legislature to provide additional support for religious institutions, more and more of the clergy gradually realized that while they needed some secular support, the expansive powers of an unreliable General Court had to be restricted in ecclesiastical affairs if the safety of God's churches was to be assured.[20]

The shift was first evident in the writings of John Cotton. The tenor and direction of his work began to change around 1643 when he stopped defending congregationalism as a workable system and began justifying it as the true church of Christ.[21] This was not the only observable alteration at this point. He also began to express the suspicions some of his colleagues long had harbored of the civil government. When Cotton had written his *Way of the Churches of Christ in New England*, probably in late 1642 or early 1643, he placed great trust in the civil magistrates, even to the extent of involving them in the selection of ministers for individual churches. In his description of the way in which New Englanders chose their pastors and teachers, he indicated that after a church had settled on a likely man, "They give notice also thereof unto the Governour, and such other of the Magistrates, as are near to them, that the person to be chosen meeting with no just exception from any, may finde the greater incouragement and acceptance from all."[22] He was almost willing to concede to the magistrates in congregational theory what they had already put into practice: the right to limit the gathering of churches. In fact, he probably would have given them this right without restriction had it not occurred to him that both in biblical times and later in situations where the magistrates were not Christians, there was no need for official approval to form a church.[23]

Cotton was also quite willing to allow the state to correct erring churches, although he noted that when both church and state were "rightly ordered, and administered, one of them doth not intercept, but establish the execution of the other."[24] In his *Keys to the Kingdom of Heaven*, written only a short time after *The Way of the Churches of Christ in New England* but during the height of the colony's presbyterian problems and in the initial stages of the most serious dispute between the factions of the General Court, Cotton was still willing to acknowledge the power of the civil magistrates in ecclesiastical matters. Reformed doctrine required him to do so, but now he carefully qualified and restricted those powers. "Yet we would not be so understood," he wrote, "as if we judged it to belong to the civil power, to compel all men to come and sit down at the Lord's table, or to enter into the communion of the church, before they be in some measure prepared of God for such fellowship. For this is not a *reformation*, but a *deformation* of the church, and is not according to the word of God."[25] So that it was clearly understood that the power of the magistrates was not unlimited, Cotton added:

> Touching the subjection of churches to the civil state, in matters which concern the civil peace, this may not be omit-ted, that as the church is subject to the sword of the magis-trate in things which concern the civil peace: so the magistrate (if Christian) is subject to the keys of the church, in matters which concern the peace of his conscience and the kingdom of heaven. Hence it is prophesied by Isaiah, that kings and queens, who are nursing fathers and mothers to the church, *shall bow down to the church, with their faces to the earth* . . . that is, they shall walk in professed subjection to the ordinances of Christ in his church.[26]

In typical fashion, when evolution in any concept appeared in Cotton's work, Mather was not one to ignore it. Years before, in an early delineation of Bay Colony church practice written in 1639, Mather had been willing to give magistrates unlimited control over doctrine and the establishment of churches in the colony. He had written, "Who must have liberty to sit downe in this Common-wealth and enjoy the liberties thereof is not our place to determine, but the Magistrates who are the rulers and governours of the Com-mon-wealth, and of all persons within the same. And as for acknowl-edging a company to be a sister Church, that shall set up, and practice another forme of Church Discipline, being otherwise in some measure . . . approveable, we conceive the companie that shall so doe, shall not be approveable therein."[27] There is no room for equivocation in this view, yet after the events of the early 1640s, Mather changed drastically. His perceptions of church and state by the time of the synod of 1646 had altered substantially, as had Cotton's, and by 1648 he was seconding Cotton's demands for the limitation of magisterial authority in church matters.

Some of the events that may have influenced Mather's change of opinion were the disputes in the General Court caused by clerical disagreements over eligibility for admission and baptism, the worry over presbyterianism at Hingham and Newbury, and the fear of English interference in colonial affairs. Many clergymen were also deeply disturbed over these difficulties, and knowing they could not resolve them alone, the elders, or at least a segment of them, followed precedent and turned to the General Court. They asked the legislature to call a synod to discuss the festering problems. The upper house of the General Court acceded to the elders' request and passed the bill, but this time all did not go according to plan. The deputies, already challenging the assistants' position, refused to follow the upper house, opposing instead the combined authority of the elders and the assistants as they had done earlier on several other questions. They denounced the action on the grounds that the civil government had no authority to call a synod or to compel churches to assemble. The true purpose of the synod, they asserted, was to create a pattern of church discipline. In denying the court's right to call a synod, the deputies were challenging precedent. The General Court had convened comparable meetings in the past, although it had done so more often by pressure than by enactment. The deputies' charge that at least some members of the colony's leadership were trying to establish an Erastian pattern of civil dominance of the church was a bit late. This pattern had already developed. The deputies' move against institutionalizing it was not a step to prevent its establishment but was another phase of their struggle against the assistants and their clerical supporters.

The legislative impasse created by the deputies' refusal was bridged when the upper house consented to ask rather than order a synod to meet at Cambridge in 1646. The request was made, the lower house gave its assent, and the synod convened on schedule. Despite the compromise between the deputies and assistants, many still expressed doubt that the General Court had authority to convene such an assembly. The Boston church refused to attend, and even after the efforts of John Norton of Ipswich to justify the manner of the calling of the synod, it was only by parliamentary skulduggery that representatives from the church were sent to Cambridge.[28]

The synod was charged with finding solutions to the problems of doctrinal deviation and baptism. They were authorized to meet as long as necessary to transact the required business. With the first winds of approaching winter hinting at the lateness of the season, Richard Mather journeyed from Dorchester to Cambridge to join representatives from the other Bay Colony churches at the appointed work. The number present was small—perhaps indicating even more dissatisfaction than was apparent—but the limited attendance did not prevent the September meeting from lasting two weeks. The participants discussed a wide variety of religious topics and agreed implicitly to preserve Mather's previously accepted 1639 statement of support for individual church independence when he had said that the colonists "dare not so far restraine the particular Churches as fearing this would be to give the *Classes* an undue power and more then belongs unto them by the Word; as being also an abridgment of that power which Christ hath given to every particular Church to transact their owne matters (whether more or lesse weighty) among themselves. . . . And for Synods, if they have such power that their determination shall binde the Churches to obedience . . . it is more then we yet understand."[29]

The report issued by the synod indicated that in addition to church government, one of its foremost subjects of consideration had been the relationship between the churches and the civil magistrates. Although the report stated that these difficult topics should be committed to further study, they were, in fact, discussed at length in the synod.[30] The clerics, sensitive to the accusations that they were being dominated by the magistrates, strove to assert their independence. The magistrates and others who were concerned with the limits of civil power were informed that the General Court could call "an Assembly, and that for the same end that a Synod meetes for, namely, to consider of, and clear the truth from the Scriptures, in weighty matters of Religion: But such an Assembly called and gathered without the consent of the Churches, is not properly that which is usually understood by a Synod, for though it be in the power of the Magistrate to Call, yet it is not in his power to Constitute a Synod, without at least the implicite consent of the Churches."[31] If the meaning of this, with its inherent proscriptions, was not clear to some, the synod added, "Churches can Constitute a Synod without the consent of the Magistrate, although the Magistrate cannot Constitute a Synod without the consent of the Churches."[32] To soothe one segment of colonial opinion, the synod declared that civil power would not be used against "godly, moderate, and Orthodox Presbyterians, if any such should desire their liberty here."[33] Thus, despite the earlier assertions of Cotton and Winthrop, and the insistence of John Norton of Ipswich that the General Court could summon a synod in 1646 as it had done earlier, the meeting rejected the action of those among them who had asked the General Court to call a synod, reserving that power for the churches. Before adjourning, the conclave instructed John Cotton, Mather, and Ralph Partridge, a cleric from Duxbury, to draw up models of church government to be presented at the next meeting scheduled for the following June.[34]

The selection of Mather to compose one of the draft platforms of church government was a recognition on the part of his colleagues of his reliability in theological matters as well as the experience he had gained in carrying out similar tasks in earlier years. His *Answer to Two and Thirty Questions* and *An Apologie* added to his various encounters with the colony's detractors had shown him to be a man of requisite capabilities who harbored no dangerous opinions of the sort that had created so many agonizing doctrinal confrontations in past years. Yet in selecting Mather, the members of the synod were apparently unaware of the resentments that simmered within the man they had chosen. Only he could recall the disappointment of being considered unfit for membership in the Boston church or the humiliation when the church he had gathered was forced to submit to examination and was then rejected by an aggregation of clerics and magistrates who doubted its worthiness. To these insults, he added bitter memories of the forced compromise with Burr, the refusal to allow him to participate, except in a peripheral way, in any defense of the colony's religion, and the failure of his "Plea for the Churches of Christ in New England" and his catechisms to gain for him the honor he was convinced he richly deserved. The host of rebuffs and degradations were all remembered, and when his colleagues sought to have him construct a model of church government, they gave him the opportunity to vent the frustration of a decade. When the synod assembled to adopt a religious statement for New England's churches, Mather would be ready.

The following spring, the council met again to consider the subjects of church government, baptism, and membership, but it was not destined to remain long in session. Shortly before it convened, an epidemic began to sweep across the country. The first symptoms of the disease were similar to those of a cold with fever, but the colonists who bled or drank cooling liquids to counter the temperature died. There were some forty or fifty deaths in Massachusetts alone, and a like number succumbed in Connecticut. Before the ravages of the disease passed, death had taken Thomas Hooker of Hartford as well as Margaret Winthrop, the third wife of the governor. Before Mather could present his work for serious debate, the fear engendered by the malady brought a precipitate closing of the meeting.[35]

In the months that followed, while Mather continued to revise his platform, the General Court gave another task to the members of the synod. The occasion for the added assignment was the news that the Westminster Assembly—still in session in London—had prepared a confession of faith for the English church. Parliament had not yet approved the work, but the Scots' General Assembly had already given its imprimatur. The New Englanders, unaware of the confession's content and suspicious of the presbyterian orientation of the Scots, knew they had to act to prevent outbursts of anticongregational feeling by those who were hostile to local church practice. The colonists decided to preempt the Assembly and issue a New England statement of faith before the English document arrived in the colony. The General Court ordered the synod to "set fourth a confession of the faith ... touching the doctrinall part of religion."[36] Since this had been the direction given by the 1646 meeting of the synod, there was no jurisdictional controversy. The court's order assigned the labor to Mather, John Cotton, and five other clerics.[37] Each man was ordered to "prepare a briefe forme of this nature, and present the same to the next session of the synode," when it reconvened the following year. Ralph Partridge, who had been appointed with Mather and Cotton to compose a draft by the synod of 1646, was not among those who received the civil government's commission.

A decade earlier, in his *Answer to Two and Thirty Questions*, Richard Mather had spoken against the casting of written platforms of church discipline. Enumerating their defects, he said that in addition to being unnecessary, they were likely to cause men to observe the external forms of religion while ignoring its spiritual and divine substance. Later, when he, Cotton, and Partridge were assigned to construct an outline of church government, he modified his position and labored unstintingly on his share of the appointed business. Although his draft model of church government contained much of what he had written in his answer to the thirty-two questions, and while he also relied heavily on the works of John Cotton, Mather's suggested platform represented a dramatic departure from earlier New England statements of faith.[38]

In August 1648 the synod reconvened at Cambridge. When the representatives turned to the work at hand, they had two drafts of suggested church governments to consider. The first of these was written by Ralph Partridge who, in the antimagisterial spirit of 1646, ignored the most recent order of the General Court that excluded him from the drafting committee and arrived at the synod ready to present his model of church government. Of the seven men actually ordered to participate in the casting of a platform by the General Court, only Mather had prepared an outline of doctrine and polity. Unlike Partridge's simple statement of faith and delineation of church practice, Mather offered a wide-ranging and full-bodied examination of almost every facet of the colony's ecclesiastical system. His "Modell of Church Government" covered the whole expanse of Bay Colony procedures, discussing at length subjects such as the general nature of the invisible and visible churches, pastors, teachers, ruling elders, deacons, intrachurch administration, and excommunication. There was even a section on the item that had occasioned Mather so much discomfort during his first months in the colony, the imposition of hands in ordination. This time he did not stumble on the issue. Although by 1648 the disagreements surrounding the laying on of hands had long been settled, he felt, nonetheless, obliged to devote two of his eighteen chapters to the topic and explain in detail not only for English readers but for his colleagues and possibly for himself the nature of the ceremony and its spiritual and logical justifications. The synod accepted Mather's description of the ordination practices and included it in the finished statement, later to be published as the Cambridge Platform, but before doing so, the synod eliminated much of his overcompensating reason and citation, compressing his lengthy discussions into one succinct chapter.[39]

If Mather was disappointed about the redaction of his segment on ordination, he must have been even more sensitive about the rejection of his ideas on baptism. Since 1646 he had come to accept the scriptural warrant for broadening the eligibility requirements for the first sacrament, thereby accepting the idea that there was divine sanction for baptizing the children of baptized but unregenerate parents. He wrote his newly accepted view into the "Modell of Church Government" saying,

> And further, such as are borne in the church as members, though yet they be not found fitt for the Lords Supper, yet if they be not culpable of such scandalls in conversation as do justly deserve church censures, it seemeth to us, when they are marryed and have children, those their children may be received to Baptisme. . . . these their children are in the covenant, they may be received to the seale of the covenant, this being the mayne ground which other children are admitted thereto: and it is scarce reasonable and equall that these being partakers of the ground of Baptisme as well as others, that nevertheless others should be admitted and these be refused . . . reason requireth that these as well as others should share in the priviledges therein.[40]

This paragraph was omitted entirely from the published platform, and the Bay Colony continued to reject all attempts to widen eligibility for baptism.

Mather's modest treatment of ordination and his acceptance of the elimination of his views on baptism indicated, perhaps, that he

was anxious to prove again his orthodoxy or at least his reasonable-
ness, but in his chapter on the relationship between civil and ecclesiastical authorities in the colony, he did not reflect any conciliatory
mood. In his concluding section of "Modell of Church Government," the full force of his years of suppressed resentment poured
forth as he denounced the subjugation of the colony's churches to
the General Court. His own caution of previous years was abandoned
and the equivocation of Cotton in his *Keys to the Kingdom of
Heaven* was rejected entirely as Mather vented his rage. He wrote:

> It is not unlawfull for Christians to gather themselves into
> church estate, and therein to exercise all the ordinances of
> Christ according to the word, although the consent of Magis-
> trates could not be had thereto; as is manifest from the
> example of the Apostles and Christians in their tymes, who did
> frequently thus practise when the magistrates being all of them
> Jewish, or Pagan, and mostly persecuting enemies, would give
> no countenance nor consent to such matters. And if it was
> then practised by them . . . in those dayes, and even under
> Christian magistrates, may have the like liberty. How if these
> things were lawfull, needfull, and profitable when magistrates
> were enemies to the profession of the Gospell . . . the saints of
> God should bee loosers and in worse condition by having
> Christian magistrates, then if they had none but professed
> enemies and so the arrest of christianity in the magistrate
> should make his power not cumulative, but privative to the
> church which may not be.[41]

To make sure that there was no misunderstanding of his view on the
role of secular authorities, he added that magistrates had no lawful
power to restrict the churches and since their consent was not
necessary to make any practice lawful, no practice could be unlawful
through want of their consent.[42]

Mather's opposition to the power of the civil authorities was not
confined only to their general superintendency of the Bay's
churches; it also challenged their interference in specific matters.
The organization of new churches was one of the areas where Mather
moved to restrict the power of the secular government. As he wrote
that "it is not in the power of magistrates to hinder the saints of god
under their government from entering into church estate, and there-

in observing the ordinances of Christ according to the rule of his word," he surely thought back to that April day in 1636 when under a newly passed law the magistrates refused him permission to gather his church.[43] Now he had his opportunity to reply and he used it to the fullest not only to deny the right of the secular powers to pass and enforce such an edict but also to prevent them from acquiescing to presbyterian demands and compromising colonial church purity by adopting the Scottish style of parish membership. To his prohibition against the restricting of new churches he added "neither is it in their power to compell all their subjects to become church members, and to partake at the Lords Table. . . . We conceive it is easye to judge how unlikely a thing it is, that both these should be the will of god, both that magistrates with the Civill Sword should compell men into the church and then the church and elders with the spiritt sword should keepe out, or cast out the same persons, whom the other one compelling or have compelled to come in."[44]

Mather's revenge against the secular authorities was a full-scale denunciation comprising a complete chapter in his draft platform, but any joy he took in striking a blow at his tormentors was short-lived. Though both Mather and his sons claimed in later years that the "Platforme agreed upon by the synod . . . and this of [Mather's] being compared, it may approve that the doctrine herein . . . expressed and delivered was well approved of by that Reverend and juditious Assembly," nevertheless, a large portion of that which made the "Modell of Church Government" a unique product of Richard Mather was removed before the finished Cambridge Platform was made public.[45] Much of the reduction was necessitated by Mather's concept of a platform which differed in some degree from that envisioned by the synod. In writing his draft, Mather, always the defender of Massachusetts Bay's religion, was bent on producing an apologia for congregational practice, while the synod wanted a more direct statement of doctrine and polity. To produce the latter, the assembly pared large sections of justifying argument and scores of examples Mather had used to substantiate every point. These, however, were only superficial eliminations. It was in his final section of the draft platform that the synod's editing changed substantially the tone and content of Mather's anti-Erastian polemic. It did not, of course, eliminate completely his attempt to restrict the power of the magistrates. The resistance of the deputies to the ordering of the synod to convene and the report of the first session in 1646 indicated there was too much support for the synod to make the elimination. But by the time the platform was agreed upon, much of Mather's anger had been removed. Although the synod accepted his dictum that "It is lawfull, profitable, and necessary for christians to gather themselves into Church estate . . . although the consent of Magistrate could not be had therunto," it eliminated the succeeding antimagisterial sentence that said "the saints of God should bee loosers and in woorse condition by having Christian magistrates, then if they had none but professed enemies" if the General Court were to be allowed, as it was in the colony, to pass judgment on the qualifications of those who desired to gather a church.[46]

At another point, when Mather spoke even more specifically and without equivocation for the limiting of the secular powers in religious matters, the assembly deleted the entire section, simply ignoring his pronouncement that "magistrates have no power from god to hinder [observance of God's ordinances] . . . . And if they may not lawfully hinder therein, then their consent is not absolutely necessary to make such practice lawfull before god. For how can any practise be unlawfull through want of their consent, who have no lawfull power by their dissent to hinder the same?"[47] When Mather spoke of the magistrates' power over church membership, the synod and the cleric were in accord in rejecting governmental authority, but the synod was more subtle, saying only that the civil government did not have the power to select church members. The point was illustrated as gently as possible with the example of the Levites who brought the uncircumcised into the sanctuary. Omitted entirely from the work accepted by the synod was Mather's blunt assertion that "it is easye to judge how unlikely a thing it is, that both these should be the will of god, both that magistrates with the Civill Sword should compell men into the church and then the church and elders with the spiritt sword should . . . cast out the same."[48]

Rather than accept Mather's uncompromising rejection of civil authority, the members of the synod retreated to the safer ground of qualification and replaced his statement with a passage designed to mitigate the abrasive attack on the magistrates. The passage, taken from Ralph Partridge's draft, assured officials that "Church-government stands in no opposition to civil government of common-welths, nor intrencheth upon the authority of Civil Magistrates in their jurisdictions; nor any whit weakneth their hands in governing; but rather strengthneth them, and furthereth the people in yielding more hearty and conscionable obedience unto them, whatsoever some ill affected persons to the wayes of Christ have suggested."[49]

Even in its rejection of civil authority, the synod of 1646-1648 could not suppress its conditioned subjugation to the secular power as Mather had tried to do. It insisted upon receiving the General Court's imprimatur. The document was presented to that body in October 1649, but it was not immediately accepted. Instead, the assistants and deputies followed a more cautious path. After some debate, they elected to "commend it to the judicyous and pious consideration of the seuerall churches within this jurisdiction, desiring a retourne from them at the next Gennerall Courte hou farr it is suitable to their judgments and approbation before the Courte proceeds any farther therein."[50] When the objections to the completed platform were returned to the synod, the elders appointed Mather as head of a committee to compile a reply.[51]

Only a small number of churches and individuals took the proffered opportunity to object to the Cambridge Platform. Three churches, those of Malden, Salem, and Wenham, formally opposed some of the platform's features, and of the thousands of church members in the colony, only three raised specific complaints. This small number could hardly have heartened Mather even though he, more than any other man, was responsible for the platform. While he had fought for his position on baptism and been defeated and seen his strong stand against secular power emasculated, none of the objections to the work of the synod concerned these subjects. For the most part, the objections consisted of presbyterian attacks, indicating that those to whom a major portion of the Cambridge Platform was directed were not intimidated by it. Even then, the complainants repeated their opposition to a congregational polity and once again asserted their support for a measure of synodical authority. They ignored all other ramifications of the adoption of a presbyterian system. When the platform with the answers to the objections was returned to the court, the upper house unanimously gave its approval to the work. The deputies, however, were not of a single mind. Fourteen of them refused to vote ratification. Two of the recalcitrants were from Salem and another was from Wenham—the churches of both towns had presented objections to the platform that were presbyterial in nature—and one of those deputies who voted earlier in the negative had offered over a dozen presbyterian protestations of his own.[52]

Certainly it was not a day of unbounded joy for Mather when, in 1651, the General Court thanked the elders for their service and approved the Cambridge Platform, stating its contents were what they "Have practiced and doe beleeve." Even in the approval there was little solace for Mather. The lower house—whose opposition to secular domination of the churches in 1646 had created the original crisis over the calling of the synod—expressed some opposition once again, but this time it was only from those who sought to establish authoritative synods in the colony. No deputy seconded Mather's calls for broader baptism and restrictions on civil power.[53]

Although Mather was profoundly disappointed at the synod's failure to accept several of the positions in the "Modell of Church Government," the Cambridge Platform, nonetheless, did not represent a complete defeat for him.[54] Although the segment dealing with the division of power between church and state was drained of Mather's venom, he had managed to make his point. The synod was compelled to explain in detail its view of how the civil and ecclesiastical governments should continue working together, and their explanation was hardly a reflection of the situation that had evolved in the colony during two decades of settlement. Instead of English-style Erastianism, the court would become the servant of the church according to the Cambridge Platform. Following Mather's lead, the synod stated, "It is lawfull, profitable and necessary for christians to gather themselves into Church estate . . . according unto the word" with or without the consent of the magistrate.

Nine articles followed, demonstrating that the elders clearly saw the state as a servant of the churches and not the other way around. "The powr and authority of the Magistrates is not for the restraining of churches, or any other good workes" and though the task of the magistrates was, among other things, to assure godliness of the subjects, they were given to understand that this did not imply authority over church affairs. In ecclesiastical matters such as gathering, excommunication, eligibility for the Lord's supper, or failure of a congregation to pay its minister, the civil government had no authority.

The synod also accepted Mather's view on the method of forming new churches. The course adopted by the synod represented a singular departure from the 1636 practice, when the General Court had caused Mather so much difficulty and humiliation by ordering all who wanted to gather a new church first to apply to the civil authorities for permission and then denying freemanship to those who were not members of approved churches.[55] In 1648 the synod entirely rejected supervision by the magistrates. When new churches were gathered, the Cambridge Platform specified only that "it is requisite for their safer proceeding, and the maintaining of the communion of churches, that they signifie their intent unto the neighbour-churches, walking according unto the order of the Gospel, and desire their presence, and help, and right hand of fellowship which they ought readily to give unto them, when there is no just cause of excepting against their proceedings."[56]

The same pattern held true on questions of admission to the Lord's supper. This had created a problem for a number of years, and although most clerics favored the exclusion of all but the regenerate from the sacrament, and had been firmly supported by the General Court on this issue, there was some uneasiness about the continued reliability of their secular support. As presbyterian sentiment grew, they worried that the court might capitulate to those who demanded an enlargement of eligibility for communion and retreat from its support of ecclesiastical purity. Cotton had already taken the initiative to forestall any movement in this direction in 1644 when he wrote, "we would not be so understood, as if we judged it to belong to the civil power, to compel all men to come and sit down at the Lord's table, or to enter into the communion of the church." Cotton, however, was unwilling to make the breach complete. He carefully prefaced his statement with remarks designed to ease the sensitivities of any civil authorities he might have offended. "Nevertheless, . . . we willingly acknowledge a power in the civil magistrate," he said, "to establish and reform religion, according to the word of God."[57]

Four years later, there was no need for Mather and the members of the synod to be so careful to propitiate the magistrates. The Cambridge Platform described at length the requirements for admission to the Lord's supper, but made no gesture in the direction of magisterial power. Even on the matter of a church that refused to provide adequate maintenance for its minister, the General Court could issue an order for payment only after the church had given its permission to the civil government to act.[58] Similarly, the clergy were no longer willing to accept interference in the affairs of individual churches. When the General Court had entered the Weymouth dispute over the doctrines of Robert Lenthall in 1637, it had been welcomed, and even in the disruption between Mather and Burr that induced schism in the Dorchester church, the civil authorities had been asked to participate. But by the time of the synod's meeting in 1648, the situation had changed. Both Mather's draft and the completed Cambridge Platform included a set of procedures to correct erring elders and members, but nowhere did it mention a need for assistance from the civil magistrates. The only issue on which the elders and messengers hesitated was on the question of the General Court's authority to call a synod. Retreating from the position taken in their preliminary report of 1646, they conceded the magistrates' right to do this. But even here they qualified their concession by adding that the churches could call a synod with or without the consent of the magistrates and, if need be, against their will.[59]

Mather's "Modell of Church Government" was an undisguised attempt to secure clerical independence from secular domination, but the platform that emerged from the synod had mitigated much of what the draft had contained. Yet the Cambridge Platform was not simply an affirmation of the status quo but also a major step in the direction of diminishing civil superintendency of church affairs. Other attempts to limit the power of the General Court had been made earlier with the adoption of the *Body of Liberties* in 1641 and the attempted impeachment of Governor Winthrop four years later, but the Cambridge Platform was at least as significant as either of these in shaping the relationship between church and state.[60] To be sure, the platform did not prohibit the General Court from participating in the colony's religious affairs. Though rejecting civil participation in many areas, Mather and his colleagues knew they needed the compulsive force of the civil authorities to enforce behavioral norms required in a Christian colony. To retain this power they included a succinct and specific list of cases where the aid of magistrates would be needed for punishing idolatry, blasphemy, and heresy. In cases of schism, where the churches had first determined the correct course to be followed, the court would be needed to eradicate erroneous opinion. But if any magistrate were to carry his power to an extreme as a result of this concession, he would be restrained not only by the pronouncements of the synod against the use of civil power to regulate essential ecclesiastical functions such as prescribing the form of church government, specifying membership qualifications, and directing intrachurch administration but also by the synod's prohibition of the exercise of secular authority against those characterized as having hardness of heart, erroneous opinions, or having committed acts that were not clear violations of scripture.

The profound effect of the Cambridge Platform as an antisecular document was not apparent to Mather and his colleagues when it was completed in 1648 or when it was accepted by the General Court in 1651, but its importance becomes clear in light of ensuing developments in Massachusetts Bay. Although there was continuing interference in church functions after approval of the platform—and a portion of it was at the behest of the clergy—this interference was limited to minor disputes.[61] On questions with far-ranging and profound religious implications, the court's role was visibly altered by the new clerical sentiment for independence. The body was no longer able to exercise powers of superintendency and arbitration.

As early as 1653, only two years after the approval of the platform, the secular powers attempted to restrict lay preaching. In its efforts to do this, the General Court met the ministerial community in a head-on confrontation. The clergy, supported by petitions from several towns, were able to protect themselves and exert enough power to force repeal of the restriction.[62] Later, on the more fundamental disagreement over eligibility for baptism, the General Court's relationship with the clergy again represented a singular departure from the pre-1648 pattern. In contrast to the pivotal position it had taken on matters of church operation in earlier years, the secular power no longer dominated the debate, and the court became instead a pawn in the ministerial confrontation between the advocates and opponents of the 1662 synod. Initially, the General Court had expressed some support for the synod's recommendation to extend eligibility for baptism and had given its support to the clerical majority, but, indicative of the new mood among the colony's ministry, those of the antisynodalian faction made it clear that they would not tolerate the same degree of interference in this division of opinion that had characterized the court's actions in the earlier disputes with Roger Williams, Anne Hutchinson, the presbyterian disagreements, and several smaller confrontations. Some of their boldness in opposing the legislature was undoubtedly due to their position within colonial society. Any attempts to restrict or censure respected members of the community such as Charles Chauncy, John Mayo, and two of Richard Mather's sons—who differed with their father and opposed the determination of the synod—would have been virtually impossible. But lest there be any misunderstanding and the court think that it could circumscribe the activities of these men, they stated explicitly they would not defer to attempts, either secular or ecclesiastical, to silence them.

The dissidents began a program of publication and agitation that was unparalleled in the colony's history. Its purpose was to win lay support and thereby pressure the court into espousing their views. The same course of action was adopted by Mather and the majority party in the synod; thus the court was subjected to the assault of two groups, each trying to gain support for its position. This sort of tactic could hardly have been used in earlier years when the legislature was accustomed to a pliant ministry willing to accept its lead. Mather wrote against the antisynodalians and he fully supported Jonathan Mitchel, the chief spokesman for the synodalians, when he abandoned any vestige of humility toward the court in his election sermon of 1667. In it Mitchel informed the legislators that they must remember their place and keep to it. "The people are not for the Rulers," he said, "but the Rulers for the people. . . . and the more aptly and fully that any do serve to their End, the better and more excellent they are." The problems of reform created by the synod's decision were part of a normal progression of events. Even in Nehemiah's time "there were faults, evils . . . sinful Corruptions and Distempers . . . among a Reforming people," he added, and then went on to prophesy, "To leave the Children of non-scandalous Orthodox Christians Unbaptized, will (I doubt not) be one day found a thing displeasing unto Jesus Christ." God, Mitchel added, would not smite a nation in the process of reform, for this was true Reformation.[63] The following year, the election sermon was less to Mather's liking. In 1668 William Stoughton, who held the opposite point of view, preached a lengthy jeremiad calling for a return to the faith of the colony's founders and warning the court, "There is no Errour in Doctrine, or in Worship and Ordinances, but it tends some way or other to alter, pervert, and corrupt the Lords Covenant with his people. By this we are to judge of the danger of Errours and erroneous practices, and answerably to watch against the infection of them."[64]

The result of this less-than-subtle persuasion was not to convince the court of the correctness of either the synodalian or antisynodalian position, but to confuse and divide it, making it less able to exert leadership in the face of determined ministerial assault. The inability of the legislature to unite against the antithetical forces seeking to influence it was made even more apparent when disagreements over the administration of baptism became the focal point for a bitter quarrel over the secession of a synodalian faction from the First Church in Boston. The situation, abrasive enough from the beginning, became explosive when the majority in the First Church called one of the leading antisynodalians, John Davenport, to be teacher of the church.

After his arrival from New Haven, Davenport attempted to persuade the General Court to support his church in its refusal to allow the synodalian minority to depart and gather a separate church. In his election sermon of 1669 he made no pretense of seeking accommodation. He warned the court that its limited support for the decision of the synod was an abuse of its civil power, stating, "The People so give Magistratical Power unto some, as that still they retain in themselves these Three Acts, 1. That they may measure out so much Civil Power, as God in his Word alloweth to them. . . . 2. That they may set bounds and banks to the exercise of that Power. . . . 3. That they give it out conditionally . . . so as, if the condition be violated, they may resume their power of chusing another." He then offered his judgment to those who sought ecclesiastical reform, saying, "Take heed of a various management of manners of Religion, to the advantage of the present postures and condition of your Civil Affairs. . . . All God's Truths are Eternal and Unchangeable by men." To the court and to those members who objected to the doctrine of the First Church he advised, "Take heed and beware that you deprive not any Instituted Christian Church . . . of the Power and Priviledges which Christ hath purchased for them by his precious blood."[65]

Davenport's sermon only divided the court more sharply, with the deputies, the governor, and a handful of assistants coming out publicly in favor of the First Church, and the majority of the assistants giving their support to the synodalian dissenters who, some days before the sermon, had actually gathered their own church. The dispute grew in intensity in the following months, and the debate over the issues became so widespread that it touched almost every person in the colony. Not since the time of the Antinomian crisis in 1637 had an ecclesiastical disagreement created so much partisanship. The heat generated by the controversy was well illustrated by the actions of the deputies, most of whom were advocates of the antisynodalian faction. Piqued by the refusal of the assistants to join them and incensed over the clerical majority's position in opposition to their own, the deputies vented their rage in a blast of anticlericalism unparalleled in the colony's history. The ministers were accused by a majority of the deputies of "declension from the primitive foundation worke, innovation in doctrine and worship, opinion and practice, and invasion of the rights, liberties, and priuiledges of churches . . . and all this with a dangerous tendencie to the vtter devastation of these churches, turning the pleasant gardens of Christ into a wildernesse . . . that these are the leven, the corrupting gangreens, the infecting spreading plague . . . the chiefe incendaries of wrath and procurers of judgment on the land."[66]

By 1669, when the controversy over the calling of Davenport was at its height, the independent-spirited clergy responded with a flurry of unprecedented political activity designed to chastise those deputies who supported the anticlerical manifesto by defeating them at the next election. The details of the ministerial campaign are obscure, but it is apparent that through the winter of 1670 and the spring of 1671, the clergy campaigned extensively to elect men sympathetic to their views. The battle was fought on the question of whether the electorate supported the right of the synodalians to secede from their own antisynodalian First Church and form the Third Church in Boston. In May the clerical candidates won an overwhelming victory and in doing so changed the complexion of Massachusetts Bay politics. In earlier years the makeup of the lower house had changed slowly, but after the election of 1671, a new majority was in command. Freshly elected synodalian deputies outnumbered the opposition by a margin of four to three. The election had so aroused passions that thirteen towns changed their representation entirely, and a number of towns that in the past had neglected to send any representatives now did so, thereby enlarging the house by one-third. A few towns increased the size of their delegations from one to two representatives.

When the General Court reconvened, the clergy, greatly buoyed by their electoral triumph, replied to the charges levied by the previous lower house. The expected rebuttal was graciously accepted by the new members, and although those deputies still in the legislature who had the year before voted to condemn the clergy insisted their negative votes on recantation be counted, this did not veil the fact that the ministers had challenged the civil power of the Massachusetts Bay Colony and won a singular victory. Confirmation of this was not long in coming. Shortly thereafter, Thomas Shepard, Jr., while lamenting the deterioration of the cooperative spirit between leaders of church and state, denounced publicly the previous attempts of the magistracy to control the clergy, saying that while the civil government needed to exert power against the Antinomians and presbyterians, this power could become dangerous when men failed to distinguish between the magistrates' legal exercise and their abuse of that power in trying to regulate the churches.[67] Later, Urian Oakes repeated the same restrictions on the General Court. After denouncing the antisynodalians as those who "gloried in their Rebellion against the Authority of Christ in his Churches," he informed the court that "it is the duty of the Civil Magistrate to tolerate what is tolerable, and that some Errors are tolerable as to the practice of them. For the Conscience [of] our persuasion about them is not immediately under the Magistrates Cognizance."[68]

The events in Massachusetts Bay that followed the synod of 1662 would have been inconceivable in the years before the promulgation of the Cambridge Platform, and although there was a complex of causes—some local in nature and others directly related to events in England—for the decline in the General Court's Erastian dominance, Mather's "Modell of Church Government" and the platform derived from it are two of the most visible and influential of these. They were officially produced statements of the direction being taken in the colony's second decade of development, and, more important, they indicated that Mather and some of his clerical and lay associates had departed from the traditional English pattern of church and state relations. The first wrenching rejection of secular dominance came over eligibility for baptism and the schism in the First Church, but this confrontation did not grow from unprepared soil. A large part of the independent clerical spirit that challenged the General Court in 1671 had been planted and nurtured in the seedbed of Richard Mather's frustrations during the 1640s, and although he did not live to see the fruition of his work in the colony, the inclusion of Mather's views in the Cambridge Platform gave it the necessary form and structure to serve as the intellectual, legal, moral, and theological underpinning for a clerical revolt that would end finally with complete separation of church and state.

VI.

The Halfway Covenant

The questions surrounding baptism were not new to Mather when he was first appointed to produce a draft platform of church government in 1646. His concern over eligibility developed during his first years in America as a natural outgrowth of the restrictions on church membership in the colony. By the time Mather arrived in Boston in 1635, church membership had already become exclusive in Massachusetts Bay, but, as he later found, this exclusiveness had created at least one problem serious enough to require the attention of several of the colony's clerics. John Cotton, Thomas Oliver, and Thomas Leverett had been asked in 1634 about the advisability of baptizing a child whose parents did not belong to a church but whose grandparents were members. They concluded that the child could receive the first sacrament only under the condition that he be committed to the grandparents for education and that the parents would endeavor to join a church.[1]

Mather arrived in the colony shortly after this decision had been rendered, and whatever his opinion of the decision may have been, he chose not to reveal it. Although it differed from the presbyterial-style of sacramental administration that he had used in Lancashire, his own difficulties with local authorities over admittance and gathering the church probably persuaded him of the wisdom of avoiding further confrontations. He had no real choice in the matter. Since he could not return to England, he had to remain in the colony with his wife and children and to support ecclesiastical decisions either explicitly or implicitly by silence. Writing to a friend in England in 1636, Mather did mention that there was some disagreement in the colony over the proper method of baptizing, but he did not see fit at this point to communicate his own position. He said only that believers and their "seed" could receive the sacrament. Prudently he did not elaborate on the definition of the term seed, thereby concealing his exact opinion.[2] Caution remained Mather's watchword on the matter, and it was not until three years later, when opinion on the question of sacramental eligibility had hardened enough to make a misstep unlikely—and after he himself had become an established member of the colony's clerical community— that he thought it safe to take a stand. Like his ministerial colleagues, he now reflected an advocacy of an extremely limited form of baptism. He wrote in 1639, "Such Children whose Father and Mother were neither of them Believers, and sanctified, are counted by the Apostle (as it seemes to us) not faederally holy, but uncleane, what ever their other Ancestors have been. . . . And therefore we Baptise them not."[3]

In the years after the unequivocal pronouncement in favor of limiting baptism was accepted by most Massachusetts Bay clerics, a number of forces began to work in a way that would eventually produce pressure for modification. The exclusive character acquired by local churches severely restricted their potential for growth. If the process went unchecked, a progressively smaller portion of the population would be able to meet the rigorous qualifications for admission, and the religious character of Massachusetts Bay would be altered significantly.[4] Many of the baptized colonials who had never been admitted to full membership in the churches wanted broadened eligibility for baptism. This sympathy was shared by emigrants to the colony who had been baptized in England but were found unfit for membership in Massachusetts Bay's churches. This dissatisfaction over baptism, when joined to the unhappiness of two other groups who rejected the common ceremonial sprinkling of infants used in Massachusetts, made the situation precarious.

The first group, led by Charles Chauncy, held that the correct form for baptism was immersion of the newborn child in water. A mere sprinkling, Chauncy argued, was inadequate. In 1642 he had done this with two of his own children in water so cold that one of them had lost consciousness.[5] Despite his insistence on immersion, the practice was not generally accepted anywhere in New England. The second group rejected pedobaptism entirely. There was no essential doctrinal connection between the two rejections of standard Bay Colony practice, but there was at least some possibility for an alliance between those who rejected infant baptism and those who advocated complete immersion. Immersing an infant was dangerous—but this was not so if the subject of baptism were an adolescent. If the two groups advocating deviant forms of baptism were to unite and make common cause with those favoring presbyterial reforms in the colony's ecclesiastical structure, what had been merely an irritation could seriously exacerbate the division already present over eligibility for baptism.

Having by this time opted for ecclesiastical conformity as prescribed by the more influential clerics of the colony, Mather supported the generally accepted colonial practice on baptism, and his reputation for orthodoxy, already well established by 1640, was further enhanced by his refutation of a work by John Spilsbury, an English Anabaptist. Spilsbury, like some Bay Colony residents, argued that only those children should be baptized who were old enough to understand the sacrament and accept or reject it of their own free wills.[6] The book did not represent a serious threat to local practice and neither the General Court nor any meeting of ministers was sufficiently alarmed by its arrival to assign a clergyman to pen a refutation. Mather, however, anxious to gain in stature among the defenders of Bay Colony congregationalism, undertook to enhance his reputation with a polemic against Spilsbury's book. The result was "An Answer to Nine Reasons of John Spilsbury to Prove Infants Ought Not to Be Baptized."

As was the case with earlier adversaries, Mather's opponent was not a formidable disputant. His lack of scriptural citations at critical points left him extremely vulnerable to Mather's opening attack, and beyond this, there were several other crumbling redoubts in his defense. The initial reason he offered against pedobaptism revealed his amateur status as a theologian and biblical scholar. He maintained that infant baptism was wrong because it was not used in the New Testament. In rebuttal, Mather needed only to cite I Corinthians 1:16, Acts 16:15, 33, and Matthew 28:19 as examples. He explained that while none of these quotations specifically mention infant baptism, the references to baptism of households and nations could not be construed in any way except to include infants. Mather refuted the remaining arguments with similar ease. The techniques of disputation and ideological substantiation that he had learned during thousands of hours of careful study and reflection were not needed to counter Spilsbury's assertions, most of which were simply opinion rather than supportable objections to infant baptism. Mather completed the demolition of Spilsbury's doctrinal views in a sixty-six page manuscript which he completed on March 26, 1646.[7]

The ease and self-assurance with which Mather dispatched John Spilsbury was deceptive. His refutation was positive, lucid, and definitive in tone, indicating a firm comprehension of all aspects of doctrine concerning baptism, but it did not reflect the situation in the colony.

The presbyterians, Anabaptists, antipedobaptists, and others who simply wanted wider eligibility for baptism were already influencing the local clerical leaders. Cotton by 1643 had withdrawn his support for Mather's 1639 statement, and he was joined in this by Thomas Hooker in Connecticut.[8] Mather, never one to lag far behind Cotton, had moved from his unyielding demand for restricted baptism, and by 1645, though he was yet to become a wholehearted convert, his opinions were clearly vacillating. This was apparent in "A Plea for the Churches of Christ in New England," where his stand on baptism varied from section to section. At one point in the lengthy work he said that children were in the same state as their parents, implying that if parents were eligible for baptism, so were the children. At another place he obscured his meaning by adding that the right to baptism could not be transferred even by the grandparents. If it were possible to skip the biological parents' generation, he said, then baptism could be extended indefinitely, and by that means, everyone would be qualified for church membership, or at least the degree of membership conferred by receiving the first sacrament. At still another place in the work, he was less certain. In reply to the question "When those that were baptised in Infancy by the Covenant of their parents, being come to age are not yet found fitt to bee received to the Lords table, although they bee married and have children, whether are those their children to bee baptised or no?" he said, "it be not fitt to be peremptorie in a matter so dark and doubtful, yet till further light appeare."[9] Then, after admitting the course to be followed was not clear, he answered with a reply that was not consistent with what he had said elsewhere in the text. He stated that children of unregenerate but baptized parents should receive the sacrament if the parents were leading lives that were in concert with Christ's teaching.[10]

By the time of the synod of 1646, Mather was no longer unsure of the proper criteria for determining who should be entitled to baptism. In his "Modell of Church Government," he attempted to persuade the clerical and secular representatives to accept the broadened eligibility previously sanctioned by Cotton and Hooker, but in the completed Cambridge Platform his suggestions were ignored and the synod affirmed the earlier doctrine restricting baptism to the children of church members.

Many of the synod participants knew that disagreement on this crucial doctrine could not be ignored. It was only a short time before the question of eligibility for the first sacrament came up again, but this time it appeared in a slightly altered context. The newest difficulty began when John Cotton received a letter positing an unusual case. An unknown writer asked the Boston cleric what should be done when a baptized but unregenerate Christian died and left his infant to a church member who then adopted the orphan. Should the child be baptized? Cotton understood the ramifications of the question, and rather than act alone in so controversial a matter he called upon John Eliot, John Wilson, and Richard Mather, asking for their opinions on the question. The selection of these three clerics indicated that Cotton was not actually seeking advice but had made up his mind and simply hoped to get confirmation of his decision. While Eliot's stance on the subject of baptism is not clear at this time, both Wilson and Mather supported the movement to widen eligibility to include children of baptized but unregenerate parents. As was expected, all three clerics returned affirmative answers to Cotton. The absence of any indecision in the case—let alone a negative answer on the part of these clerics—meant that by 1648 there was genuine ministerial support for extending the definition of "seed" beyond the biological parents.

Eliot, Wilson, Mather, and Cotton were not the only clerics in the colony who had rejected the carefully prescribed limits on administering baptism by this time. As Cotton had indicated by his choice of the three men, the fraternity of Massachusetts Bay clerics was in the process of doctrinal change. Sometime between 1646 and 1648,

Mather had sensed the direction being taken by the ecclesiastical leaders and had become one of the most ardent advocates of the change. He campaigned among his colleagues in the Bay Colony and other New England divines, discussing the problem and making known his opinions on the subject. Shortly before the adoption of the Cambridge Platform, Henry Smith of Wethersfield in Connecticut had written to Mather asking advice and informing him that the Wethersfield church favored baptizing the children of baptized but unregenerate parents. Mather's answering letter to Smith has not survived, but a short time later he replied to another inquiry saying that he openly favored broad baptism as early as 1646.

Samuel Stone, another Connecticut cleric, confronted Mather with the same problem in 1650, noting that both he and his fellow minister John Warham agreed that baptism should be more widely available. In his letter he mentioned the growing discontent among his congregants and suggested the calling of a conference to deal with the problem. The following year Peter Prudden, pastor at Milford in New Haven, exchanged letters with Mather on the same subject. Prudden lamented the division of opinion, believing it aided those with presbyterian inclinations in their efforts to subvert congregationalism. He favored extending baptism to infant children of unregenerate Christians as did Warham and Stone. Mather continued to work for wider admittance to the sacrament. He was successful in his efforts with at least one of his fellow clergymen. A letter he sent to Nathaniel Rogers in 1652 probably induced him to join the growing number of colonial clergy who supported a widening of eligibility for baptism.[11]

Mather's role as a member of the ministerial community was clearly defined by the time he was engaged in persuading his fellow divines to support the revised view on baptism. He was an accepted associate of the colony's ecclesiastical fraternity, willing to follow the courses of action determined by his more influential colleagues; when that course of action had been set forth, he gave it the best of his limited talents. Unfortunately, his activities and the nature of his operations within the church and in the town of Dorchester are not so easily observed or delimited. In his role as a leader, Mather's performance was affected by a myriad of factors. In his dealings with parishioners, he exerted the same enthusiasm for the true faith that he exhibited in his theological polemics, but when called upon to provide inspiration and direction rather than enthusiastic acquiescence, he fell short. The consequences of his performance were determined less by his abilities or by the merit of the doctrines he propounded than by the nature of the human relationships in his village.

A signal factor in making determinations about Dorchester and its people, and an element without which an understanding of the dispute over eligibility for baptism is impossible, is the knowledge that while the residents of the town undoubtedly thought of themselves as Englishmen—and as residents of Massachusetts Bay—they did not evolve their orientation toward society by reference either to the homeland or to the colony. The measuring points on their scale of relationships were located rather within the complex of social interactions in their own village. These Dorchester folk were a special type of Englishman, but those features that made them special did not distinguish them from the settlers at Roxbury, Watertown, Hingham, or Charlestown, nor did they set them apart from residents in a thousand of the mother country's hamlets. As was the case with most of the world's population in the seventeenth century, the people of Dorchester were inhabitants of a small rural agricultural community with problems and concerns separate and often antithetical to those that occupied the residents of the preindustrial urban centers.

The residents of Dorchester were peasants, a group long recognized as having special and identifiable characteristics. Peasantry is a broad and inclusive term; it is not tied to a geographic or historical mooring, but identifies instead groups who live in a manner with certain social, economic, and personality features. They are communities of producers on a small scale with simple equipment and market organization, often relying on what they produce for their subsistence. Their communities possess many common traits of preliterate societies: intimate local groupings, strong kinship ties, periodic ceremonial gatherings, and, occasionally, a strong emotional attachment to the soil. This does not mean that they are independent of other distinct units. Peasant societies like Mather's Dorchester were not isolated and unregulated groups of agriculturalists, independent of the world beyond the bounds of their village.

Though Dorchester was the primary unit of societal orientation, its limits did not circumscribe the whole of the inhabitants' activities. The villagers were linked to the outside world by the obvious bonds of language and kinship and by the economic, social, and intellectual ties that were also vital to their physical and psychological well-being. The elements that augmented Dorchester's part-society and part-culture came from a wide variety of sources ranging from England and the whole of the English and English-continental tradition to the nearby markets in Boston. The proximity of Boston meant that it was a major source in supplementing Dorchester's society and culture. It provided the market for surplus production and supplied needed goods, either made locally or imported from Europe.

The town also was the seat of government, whose legislation regulated important phases of the villagers' lives, and it was the focus of their religion. Though the spiritual life of the villagers was centered in the local meetinghouse and was congregational, the First Church in Boston was their colonial Canterbury; and though he preached clad in a cloak instead of a gown, John Cotton was their archbishop. Yet while the Dorchestermen were bound inextricably to Boston, they remained villagers, distinct from the residents of Boston and alien, in many respects, to the attitudes, perceptions, and aspirations of its citizens.[12]

The peasant character of Dorchester is particularly visible in the nature of the intellectual and religious divergence between Mather and the members of his church. The divergence, in the words of Robert Redfield, is "the difference between a great tradition and a little tradition. . . . In a civilization there is a great tradition of the reflective few, and there is a little tradition of the largely unreflective many. The great tradition is cultivated in schools or temples; the little tradition works itself out and keeps itself going in the lives of the unlettered in their village communities. The tradition of the philosopher, theologian, and literary man is a tradition consciously cultivated and handed down; that of the little people is for the most part taken for granted and not submitted to much scrutiny or considered refinement and improvement."[13] Like peasant society and its complementary greater society, great and little traditions are coordinates; they remain segments of the same whole with the great tradition carrying forward cultural norms and values already contained in the little tradition.

In peasant communities, the great tradition is bound to the little tradition through a shared body of sacred literature and a mythical-historical past, a common ritual, and a class of literati charged with coordinating, directing, and interpreting ceremony and tradition. Those people who carry the little tradition and those who maintain the more sophisticated elements of the great tradition recognize the same priority of levels, a higher and a lower. Characteristic of this separation of the cultural elements is the development of hierarchic traditions supervised by a specialized elite who possess sacred and secular powers for the cultivation of portions of the intellectual or religious life. In any of the thousands of ethnographic units where a peasant population forms part of the larger civilization, the distinction between a little and a great tradition appears in the control of certain members of a religious or intellectual coterie, recognized by the masses as possessing special knowledge and understanding of matters of the mind and spirit.[14] It is the task of this group to relate the peasants' cognitions of the sacred and their techniques for coordinating those cognitions with the beliefs and techniques of the total society. In Dorchester, Mather was the religious specialist who was charged with seeking "meanings behind meanings, [and engaging] in the labor of examining symbols and rituals, exploring meanings behind meanings, [and] striving to render meanings and actions more consistent."[15]

It is not unusual in these peasant communities to find differences in doctrinal outlook between the peasant and the religious specialist. Typically, the peasant responds only to the situation within the village community, while the religious specialist is required by the demands of his own societal identification to take a broader view. The restricted outlook of the peasant effectively prohibits him from fomenting religious innovation; thus, there is frequently a time lag in the peasants' adoption of the concepts and innovations advocated by the religious elite. Peasant groups struggle to retain traditional forms of religion, while the elite press for religious systems of wider scope. This tension between the peasants and the religious leaders often produced sufficient friction to isolate the religious specialist from the villagers.[16]

Although there are exceptions to the presence of great and little traditions within peasant societies, as Redfield freely concedes, Dorchester in the seventeenth century was not one of these. The ministerial elite with which Mather was associated by 1640 had been an esoteric and cohesive group since the middle of the sixteenth century in England when it had led what began as a band of radical revolutionary Calvinists. In later years, this movement matured and enlarged as it acquired allies among the gentry and even among the nobility, but no matter how numerous or highly placed the recruits, ideology remained entirely a clerical creation, and the ministers continued to direct their brand of reformation. Even under Elizabeth, courtiers like Leicester sought to solicit support by proclaiming a type of militant Protestantism, but Leicester and his supporters could not consistently pursue policies in opposition to the queen, and the leadership of the movement remained in the hands of the ministers.[17]

By the time Mather was well established as a cleric in Massachusetts Bay, the colony's religion had come of age. The faith that once had been confined to a tiny group of exiles a century earlier had matured under the guidance of the colony's clergy into a congregational pattern dominated by and adjusted to the needs of an intellectually sophisticated priesthood. The work of the fellowship in controlling the great tradition was a continuing process, as the clerics year after year confronted new doctrinal and theological difficulties. In most circumstances, when the clergymen fashioned solutions in response to new problems, they did so without seriously violating the psychological and social sensibilities of the laity. Church membership was restricted to the justified, Antinomianism was extirpated, presbyterians were tolerated, Quakers were banished, and separatism was suppressed, all with the eventual concurrence of Bay Colony laymen.

The ability of the clerics to emerge from these encounters with victory secured was due to the successful employment of any number of techniques for the management of the people. Reference to their superior knowledge of the sacred, influence with the civil authorities, superior social position, and even the threat of force were all employed singly and in combination by the clergymen to persuade laymen and occasionally deviating clerics of the wisdom of their policies. In Dorchester, Mather was generally successful in achieving his goals by persuasion and by preaching a religion that was devoid of much of the academic sophistication that formed a central part of the faith held by members of the clerical brotherhood. He skirted the complexities of John Calvin, Theodore Beza, William Ames, and William Perkins, and while he did stress the stages in the nonconformist pattern of conversion, his sermons avoided the precision and continuity that was essential in his debates with ecclesiastical associates. Instead, his sermons provided an acceptable and comprehensive explanation of God's ways, a guide for living, a practical code of conduct, and, at least before the employment of the jeremiad in later years, they emphasized the regulation of human interaction and provided a set of prescriptions for daily life. In this respect, the religion Mather presented to his Dorchester parishioners was truly a peasant's faith, highly utilitarian and moralistic with little latitude for questioning or for ethical consideration. It was also a faith that contrasted with that at Boston and Salem where accessibility to the outside world was greater than in Dorchester. In both of these villages, where the peasant character was much less pronounced than in Mather's town, repeated religious disagreements and constant questioning disrupted the operation of the churches with a frequency and intensity unmatched in Dorchester.

As Mather was to find during his attempts to introduce to his church members the newly accepted view of eligibility for baptism, the unlettered peasant qualities that had once helped him resist Antinomianism and preserve the peace in Dorchester could present formidable resistance when his intellectual elitism and the ideology of the brethren clashed. Though he labored to explain the doctrines to his church, he would discover again and again that while he might spend endless hours illuminating the meanings and true intent of symbol and ritual, and attempt to make precept and action consistent, his peasant church members sometimes would not respond. Unlike Mather whose concerns went far beyond the bounds of Dorchester to other village clerics and to like-minded ministers in England and who was dependent on maintaining clerical harmony to preserve his own status, the members of the village church were responding to the local requirements of their own group. Thus, in Dorchester, the people clung to their traditional concepts; for men with the abiding faith of Mather's brethren, the sacred was a thing uniquely inalienable. The peasants, unsure of themselves in matters of religion, preferred the security of the familiar. While a system of greater scope was designed by a fellowship of like-minded intellectuals to deal with the problems of the colony, the peasants chose to retain a faith that was eminently suited to local needs. It is hardly surprising that this disparity of orientation existed between cleric and church members, producing tension and later a break over the limits of eligibility for baptism. In almost every part of the world, peasants, generally speaking, have been a conservative social force, and there is no reason to suppose that seventeenth-century peasants in Dorchester differed in this respect.[18]

Mather probably encountered resistance among his church members to his views on baptism as early as 1648 or 1650, and when this occurred, he found it difficult to understand. The brethren had accepted his views on numerous occasions in earlier years, and by all indicators he was deeply admired not only by his colleagues but also by the residents of the town. They had shown their esteem year after year by granting him large amounts of land and by awarding him one of the largest clerical salaries in the colony. Although ministerial maintenance had repeatedly been a problem in many villages in the Bay and had received the regular attention of preachers of the stature of John Cotton and John Wilson, Mather had never experienced any difficulty on this account. During the latter years of his ministry, he usually received £100 per annum, probably a share of the substantial weekly collection, and an income from the several hundred acres of land he owned.[19] Thus it is fair to speculate that when he reflected on the reasons for the failure of the church to follow his lead on sacramental administration, Mather's own overestimation of his abilities as well as the regular generosity of the townsmen caused him to rule out personal unpopularity as a reason. But it is also fair to speculate that he ignored the profound social implications inherent in a broadening of baptism and instead saw in the refusal to accept his new perception only the intransigence of many of his church members.

As he had done when his new church was denied official sanction in 1636, Mather sought to lay the blame on the ordinary members who had gained, much to his chagrin, a pivotal role in the governing of the church by the mid-years of the seventeenth century. Distinction between cleric and members had always been emphasized by Mather, and over the years he had regularly expressed an abiding distrust of the ordinary saint's judgment in ecclesiastical matters. When his first church was denied official recognition during his first months in America, he decided that the onus of failure lay with those prospective members who had given him advice on how to proceed. Since that time nothing had happened to alter his view. It had been he, not the membership, who had preserved the true doctrine during the Antinomian crisis; it was he who had prevailed against a minor outbreak of separatist sentiment in Dorchester; and now, in 1650, it was he who carried God's word on baptism.[20]

Mather had learned from bitter experience the result of allowing members to gain even a limited measure of power in his conflict with Jonathan Burr, who had roused a portion of the membership against him, almost sundering the church. Clearly, the members could not be trusted, and even though many of the colony's ministers had advocated a form of church government in which power was shared by the elders and members, Mather had always thought otherwise. In his sermons he expressed the need for harmony that could be attained only when the ordinary members submitted to the elders' judgment, and he repeated this in his writings.[21] "Ministerial and delegated Government," he wrote, "belongeth only to the Elders. . . . So all are not Governours, but some only; and therefore it cannot be that the Power of Church Government should be in all the People. . . . The People are especially commanded to Obey their Elders as their Rulers, and to submit themselves. . . . Which plainly sheweth that the Power of Government and Rule is not in the People at all, but in the Elders alone."[22]

Although many of Mather's clerical colleagues had attempted to soften his restrictive approach to church government, holding it was a mixed form "in respect of the Elders, Aristocratical, and in respect of the People Democratical; and therefore the People have some Share in the Government," Mather remained suspicious of this approach, preferring the same system of church government practiced in the diocese of Lancashire. "They that so speak," he answered, "do take Democracy in a large sense, to note that Liberty, and Interest and Consent which the People have in Elections and

Censures, and the like: which tho' in Propriety of Speech, it be not Government or Rule. . . . And . . . it may be granted, that Church Government is not without some Democracy therein: Only heed must be taken, that under a color of a mixture . . . we do not Establish . . . meer Democracy, and so destroy that mixture which we seem to plead for. . . . The Elders must have at the least a Negative Voice, and no matter pass Judicially without their Authoritative Concurrence in the same."[23] Understandably, Mather never mentioned the negative voice for the members, but by 1650, as a result of congregational insistence on near unanimity in church matters and his own unwillingness to challenge doctrine or polity sanctioned by those he chose to emulate, the members gained that negative voice; later, on baptism they used it with full effect to thwart the will of the teacher.

There is no indication of a causal relationship between the negative voice and the rejection of the Halfway Covenant by the members of Mather's church. The negative voice was only a mechanism for expressing dissatisfaction or questioning the direction taken by Mather and any who made common cause with him, but the disagreement serves to emphasize the existence of disparate sets of interests in the church and to provide fuel for the distrust of the clerical brotherhood that could already be discerned in Massachusetts Bay by 1648.[24]

During the years after the adoption of the Cambridge Platform, while the discussion of baptism and eligibility continued among clerics, Mather preached to his own flock in favor of baptizing infants of baptized though unregenerate church members, but it was not until 1655 that he felt secure enough to ask his Dorchester church to consider modifying the eligibility requirements. The discussion that followed indicated Mather was correct in discerning support for his position, but even at this early date, the members' distrust of their teacher on this issue was made apparent when they requested the opinions of the churches in four neighboring villages. The answers they received were of little help. The three churches that replied to the request were as divided on the question as was Dorchester. Rather than accept Mather's determination without further doctrinal buttressing, the church made no decision, thereby rejecting implicitly their teacher's advocacy of broader baptism and retaining their practice of baptizing only the children of church members.[25]

While Mather and his church debated the proper manner of administering the first sacrament, a series of events was taking place that though only partially connected with baptism would force the colonial ecclesiastics to confront directly the question of eligibility for baptism. Between the years 1653 and 1659, a bitter quarrel raged in Hartford over the selection of a cleric to replace the deceased Thomas Hooker. The disruption brought about by the disagreements emboldened a few nonmembers of the church, and they petitioned the General Court of Connecticut, asking for a relaxation of the restrictions surrounding baptism. The Connecticut governing body deputized a committee to examine the petitioners' request, and to aid in making a decision, the opinion of the Massachusetts Bay General Court was sought in the summer of 1656.[26]

During the autumn following the inquiry, the court, realizing the full extent of the problem, called for a meeting of the colonies to discuss the points at issue. The date was set for the first week in June 1657, and representatives were appointed from all sections of Massachusetts Bay. Richard Mather, John Allin, John Norton, and Thomas Thatcher were selected to speak for Suffolk; Middlesex was to send Harvard's president Charles Chauncy, Jonathan Mitchel, Zechariah Symmes, Peter Bulkeley, and Edward Norris; Ezekiel Rogers, Samuel Whiting, and Thomas Cobbett were to represent Essex. Some idea of the seriousness the General Court attached to the meeting was indicated when it ordered Robert Turner, a Boston innkeeper, to "provide convenient entertaynment for the said gentlemen during their attendance on the said meeting" with the cost to be borne by the colony.[27]

The invitations sent out by Massachusetts Bay were received with mixed feelings by the other colonies. Connecticut accepted and sent four ministers to the conference.[28] Plymouth took no action on the communication, and the New Haven colony refused to participate.

The ministers from Massachusetts and Connecticut, some twenty in all, convened in June. No record of the debates survives, but with Charles Chauncy present to articulate his views on baptism, those assembled surely knew there would be no unanimity. It took the conference nineteen days of discussion before they agreed to sanction the Halfway Covenant. Mather was one of those who stood with the majority. The support of the clergymen on this important issue strengthened Mather's position in his church. He now had the combined authority of the Connecticut and Massachusetts Bay ministry behind him—and he was to need it. Soon after the meeting ended, his Dorchester church was confronted with a dispute over baptism when Martha Minot, the newborn granddaughter of elder George Minot, was presented for the first sacrament by her baptized but unregenerate father. This represented a perfect opportunity for Mather to explain clearly to his church the need for broadened baptism. He had already drawn up a manuscript compendium of the June meeting, which included justification for the decision to broaden eligibility for baptism, and now he could offer the arguments to his church.

Mather knew that on so divisive an issue he would have to structure carefully his arguments to assure total understanding by his church. He began with the initial premise used by most of his colleagues when they argued for broader baptism. "Some Children of confederate Parents," he asserted confidently, "are by meanes of their Parents Covenanting, in Covenant also, and so Members of the Church by divine Institution."[29] Such a statement was difficult to establish as fact, but it was necessary to do so, for without it Mather's case would crumble. He began his defense of the premise by insisting that the covenant established in the Old Testament was applicable to the seventeenth century. He patiently explained, "some children are in that Covenant for substance which was made with *Abraham*, Gen. 17.7 as appears by sundry Scriptures, which being rightly considered, and compared, do inferre the continuance of the substance of that Covenant, whereby God is a God to his People and their seed, under the New Testament." He confirmed this with a flood of examples from the Old Testament, from the life of Christ, and with a host of citations ranging from Genesis almost to the book of Revelation.[30]

As Mather moved from example to example and from premise to premise, there were repeated demands from the brethren to clarify minor points on which confusion had already arisen. What of children of various ages; were they in covenant as were their parents? What of children never brought to the church? What of children born before their parents had covenanted? What of incorrigibles of seven, or eight, or twelve years of age or of children who did not desire to be associated with the church? These issues were often difficult and troublesome for Mather. They took time, patient and involved explanation, and served to divert attention from the argument he was attempting to construct, but before he could complete the line of logic, he was forced to answer such queries. Only then could he bring the debate back to the central issue, the question of "Whether the child admitted by his Fathers Covenant, be also a Deputy for his seed, without or before personal Covenanting, or without and before like personal qualifications in kind, as his Father was to enjoy when he became a Deputy." Mather retreated continually to his firmly established opening premise to provide unequivocal proof for this statement. He insisted "Infants either of whose immediate Parents are in Church-Covenant, do confaederate with their Parents, and are therefore Church-members with them." These children, then, "In case they understand the grounds of Religion, are not scandalous, and solemnly own the Covenant in their own persons, wherein they give up both themselves and their children unto the Lord, and desire Baptism for them, we (with due reverence to any Godly Learned that may dissent) see not sufficient cause to deny Baptism unto their children."[31] This last statement, diffidently offered with a provision to avoid giving offense to those in opposition, was supported by a half-dozen arguments and reasons. "Church-Members without offence and not baptized," Mather explained, "are to be baptized. The children in Question are Church-Members without offense and not baptized. Therefore the children in Question are to be baptized." The teacher added more premises and deductions in quick succession to support his logic. "Children in the covenant of Abraham, as to the substance thereof . . . are to be baptized. The children in Question are children in the covenant of Abraham. . . . Therefore the children in Question are to be baptized." "Children in the same estate with those children under the Law . . . are to be baptized. . . . the children in Question are in the same estate . . . with those children under the Law. . . . Therefore the children in Question are to be baptized." Several more syllogisms of this nature followed, and then the teacher closed with an attempt to assuage fears that the sanctuary would be corrupted by the

admission of a host of unworthies. "Though the persons fore-
mentioned own the Covenant according to the premises," he assured
his listeners, "yet before they are admitted to full communion . . . they must so hold forth their Faith and Repentance, unto
the judgment of Charity by way of confession in the congregation,
as it may appear unto the Church, that they are able to examine
themselves and to discern the Lords body."[32] Even with all his
reasoning, examples, citations, and exhortation, Mather was not
sufficiently convincing. The Dorchester church refused to give its
assent, and baptism was denied the infant Martha Minot.[33]

The rejection of the Minot child did not end the difficulties over
the administration of the first sacrament, and the church was again
confronted with the problem when, in April 1660, Hannah, the
daughter of Thomas Andrews, made known her desire to leave
Dorchester and join the church at Roxbury. She was not a member
in full communion, having achieved membership through her
parents' covenant, but the woman asked for a formal letter of
dismission. The usual practice was to issue certificates of dismissal
only to full members, but the church relented and granted her
request. A letter of dismission was written, and, although the Dorchester church had not adopted the Halfway Covenant endorsed by
the synod of 1657, the letter explained to the church at Roxbury
that the woman was formally dismissed because she had been baptized as an infant and since she had not been excommunicated, she
was still joined to the church. The letter, in an obvious attempt to
avoid misunderstanding, added she had not been admitted to the
Lord's supper in Dorchester. The explanation of the status of Andrews's daughter was necessary, for though the Roxbury minister,
Thomas Allen, was a supporter of wider baptism, his church, like
Mather's, had refused to accept any broadening of eligibility. The
Roxbury church was not, however, so strongly opposed that it
rejected the woman from Dorchester. A week after her dismission,
she was admitted to the Roxbury church, though not in full communion.[34]

By the time Hannah Andrews had asked for the letter of dismission it was evident that while Mather had not been able to persuade
his church to accept the Halfway Covenant, he had developed a base
of support within the church on the issue. It is not precisely clear

how strong his support was, for the position of all voting members on the baptism issue cannot be ascertained. But a tabulation of those who were known either to support or to oppose the measure indicates Mather was successful not only in gaining support of the elders but also in persuading many of the more influential residents of the town to accept the measure as well. In fact, by this time he was able to enlist as supporters of the Halfway Covenant almost the entire village aristocracy, and while this higher status group was surely joined by some of the ordinary folk, the records of the church make it plain those of elevated social position dominated the discussion.[35] On the other hand, the names of those few that are known to have opposed the extension of baptism, for the most part, were drawn from the less affluent segment of the church's membership. This is apparent from the Dorchester town records which indicate that those who favored the Halfway Covenant tended to be larger landowners than those who opposed it.[36] The sample is small, however, and the nature of the Dorchester town records and the incomplete evidence of land transactions in the village during the seventeenth century should induce caution in drawing substantive conclusions. Although the settlers began keeping careful accounts from the time of their arrival, the first four pages of their registry have not survived. There is therefore no record of the distribution of land to colonists who arrived in 1630. Extant records of land ownership begin in 1633, however, and from that point, a number of projections can be made.

Most important in determining relative wealth among Mather's parishioners is a land distribution chart compiled in 1637. In that year, the town council voted to divide more than five hundred acres of pasture within its jurisdiction, and at least part of that land was distributed on the basis of previously acquired holdings. The land was divided by giving every resident owner of a house lot one acre and every nonresident lot owner half an acre. Of the land remaining after this apportioning, two-fifths was divided equally among approximately one hundred claimants who included almost every adult male and widow in Dorchester. The remaining three-fifths was apportioned according to previously acquired holdings. Careful account was kept of the amount of land given to each person, and on the basis of the number of acres distributed to known supporters and opponents of the Halfway Covenant an estimate of their total and proportional wealth can be made with some degree of accuracy.[37] After Richard Mather had received one acre of land for his two-acre house lot and another acre as part of the equal shares given to all claimants, his proportional share for the one hundred additional acres he already held was ten acres.

In like manner, Israel Stoughton was first granted one acre for his house lot, an additional acre from the pastureland that was divided equally, and then twenty-four acres for his holdings of almost two hundred and fifty acres. Mather and Stoughton were two of the wealthiest men in the village. Stoughton's twenty-four-acre parcel was the largest segment of pasture given to anyone. Of the three grants that followed Stoughton's in size, one was of eighteen acres and three were of eleven acres. Then followed Mather's portion of ten acres. The other ninety-nine grants were all smaller than these, most of them considerably smaller. The average portion given out on the basis of land already held was slightly more than three acres, indicating that Stoughton and Mather were among a few who held substantial wealth.[38]

The summary above was composed from data generated two decades before the division in the village over the Halfway Covenant, and thus allowance must be made for fluctuations in the degree of relative affluence among these men. Land was an item of trade and commerce in Dorchester like corn, tools, livestock, or any other form of property; and parcels were regularly exchanged for other land, goods, and cash or transferred by testamentary bequest. Many of these transactions were entered in the town records, but some were not, and even an examination of existing wills and deeds does not give a completely accurate picture of the distribution of real property between 1657 and 1667. The records reveal that the financial position of those in Dorchester whose stand on the Halfway Covenant can be determined did not change substantially over the two decades. If there was any meaningful change, it would appear that the economic gulf between the two groups actually widened.

Some who had received large grants of pastureland had sold their holdings and departed Dorchester before the disagreements over the limits of eligibility became a critical issue, but several remained in the village, and as the population grew, the aggregate wealth of this landowning aristocracy was multiplied by each acquisition made from grants of previously unassigned land, purchases from departing townsmen, and regular increases in the price of village property.[39] The accounts of land transactions, when considered along with records of public offices held and the various commercial concessions or monopolies granted over the years, indicate that those who dominated economic life in Dorchester during the town's first decade of settlement and who remained in the village continued to control its economic affairs in 1660. This is apparent from an examination of the activities of the families on the 1637 list who resided in the town two decades later. The Dorchester records indicate Edward Brecke, an advocate of the Halfway Covenant, continued to acquire land and business concessions, and Mather not only increased his holdings almost 100 percent in the two decades after 1637 but all the while drew his customary salary and supplemented his income from a variety of sources.

Like Brecke and Mather, George Minot shepherded his estate carefully, adding land and transferring it to his sons over the years. It was his third son, Stephen, who wanted his infant daughter, Martha, baptized under the grandfather's covenant. Later, Minot's second son, James, would also attempt to gain baptism for his children by the right conferred by the grandfather's church membership. James Minot's application was fully supported by his wife, the former Hannah Stoughton, a daughter of Dorchester's wealthiest family. Although Israel Stoughton, the family patriarch, had been dead for some time before the disagreements arose over eligibility for baptism, his descendants in the village had inherited his extensive properties, and his widow, like her daughters, Hannah Minot and Rebecca Taylor, was an ardent advocate of the Halfway Covenant. Elder Henry Withington, a supporter of widening eligibility for baptism, was known as a man of "good estate." He was related to Elder John Wiswall, who, although the man with the least amount of wealth among those known to favor the doctrinal modification, was the founder of a leading Dorchester family, was related to Elder Richard Eliot of the Roxbury church, and was the father-in-law of Thomas Danforth, a member of the Court of Assistants and a future governor.[40]

While those who were known to favor the Halfway Covenant were all part of a village elite, there was no indication of similar elevated status among the opposition. One of the opponents, Hopestill Foster, did hold a number of minor local offices and commissions, but he never amassed large amounts of land or extensive commercial interests. In the twenty-five years after the distribution of the pastureland, it is equally certain that neither Gabriel Meade nor Goodman Wayles ever acquired any amount of wealth. The atypical opponent, of the four who can be identified, was Increase Mather, who was not wealthy at the time he chose sides against his father, but who was still young and surely could consider himself a man with exceptional prospects. His theological justification for taking such a stand was presented in his writings, and beyond that there may have been other compelling considerations that dictated his opposition. He had just returned to New England after a sojourn in Ireland and England, and after having been forced out of Britain by men whom he considered to be ecclesiastical reactionaries, he may not have been enthusiastic about any modification that could be construed to contain even the remotest hint of compromise with either Anglican or presbyterian practice. Furthermore, he had not participated in the intense debates that had preceded the synod and may not have realized all the ramifications in the question at issue. Or perhaps his opposition was merely a response to his father's advocacy. Whichever of these or other reasons influenced his decision, Increase soon left Dorchester to take charge of his own church and in a short time reversed his stand and became a spokesman for the Halfway Covenant.

The data on land ownership and the amplifying considerations suggest some measure of economic division on the issue of the Halfway Covenant. It is unfortunate that the statistical breakdown on the way the majority of the church members cast their votes on the issue, the piece of information vital for any substantive quantitative conclusion, is simply not available. Approximately sixty church members were eligible to vote in Dorchester at any given time between 1657 and 1665, but on this issue the alignment is known for less than a dozen. Even if it were inferred that the husbands of women favoring the measure held the same views as their wives, the number would still be less than fifteen. As a result of this paucity of information, there is no way of establishing statistically whether the modification requested by Mather and the town's more affluent residents was opposed by the majority of the people or if there was wide acceptance of the Halfway Covenant but that adoption was prevented by a core of reactionary or recalcitrant members.

Eligibility for baptism was finally broadened by the church in 1677, but only after a period of severe trial at a time when the membership and the whole village were deeply concerned with the threats to the colony's institutions posed by Stuart policies and by the struggle against King Philip and his native allies. Thus, the vote to accept the Halfway Covenant at that time cannot be interpreted as an indicator of broad support in 1662. Even without this information, the grants of pastureland in 1637 and the certainty they anticipated similar holdings twenty-five years later strongly suggests that with most of the village's wealth, including the teacher of the church and the whole of the ruling eldership, on one side of the question, there was at least a very apparent status division in Dorchester on the doctrinal question. With Stoughtons, Minots, Edward Brecke, Henry Withington, John Wiswall, and Richard Mather united in support of one particular view, there were few of this same status level in the village to oppose them. Under these circumstances, it is difficult to imagine the leaders of the church and the village being resisted on this crucial matter only by a handful of ordinary members. Since the village was peasant in character, it is more likely that the known opponents of the Halfway Covenant did not stand alone. Since those from the highest levels in the village were already committed to advocacy of the modification in doctrine, most of those joining Foster, Meade, Wayles, and the younger Mather could only have been ordinary church members.

The status division within the Dorchester church was not the result of Mather's ability to construct a series of arguments that were persuasive enough to carry the leaders with him even though they failed to sway many of the church members. The upper level of villagers joined him for other motives. Unlike the minister, they were not driven by a long-developed habit of striving for association and acceptance by a clerical elite nor did they share the peculiar perceptions Mather had acquired as a result of his education, the brief stay at Brasenose, or his lengthy and continuous contact with ecclesiastical associates. It is likely that most of these men had grammar school educations and one or two may have attended a university, but they were, nonetheless, disassociated from those things that determined the minister's course of action, and their decisions to support the Halfway Covenant were made for reasons other than his. They could join Mather in his position on baptism even though they differed from him in terms of motive not only because their status gave them a broader view of colonial and congregational needs, and thereby brought them closer to the perspective of their teacher and his clerical associates, but also because there was no compelling reason why they should not follow his lead as they had done in the past. They respected him and had generally accepted his leadership in ecclesiastical matters. The extension of baptism in no way represented a threat to their social, secular, or theological security. These were men from a qualitatively distinct status level, association with which was determined by wealth, occupation, service, and education. Increased church membership would not damage their self-esteem or lessen the regard in which others held them. More likely, it would enhance their status by making them leaders of a larger ecclesiastical body.

The factors that brought the views of Dorchester's leaders into harmony with those of Mather were the same factors that forced many of the members into open opposition. For those in the lower strata, the only security they were able to attain came largely as the result of severe restrictions on church membership that had been instituted in the colony. By the time Mather had arrived in the village, all individuals were required to demonstrate evidence of justification before being admitted into the church. Membership in this exclusive body gave them an identity with at least one institution in the colony and secured for each of them a portion of distinction.

Initiation into a formally constituted body of saints naturally altered perceptions sufficiently to make many members understand their newly acquired status (recognized saint as opposed to suspected reprobate) was secured by the perpetuation of a static social order. They had proved, according to church doctrine, that they were of God's elect by demonstrating the works of grace within them. The steps they had followed to sainthood—the public confession of faith, the witness of neighbors, and the recounting of the conversion experience—had all become sacred. To tamper with these was to tamper with the basis of their sainthood, their admission to the church, and their assurance that they had received God's grace. Even when the clerics sought to mitigate the rigid insistence on purity by dividing the covenant into two parts, the first a covenant between men to gather a church and the second between the saint and his God as a seal of salvation, they made this separation only by inference rather than through institutional reorganization.

When a specific step was under consideration which would explicitly alter such institutions and thus disrupt the moorings of the people's religious identity the result could be, as it was in Dorchester, continuous strife. When Mather moved to do this by extending baptism, he challenged the identity and security of his peasant church members. By adopting the Halfway Covenant, the church would be weakening membership requirements, thus making it possible to increase the numbers admitted to the fellowship. For those whose only distinction was having received God's grace, an enlarged religious body—even though the members were not all voters or communicants—would tend to decrease the worth of their own election and thereby diminish the value of their claim to distinction. This had to be resisted and the way to do it was at hand. In an intimate peasant community where face-to-face relationships dominated social intercourse, the will of the upper status group could be thwarted.

Mather was deeply discouraged by the division within his church over the question of Martha Minot's baptism, and it was not until three years later that he had another opportunity to persuade his Dorchester saints to accept broader eligibility for baptism. In May 1660 he again brought the matter before his church. After an evening service he told the members he wished to speak on an important matter. He informed them that he had conferred earlier with other elders of the church and they agreed with what he was about to say. Then he explained to those assembled, as he had explained on previous occasions, "Such children as are [the seed of church members] affirmed to have a place and portion in the Kingdome of Heaven, they have a place and portion in the visible Church, and so consequently are members thereof. . . . If children were once Church-members and do not continue to be Church-members still, then their Membership must have been repealed by the Lord, who alone could make such an alteration: And if any should affirm that the Lord hath done it, it lieth upon them to prove it."[41] It followed from this, he maintained, that though some children of members had yet to be admitted to the privilege of voting and to the Lord's table, they were nevertheless members, they should be treated as such, and their children should be baptized.[42]

There were no immediate repercussions from Mather's announcement, but a few months later the church was in the midst of another dispute. It began in the autumn of 1660, when the teacher again asked the members to remain after the conclusion of services. He then informed them that the wife of James Minot had requested baptism for her children. Neither of the Minots were full members of the Dorchester church, though both had been baptized under their parents' covenants. The church members discussed the matter but reached no conclusion.

The following week the subject was broached again, but the opposition was strong, and once more the members failed to reach agreement. After letting the matter rest for several weeks, the church leaders decided to press for a decision on baptism. Elder Henry Withington rose before the entire congregation and said he had discussed Mather's proposal with members of the church over the past several days and found many wanted more debate on the subject. One by one the arguments surrounding baptism were voiced.[43] Opponents of expanding sacramental administration argued that the children of baptized parents who were not members in full communion were deficient in glory, mercy, and other blessings and should be denied the sacrament. Other opponents would deny baptism to the child because the parents were not members in the truest sense.

Mather countered these arguments, saying, "The Church-act onely, and not any other act (much lesse defect) of the Parent is by Divine Institution, accounted to the child. The membership of the child is a distinct membership, from the membership of the Parent. In case the Parents membership ceaseth by death or censure, the membership of the child remaineth still. . . . The child is baptized by vertue of his own membership, and not by vertue of his Parents membership."[44] This was not sufficient to persuade the members, and the debate continued. One Dorchesterman said since the children of members such as the Minots were circumcised in the Old Testament, they should receive baptism in a Christian church. Another added that because the Minots were made members by their parents' covenant and had not left the church or been excommunicated, their children should receive the sacrament. At least one person argued that since New Testament churches were merely improvements over Old Testament congregations, baptism was, therefore, only an improvement over circumcision and could be administered. Many in the church remained unconvinced, and again no decision was reached. After this discussion, the intensity of the debate made it clear that nothing approaching unanimity could be achieved, and the question of eligibility for baptism was dropped.[45]

The Dorchester disagreement over who should receive the first sacrament was soon complicated by events in England. With the passing of the Protectorate and the restoration of Charles II, the future of the colonial churches and governments was uncertain. Even though the new king had made many promises in the Declaration of Breda, there was much suspicion surrounding a Stuart on the throne. Since the death of Cromwell, Mather's church had proclaimed a continuing series of fasts. Often they were brought about by some difficulty in the colony, but in almost every case, the disruptions in England were included as one reason for their proclamation. Usually the fasts were local, proclaimed by the authority of the church, but by May 1662, concern in the colony grew so great that the General Court announced a day would be set aside for fasting and prayer because of sickness in the colony and the adverse events in England.[46]

With the situation in the homeland growing more unfavorable as time passed, the Bay colonists knew that they must have uniformity at home, but the meeting in 1657, while it had endorsed halfway covenanting, had not settled the question to the satisfaction of enough settlers to insure an absence of serious disagreements. There was also the agonizing theological problem created by the very presence of divergent views on baptism. There had never been any attempt in the colony to insure absolute ceremonial uniformity among the churches. Deviations on minor points were tolerated, but on something as important as baptism, disagreement could not be permitted indefinitely. God prescribed only one way; that way had to be discovered for the benefit of all. A meeting was needed to resolve the problem permanently.

The synod was scheduled to convene on the second Tuesday of March 1662. Some two weeks before the meeting, the Dorchester church received official notification that they were to send representatives to Boston for the deliberations. The two men chosen to speak for the church were Richard and Increase Mather. On the appointed day in March, the father and son gathered with representatives of the other churches of Massachusetts Bay at the meetinghouse of the First Church in Boston. The ecclesiastical leaders of most if not all the villages were present. Their somber mood intensified the atmosphere of urgency and the feeling that the success of God's experiment in New England would depend on their deliberations. The two titans of the New England churches, Hooker and Cotton, were both dead, but the assemblage of clergy was still an impressive array. John Wilson, the aging pastor of Boston was present as was Charles Chauncy, the president of Harvard College. Even Eleazer Mather had journeyed from his church at Northampton to join his father, brother, and the other delegates for the meeting. In all, some seventy men came to the conference to test arguments and to extract a solution from the theological interplay. The assembly was divided into two camps from the beginning, those who supported the solution put forth by the 1657 meeting of ministers and those who opposed it. The clerics who favored restricted baptism numbered a few more than ten, while the remainder favored enlargement of eligibility. Among those who composed the smaller faction were Chauncy, John Mayo of the Second Church in Boston, and both of the Mather brothers. Numbered with the advocates of extended baptism was Richard Mather.[47]

The synod lasted until autumn, though it did not meet continuously for the six months it was in session. The clerics conferred in three relatively abbreviated conferences during the spring and summer before they made a decision. On September 27 the Dorchester church was notified that agreement had been reached. The advocates carried the day. Nevertheless, in spite of their victory, they had failed to convince the minority of their errors, and so their view was not accepted unanimously. After adjournment, the General Court was notified of the synod's decision, and acting according to the precedent established with the Cambridge Platform, it ordered the work printed and sent to the churches of the colony for objections or approval. As an afterthought, the court asked Richard Mather, John Wilson, John Allin, and Zechariah Symmes to compose a preface for the printed form. Jonathan Mitchel was deputized to examine their introductory remarks for errors.[48]

The work of the synod was not binding, and since the General Court could not impose the decision on the churches, they were left to their own judgment on whether to adopt broad baptism. Often the same battle waged in the synod was fought again on a smaller scale among the members of individual churches. In Dorchester once again there were difficulties when Mather's flock was confronted with the synod's work. The halfway solution now had the support of the minister, the elders, the town's most influential citizens, and the authority of a large majority of the colony's clergy, but even this did not persuade the church members that God's command was at last unequivocal. After another round of debate in which many of the same premises, deductions, and conclusions were reexamined, the Dorchester saints again rejected the teacher's arguments and refused to accept the recommendations of the synod.[49]

Despite the refusal of Mather's church to adopt the Halfway Covenant, the synod of 1662 was not without effect in Dorchester. In fact, the aftermath of the most recent round of deliberations considerably increased the strength of the opponents in resisting Mather and the determinations of the synod. After 1662 the church members were no longer forced to stand alone against their educational, economic, and social superiors. They gained considerable outside support from the minority dissenters, and it was this infusion that distinguished the Dorchester disagreement from a simple clash between the intellectual and the unlettered mob. In peasant communities like Mather's village when the representatives of the ecclesiastical elite become ideologically detached from the members or fail to interpret the essence of their perception of the faith to their flocks, the typical reaction is not usually a rejection of the elite but a maturing of a counterinterpretation by the members.

This type of counterinterpretation or lay intellectualism was not new to the Bay Colony by 1662. In the first years of settlement it had been manifested in the disagreements over prophecy, membership, and Antinomianism. On these issues, the clerics were involved, more or less, as a coherent unit in opposition to one dissenter or a small group of clerical dissenters. Wheelwright and Cotton, at least temporarily, had stood with Anne Hutchinson. Robert Lenthall, Thomas Hooker, John Warham, and Parker and Noyes were also involved at one time or another in separate disputes over membership and they too stood almost alone against the massed authority of their fellows.

The dissension over prophecy and presbyterian intrachurch organization followed the same pattern with the weight of the ministerial fraternity being used to press a dissenter or a handful of recalcitrants either into silence or into a more agreeable stand. But this was not the case in the dispute over the Halfway Covenant. Even by 1657 the issue had deeply divided the fellowship, placing respected and highly esteemed members on both sides of the question; but by the end of the synod in 1662, the vanquished were strong enough and sufficiently confident in the rightness of their stand so that they did not have to accept the minority position as an indication of total defeat. Despite being outnumbered and outvoted, they remained a cohesive and articulate segment of the colony's ecclesiastical community, and, most important, they were able to make an attempt at gaining support for their cause by using the traditionalism of peasant communities to foster the growth of a lay intellectualism that would counter the sophistication of the synod's majority party. This was particularly evident in the pamphlet battle over the Halfway Covenant which followed the dissolution of the synod.

As soon as the participants in the conclave had returned to their homes, the debate began. Charles Chauncy composed his *Anti-Synodalia Scripta Americana* to express the dissident view, and he was answered by John Allin of Dedham, the spokesman for the majority. Increase was the first of the Mathers to enter the fray. He wrote an unsigned preface to a book by John Davenport opposing the synod's decision. A reply to the work by Mather and Davenport was composed by another pair of theologians: Jonathan Mitchel, the guiding force of the majority party in the synod, and Richard Mather. Mitchel wrote the rebuttal to Increase Mather's preface, and Mather, again writing in advocacy of the doctrine, replied to Davenport. Mitchel's effort, *An Answer to the Apologetical Preface*, was published under a single title page with Mather's work as *A Defense of the Answer and Arguments of the Synod*.[50]

The battle waged by Davenport, Chauncy, Mitchel, the Mathers, and others who joined the exchange was over control of the peasant mind. This was a different approach than that of the earlier polemical confrontations which were fought only among accepted members of the clergy. Much of what the dissenters had lost in the synod, they hoped to regain by turning the colony's ordinary church members against the clerical majority who favored the halfway solution.[51] This tactic was particularly evident to supporters of the synod's recommendations such as Mitchel who wrote to one of the dissenters, "For the People in the Country have in a manner no Arguments to object but this, some of yourselves, some of the Ministers are against it."[52] In *Another Essay for the Investigation of Truth*, John Davenport had tried to deny the nature of the antisynodalian arguments by insisting he was only seeking "Truth with Peace," but the inaccuracy of his assertion was apparent in Increase Mather's preface to the same work. The younger Mather admitted the purpose of the book was to gain a wide audience for the antisynodalian argument. He said, "We are willing that the World should see what is here presented. But especially, being perswaded that the Honor of God, and of his Truth, require this as a duty at our hands, We durst not hinder what is here maintained from coming into light, lest we should one day have it laid unto our Charge, that we did withhold the Truth in unrighteousness."[53] The measure of their success is evident not only in the damage the disagreement brought to the status of the clerical community but also in the reluctance of the majority of the colony's churches to adopt the Halfway Covenant.[54] This was particularly true in Dorchester where Mather's position on the issue should have been strengthened by the result of the synod, but it was not, or, if it was, it was not strengthened sufficiently to overcome peasant resistance, strengthened opposition, and diminished clerical prestige.

The first confrontation in Dorchester after the synod of 1662 began when Mrs. Israel Stoughton, the town's leading matron, and her daughter, Rebecca Taylor, requested baptism for the Taylor children, even though the mother was a member of the church only through the covenant of her parents. Mather, whose hearing was failing noticeably and who was now sightless in one eye, could not have been cheered by the bitterness the request generated, and he attempted to avoid a direct clash of factions similar to that which had followed the request of James Minot's wife for modification of the procedure on baptism. At the request of the elders and brethren, he asked the mother if she would join the church and thereby remove the impediment to her children's baptism. On October 24, 1688, he reported that the woman had refused the request. Mather related, "She did not Judge her self worthy or as yet fitt for the Lord's supp and therfore durst not adventure ther uppon but yet did desier baptizme for her Children." The question was debated again, but neither side would relent. Consensus was not to be gained, and the Dorchester church was prevented from taking any action. The restrictions on sacramental administration were retained, and the children were not baptized.[55]

This was Mather's last attempt to persuade his church to accept the results of the determinations of 1657 and 1662, and he had failed. His disappointment at the rebuke from those he had served so long was a painful thing to the aged minister. Long the champion of expanded baptism, he had worked hard for its acceptance. Then, after it had received approval by most of the colony's leading clergymen, some of the local churches, and many of the churches in Connecticut, he remained unable to persuade his own members to accept it.

As three centuries of investigation have shown, an understanding of the struggle over the Halfway Covenant is an elusive thing. When the heat generated by the struggle was beginning to subside, Cotton Mather became the first commentator to attempt to make sense of the difficulty. He informed readers of the *Magnalia* that those who dissented from the pronouncements of the synod did so because they "feared that if all such, as had not yet exposed themselves by censurable Scandalls found upon them, should be admitted unto all the Priviledges of our Churches, a worldly part of Mankind might, before we are aware, carry all Things into such a course of Proceeding, as would be very disagreeable unto the Kingdom of Heaven."[56]

Since Mather expounded his view, large numbers of historians and

chroniclers have agreed with him. Others have opposed his interpretation or offered explanations of their own, and as the controversy has continued up to the present time, the variety of viewpoints
expressed has continued to expand. James Truslow Adams, for
example, writing some fifty years ago, maintained that the clerical
insistence on modifying the eligibility requirements for baptism was
the result of the ministers' declining influence in the colony and
"the fact that they felt the need of lowering the requirements for
admission to the church is the strongest sort of evidence as to the
extent to which liberal opinion had developed among the mass of
laymen." Perry Miller agreed with Adams, at least in the opinion
that the Halfway Covenant was designed to stay the decline of
religion in Massachusetts Bay. "On the face of it," he wrote, "the
Half-Way Covenant, instead of being a concession to worldliness,
purported to be a device for preventing worldly children from
invading the sanctuary; yet underneath, the real motive was a determination to keep actual control a monopoly of those who could be
relied upon." The fear that a large segment of the colony's population would be unbaptized, he added, also contributed to the uneasiness that troubled the clergy in the years after 1645. Unlike
Adams, Miller did not attribute the members' refusal to accept the
innovation to an excess of "liberal opinion." He discerned a polariza-
tion between the mass of church members and their clerical leaders
and attributed it to the outgrowth of the threat such an innovation
posed for the ordinary members. In the advocacy by a closely knit
ecclesiastical brotherhood, the members saw the sinister outlines of a
clerical plot, and to a generation raised on tales of Jesuit intrigue and
machinations, the residual sensitivity to secret combinations and
clandestine cabals was enough to move their thoughts in this direction even if the motive for such a plot remained obscure.[57]

More recently the division between clergy and members has been
examined by Robert G. Pope, who agrees with Cotton Mather and
Perry Miller that the members' refusal to accept broader baptism was
a symptom of traditionalism rather than proletarian liberalism. The
same pattern of conflict that prevented twenty-nine of the Bay
Colony's thirty-four churches from accepting the Halfway Covenant
was also present in Connecticut. Like Mather's flock in Dorchester,
churches at Hartford, Windsor, Wethersfield, and even Peter Prud-

den's church at Milford refused to alter their stand on membership and the qualifications for baptism. The forces behind the rejection were manifold, according to Pope, but first among them was the failure to find accord on matters of polity. "The controversy over baptism only hid the fundamental disagreement over membership and structure," he noted. "The superficiality of the half-way covenant as an issue was apparent in several churches; when schism finally occurred, both factions adopted extended baptism. The basic cleavage was presbyterial versus Congregational polity."[58]

If events in Dorchester were typical of those in nearly fifty other New England villages, the analysis of the dispute made by Perry Miller is probably the most accurate of those that have been made. The split he discerned between clergy and ordinary members was indeed the result, at least in part, of what he labeled traditionalism, but this was not the sole result. More factors were involved in the churches' rejection of broadened baptism. The divergence within Mather's community of saints offers information on at least a few of these. It involved a three-part division, with the church members opposing the combined strength of the village aristocracy and Mather, whose motives varied considerably from those of his allies. This tripartite division in the church was more than the result of the persistence of traditional values or standards and cannot be dismissed simply as anti-intellectualism.

The division was inherent in the peasant character of the village, the result of the limited number of points of societal reference available to the Dorchester residents. Questions involving broad-based or restricted baptism, congregational or presbyterial polity, or democratic versus aristocratic control of the churches were only expressions of the conflict. Ample testimony to the true nature of the dispute was given by the minority members of the synod who were candid in admitting that their attacks were not directed at ideology or at their ministerial colleagues—a tactic that had been found to be ineffective. Instead, they aimed their assault at that segment of colonial society whose interests were most threatened by the proposed modification. The success of their tactics was revealed in their ability to prohibit the general adoption of the synodalian prescription for nearly fifty years.

Epilogue

In the two decades that Mather labored to find a solution to the problem of baptism, he did not neglect his studies or fail to engage in his full round of clerical activities. Early in 1648 he borrowed some ninety books from John Johnson and William Parks of Roxbury. Since they were largely concerned with theology, Mather probably used them extensively in the preparation of his sermons and lectures.[1] Another of his activities during this period was a visit to an Indian village. This was not his first experience with the natives. Earlier, in 1646, he, John Eliot, and John Allin, accompanied by an interpreter, probably visited Cutshamekin, a local sachem.[2] On this second occasion, however, he traveled to a settlement of Indians that had been subjected to Eliot's proselytizing zeal. Under the missionary's direction, the Indians had been forming towns to practice their newly received religion, and Natick, the largest of these communities, was only a short distance from the older English settlements. The Indians had decided to gather their own church, and it was for this reason that Mather and many other clerics had journeyed to the village.

Wearing a white armband designating him as a visiting minister, Mather was a fascinated observer at the solemn ceremony. He was deeply impressed with the meetinghouse and recorded that it looked like it had been built by English carpenters. What further proof could there be, he asked, of the blessings Christianity was bestowing on the Indians?[3] The thing that impressed Mather more than the meetinghouse, however, was the sight of the Indians at prayer. He lamented that there were some English who made light of the attempts to convert the natives, saying:

To see and to hear Indians opening their mouths, and lifting
up their hands and their eyes in solemn Prayer to the Living
God, calling on him by his Name JEHOVAH, in the Medita-
tion of Jesus Christ, and this for a good while together; to see
and hear them exhorting . . . from the Word of God; to see
them and hear them confessing the Name of Christ Jesus, and
their own sinfulness, sure this is more than usual. And though
they spake in a language, of which many of us understood but
little, yet we that were present that day, we saw them, and we
heard them perform the duties mentioned, with such grave and
sober countenances, with such comely reverence in gesture,
and their whol carriage, and with such plenty of tears trickling
down the cheeks of some of them, as did argue to us that they
spake with much good affection, and holy fear of God, and it
much affected our hearts.[4]

The Indians had to follow the same procedure as the colonists to
form a church. Personal professions of faith were required and the
visiting officials had to be satisfied that the congregation was indeed
a true church. In this case, the observers seem to have been convinced the Indians were regenerate, but they were not given the
needed endorsement. The reason for the refusal was that no qualified native was available to serve as pastor or teacher to the congregation. It was deemed inadvisable by the magistrates and elders in
attendance to give their approval in that circumstance. Though no
church was formed, Mather was optimistic about the attempts to
bring the natives to Christ. Shortly after his visit to Natick, he wrote
a preface to a book by John Eliot and Thomas Mayhew, Jr., on the
conversion of the Indians. In these few pages, he told how Christ had
effected marvelous changes in the Indians' way of life and how
Christianity had brought joy to their souls.[5]

The first decades in Massachusetts Bay were busy for the Mather
family as well as for the patriarch. Samuel had graduated from
Harvard in 1643 and Nathaniel in 1647. Both sons continued at the
college after finishing their degrees; Samuel served for a time as a
fellow of the institution, and Nathaniel received his master's degree
in 1650. The two younger boys, Eleazer and Increase, also entered
the college at about this time, and the education of four sons
exerted at least some strain on the cleric's purse, for when Nathaniel

finished at Harvard he owed more than £3 in commencement charges and £1 to the president. In three years following his son's departure, Mather repaid part of the debt in silver, but there is no record of his making payment in full. The education of Increase provided a number of problems, for although he had been dedicated to the service of God by his parents, he was, by his own admission, a less-than-devoted scholar. Neither did the meals at Harvard agree with him. In 1652 he left the college and went to live with John Norton of Ipswich where he continued his education. Eleazer was a bit sturdier and continued his studies at the New England Cambridge. He received his master's degree in 1656.[6]

While his sons studied for the ministry, the elder Mather's connection with Harvard became more than that of a concerned parent. He served for a time as a member of the college's board of overseers, and it was as a member of the board that he and John Norton were sent to ask Charles Chauncy to become president of the college. Henry Dunster had resigned over the controversy caused by his views on baptism, and so to avoid a repetition of the difficulties that brought about Dunster's departure, Chauncy was offered the post at £100 per annum on the condition that he "forbeare to disseminate or publish any Tenets concerning the necessity of immersion in Baptisme and Celebration of the Lords Supper at Evening, or to oppose the received Doctrine therein." Mather and Norton were successful in their mission. Chauncy accepted the offer and was inaugurated shortly thereafter.[7]

Difficulties and tribulations of the sort concerning the presidency of Harvard were of a minor nature to Mather, however, compared to his own personal tragedy. After three decades of marriage and six sons, he was left alone on the death of his wife in the early spring of 1655. In the following months, the minister submerged himself in study, but the rewards of scholarship were not enough to assuage his loneliness. Bachelorhood was not a cordial state for a seventeenth-century New Englander, and eventually his thoughts turned toward remarriage. His choice was a woman who had been the wife of a minister for many years. The widow of his old friend John Cotton, who had died in 1652, was selected to be the second Mrs. Mather. Sarah Cotton and Richard Mather were married on August 26, 1656, in a ceremony performed by Governor John Endicott, and Sarah moved to Dorchester with her daughter, Maria Cotton.[8] After raising a family of sons, Mather must have found it to be a new experience to have a young woman in his home. Increase undoubtedly took some interest in sixteen-year-old Maria when he left John Norton's house to make his periodic visits to Dorchester, but if he was ever filled with thoughts of her, the visions were not regular enough to keep him from his studies. He received his degree from Harvard in 1656. Samuel, who had some years earlier accepted a nonconformist pulpit in Dublin, had written asking that his youngest brother be sent to him for training. The father agreed, and the boy sailed from Massachusetts Bay in 1657.[9]

The departure of Increase may have turned Mather's thoughts to the day when he would no longer be able to fulfill his function as a teacher to his church. Considering the possibility that God could call him suddenly, he prepared *A Farewell Exhortation to the Church and People of Dorchester*, a volume published in 1657. In it Mather pointed to a decline in the colony's religious fervor, but it was not the first time he had done so. Earlier, he had written two catechisms in an attempt to install the piety of Massachusetts Bay's founders in the second generation, but just as the catechisms were composed with thoughts of England in his mind, *A Farewell Exhortation* also indicated Mather had not forgotten his mother country. While sectaries multiplied and liberty of conscience held sway in Cromwell's Protectorate, he exhorted his parishioners against toleration, labeling religious liberty as one of the "divises of Satan, that so pernicious errours might more easily be entertained."[10] When the book was printed, Mather had copies distributed to the church members by his deacons, hoping in that way they would remember his words after death had claimed him.[11]

The tenor and style of *A Farewell Exhortation* were similar in many respects to *An Heart-Melting Exhortation*, a polemic Mather had written in 1645, but while almost a decade separated the two works, both were fine early examples of the form that later became known as the jeremiad. The use of this form was more characteristic of New England's second generation, but Mather and several of the founders had used it before 1650. The Dorchester cleric's two books differ in many respects from the stylized products that became standard by 1660, but they included, nevertheless, the ingredients that made them genuine examples of the form. Each contained, to some degree, the idea of divine visitation for sin, an analysis of the faulted relationship between God and the group, a catalog of future judgments, and a plea for reformation. Both works were lamentations for a people fallen from grace.[12] The jeremiads by Richard Mather carried an authority that was missing when the younger clerics used the same form. Over the years death had claimed many of those who first challenged a wilderness to reform the world. He was one of the few who survived as a last witness to what had been the city on a hill. He had watched four decades of change in England and America, and in the change he saw decay. The two exhortations embodied Mather's sorrow for fallen nations, yet in the pattern that was to become standard in later jeremiads, they also revealed his hope for redemption.

While Mather pondered what he saw as a decline in Bay Colony piety, events in England only served to intensify his concern for the future of Christianity. The death of Cromwell, the return of a Stuart monarch, the reestablishment of Anglicanism, and the renewal of some measure of persecution for nonconformists all boded ill for the church. The seriousness of the problems was made clear to Richard Mather when Increase, after being harried from parish to parish by agents of the restored king, decided to return to Massachusetts in 1661. The young cleric arrived at Boston on a Saturday and was at his father's house by nightfall. There he met his older brother Eleazer who was visiting from his own church in Northampton. The three clerics probably had much to discuss on that first evening together. Besides the usual theological topics there was the religious situation in England, and the conversation could not have been optimistic as they sat and talked. As the fire flickered and the hours passed, they could only decry the evil times that had come to the Reformation. The following day the gloom over events in the homeland was dispersed temporarily and there was much joy for the father: "The Comforted Old Patriarch, sat Shining like the Sun in Gemini, and hearing his two Sons, in his own Pulpit entertain the People of GOD, with Performances, that made all People Proclaim him, An Happy Father."[13]

The following month, Increase, now a Master of Arts from Trinity College in Dublin, was admitted as a member of his father's church.[14] He preached alternately in Boston and in Dorchester. The young man recorded nothing of his romantic thoughts during these months, but the winter days at Dorchester were surely pleasant for him. Maria, the daughter of his father's second wife still resided with the Mathers, and Increase wasted no time in beginning a courtship. On March 6, 1662, they were married.[15]

At the time his youngest son took a bride, and while the controversy over baptism was at its height, Mather was remarkably active for a man of nearly seventy years of age. Beyond taking part in the colony's internal squabbles, he preached to his congregation, attended the additional spiritual needs of his church, and devoted time to many other duties. In 1660 he went to Taunton to confer with other elders about the difficulties then besetting the village church, and the following year he briefly gave his talents to the cause of civil government when he and other leaders, both secular and ecclesiastical, met to discuss patent laws and report their findings to the General Court. The year Increase became pastor of the Second or North Church in Boston, the elderly teacher and Deacon John Capen journeyed to Weymouth to witness the gathering of a new church. In the same year, 1664, a petition from the town of Dorchester was written in his hand and presented to the General Court. Along with petitions from other towns, the document affirmed Dorchester's support for the colony's mode of government and enjoined the court to make no changes, since the original Massachusetts Bay patent had been newly confirmed by Charles II.

Yet the strain of constant labor could now be seen on Mather. He often shared his pulpit with visiting ministers, and since Increase's return from England, the young man had aided him on an irregular basis. This was not enough, and the Dorchester church sought more assistance for him. In December the church invited William Stoughton to preach periodically in the village meetinghouse; the following week he accepted.[16] Though he had agreed to take the pulpit, Stoughton refused ordination, preferring to preach as a layman.

Further evidence of Mather's physical decline is found in the notebook of John Minot, the elder son of George Minot, a founder of the church. The shorthand notes he took on sermons delivered in the Dorchester meetinghouse provide a valuable record of the men who preached in Mather's pulpit from December 1663 to the end of the following June. During that period Minot heard approximately seventy sermons. The record was far from complete, since there were days when he attended only one sermon and other days when he missed church altogether, but it shows that in his sixty-seventh year, Mather's vigor had diminished considerably. Of the sermons recorded by Minot, Mather preached only thirty. Stoughton, who had been engaged to lighten Mather's preaching load, evidently had other business during the period. The record indicates he preached only twelve times in the seven months, and at one point, he missed fourteen sabbath services in a row. The only other man who preached with any degree of frequency was Samuel Torrey who occupied the pulpit more often than Stoughton. The remainder of the sermons were divided among a large group of men, though none on a regular basis. Increase and Eleazer Mather delivered a combined total of three sermons in the months recorded in Minot's book.[17]

As Mather's share of the preaching was reduced, the irritations connected with church management did not decline proportionately, and the little incidents that are the bane of clerics' lives continued apace in his church. In 1653 he and thirteen others were present at a meeting called to decide what course of action to take with one of their number, "Dorcas the blackmore," who was incarcerated in Boston. Dorcas, the servant of a church member, had joined the church in 1641 and at the time of her admission and baptism was regarded as a woman of sound knowledge and godliness. The meeting called to discuss her fate decided the hapless woman should be "redeemed" and Ensigne Foster and two deacons were sent to Boston to secure her release. An ox and a cow were placed in the custody of a Mr. Howard for partial payment to gain her freedom, and the church agreed to contribute the remainder of the amount.[18]

There were many incidents of this nature to distract Mather from the work of God. One of his nagging problems was maintaining the Dorchester meetinghouse in good repair; although this was the task of the deacons according to the division of labor specified in the congregational plan of ecclesiastical order, much of the problem ultimately devolved on Mather for solution. The structure required periodic maintenance, and repairs were rarely made without some measure of prodding. "William Blake is appointed to warne Thomas

Andrews to daube the meeting house" in 1661, and this was only one such case where the deacons were remiss in their duties and the church was required to issue a warning.

Only four years after the repair work, more controversy centered on the building. The difficulty began when three members decided the meetinghouse needed a gallery. Uncertain that they could obtain the necessary support from the church officers as a group, they approached them singly and gained their consent. They then ordered the gallery built even though no official permission had been given. During construction the officials were silent, but when the gallery was completed, they denied having given approbation to the project and complained the gallery was poorly designed. They accused the planners of having committed the most egregious error possible in meetinghouse architecture; they had built a gallery that darkened the pulpit.[19] A town meeting was held to discuss the matter in August 1665. The assembled villagers decided to allow the gallery to remain since it was already built. But they demanded a public apology from the three men who commissioned the construction. Filled with contrition, the men said:[20]

> We whose names are vnderwritten doe acknowledge that it was our weaknes that we were so inconsiderate as to make a small seat [gallery] in the Meeting house, without more cleare and full approbation of the Towne, and Select men . . . . Therefore we desire, that our failing therein, may be passed by: And if the Town shall grant us our seat, that we haue been at so much cost in setting vp, we thankfully acknowledge your loue vnto us therein; and we doe herevpon further engage ourselues, that we will not giue vp, or sell any of our places in that seat, to any person or persons, but whom the Elders shall approue of, or such, as shall haue power to place men in seats in the assembly.

	Increase Atherton
signed	Samuel Procter
	Thomas Bird

One of the reasons the gallery caused difficulties in the town was that it necessitated a new seating arrangement. Since seating was done on the basis of status, any changes were bound to occasion disruption. Those responsible for the seating order were also in an awkward position. They were certain to incur the enmity of both those who found they had been demoted and those who insisted they deserved a more dignified position. The strain on members of the committee was well illustrated in the action taken by Henry Withington at the time the gallery was under construction: "That (he being formerly appointed (with the other elders) for to seat people in the seats of the meeting hous) he was not willing to doe that worke any longer but was resolved to lay it down the other elders not acting in that thing with himself but left it to him only."[21] Withington was not interested in winning the opprobrium of his fellow church members while the other elders escaped their wrath.

It is not known how the seating arrangements were made in the new gallery, but the motives of the three men who commissioned its construction were obvious. Their apology indicated they had been assigned places in the gallery. Although the most sought-after seats were in the front rows on the main floor, the first row of the gallery was next in prestige. This meant that Atherton, Procter, and Bird probably moved themselves into very desirable seating by instigating the project.

In the same months that the gallery controversy was raging, Mather was harassed with even more details of administering a church. In the closing months of 1664, Deacon Edward Clap, who had given twenty-six years of service to the church, died. His position remained open for a time, but in May, a few members suggested someone be appointed to fill the vacancy. The job carried a certain amount of prestige, but the duties of the position required more time and effort than the honor was worth. The deacons managed the temporal affairs of the church, handling the finances, aiding the elders, and serving at the Lord's table. An argument began over the position. One segment of the church opposed filling it, arguing that the church's two remaining deacons, John Capen and John Wiswall, were sufficient. The other segment insisted that the position be filled because Wiswall was a deacon in name only—that he paid no attention to church business. The disputants chose not to debate the matter at length until Wiswall could be present to defend himself. The following week he appeared, was questioned about his performance, and was reprimanded for delinquency. Wiswall was not intimidated by the censure, and he refused to resign. Not wanting to create more ill will by pursuing the inquiry further, the congregation dropped the matter.[22]

Another unpleasant incident occurred in the church at approximately the same time as the disagreement over Wiswall. The elders ordered the wife of Captain Thomas Clark to appear before them to answer charges of slandering the governor and the General Court. The woman was no longer a participating member of the Dorchester church, having been dismissed some time before the alleged offense. But since her dismission, she had not joined another church; hence, her objectionable conduct fell within the jurisdiction of the Dorchester church. Clark failed to appear before the elders on the appointed day, but the following month she was present. She freely admitted her guilt, but refused to recant. As penalty she was admonished by the church. Six months later, on April 13, 1667, she was again called before the church members and given another chance to retract her remarks; again she refused. As penalty for her incorrigible behavior, she was excommunicated from the Dorchester church.[23]

While his church debated Wiswall's qualifications and Clark's answers, Mather received a letter from Taunton asking for assistance in settling a new set of differences. Five years earlier he had journeyed to the town to give similar aid, but was now physically unable to make the trip. William Stoughton and Lieutenant Foster were sent in his place. Mather's health continued to decline, and the church again asked Stoughton to accept ordination and become a teaching elder. They made the request three times in as many weeks. Each time he refused, but he agreed to continue helping with the preaching.[24]

Stoughton's refusal, the teacher's diminishing vigor, and the death of his colleague John Wilson of the First Church in Boston were all part of a series of events that saddened Mather's days. One after another, the men with whom he had worked and endeavored to build a land according to the revealed will of God were dying. John Winthrop passed away in 1649 and Thomas Hooker shortly before. Gone, too, were John Cotton, Thomas Shepard, Peter Bulkeley, and John Norton, his friend and confidant of many years. Mather was deeply grieved by Norton's passing, and at his funeral "wept over him . . . a Sermon most agreeable to the occasion."[25]

In 1668 Mather was asked again to participate in the adjudication of another ecclesiastical controversy. As with many of his struggles in the past, the most recent confrontation was related to baptism. The First Church in Boston had called John Davenport of New Haven to fill the vacancy created by Wilson's death, but a minority within the church opposed his selection. The objections centered on Davenport's advanced age and his continued opposition to the Halfway Covenant. Under Wilson, the sophisticated semiurban Bostonians had accepted broadened eligibility for baptism, but Davenport was determined to return to the church's earlier regulations. A further complication was that those opposed to Davenport were involved in agitation for permission to leave the First Church and form their own religious body.[26]

In August 1668 the church members at Dorchester received an invitation from Boston asking them to send elders and messengers to advise on Davenport's appointment. They complied with the request, and a delegation headed by Mather made the trip to Boston. There they met with representatives of other churches from the sixth to the eighth of August. Three days later, Mather reported the results of the conference to his own church. The Bostonians were advised to call Davenport as their pastor and to allow the dissident members to depart and gather their own church. The recommendations were accepted in part, and Davenport and his family were admitted to membership in November. The next month he was ordained pastor of the church. The church at Dorchester was invited to send its elders to the ordination, but Mather was unable to attend. Two deacons and two members represented the town.[27]

The second part of the recommendations made by the August meeting of elders was not followed by the First Church in Boston. When Davenport became the pastor, he joined the majority party in refusing to allow the dissenters to depart and gather their own church. The dissidents, thwarted by the new teaching elder, made another attempt to gain dismission. They asked the elders to convene again at Boston, reexamine the case, and make a new recommendation. Mather had been in better health than usual when the request arrived, and he was chosen as a member of the Dorchester delegation. The conference began on April 13, 1669, and because of his "Age, Grace and Wisdom," Mather was chosen as moderator. After three days of deliberations, the assembly adjourned after recommending once again the dismission of the dissenting brethren.[28] On the final day of the conclave, Mather became ill while visiting the house of his youngest son. In extreme discomfort due to urinary blockage, the septuagenarian was moved by coach from Boston to his home in Dorchester the following day. Mather had experienced difficulties with kidney stones on previous occasions, but this time the problem was more serious. The pain continued to grow in intensity, but the only indication of his agony was an occasional groan he could not suppress. He read from Goodwin's *Patience* to mitigate the pain and at one point confessed to Increase that while he was distressed by the refusal of his church to accept the decision of the synod of 1662, he remained convinced the Halfway Covenant was valid according to the will of God.

On the morning of the twenty-second, he asked friends to help him get to his study, for he had been away from his work for several days. They did as he requested, but even with their aid he could not manage the move. The pain continued and later in the day he lost his voice.[29] That night "he quietly breathed forth his last; after he had been about Seventy Three Years a Citizen of the World, and Fifty Years a Minister in the Church of God."[30] His demise was duly entered in the church record with the following brief notation: "The 23 of the (2) [April] 69 Mr. Mather the teacher of this Church departed this lif about 10 of the Clock on the evening before being the first teaching officer that have been taken away by death since the first gathering of the Church which is now 32 yeers and 8 months Compleate."[31]

Notes

CHAPTER   I

1. William F. Irvine, "Parents of Rev. Richard Mather," *New England Historical and Genealogical Register* 54 (July 1900): 348-49.

2. Increase Mather, *The Life and Death of That Reverend Man of God, Mr. Richard Mather* (Cambridge, Mass. Bay, 1670), p. 2; J. Paul Rylands, "Abstracts of the Wills of the Mather Family, Proved in the Consistery Court at Chester from 1573 to 1650," *New England Historical and Genealogical Register* 44 (January 1893): 39; Lawrence Stone, "Social Mobility in England, 1500-1700," *Past and Present* 33 (April 1966): 17-18, 33-34.

3. Kenneth Murdock, *Increase Mather: The Foremost American Puritan* (Cambridge, Mass., 1925), p. 2. In his will, Mather mentioned Ellin Worseley and referred to her as "sister." Whether the reference meant sibling is not clear (Richard Mather, "Will," printed in full in the *New England Historical and Genealogical Register* 20 [July 1866] : 248-55). Increase Mather, *The Life of Richard Mather*, pp. 2-3; Samuel E. Morison, *The Intellectual Life of Colonial New England*, 2d ed. (Ithaca, N.Y., 1956), pp. 59-60; Foster Watson, "The Curriculum and Text Books of English Schools in the First Half of the Seventeenth Century," *Transactions of the Biographical Society* 6 (February 1903): passim; J. S. Purvis, *Educational Records* (York, Eng., 1959), p. 5; Cotton Mather, *Magnalia Christi Americana* (London, 1702), 3:123.

4. Increase Mather, *The Life of Richard Mather*, p. 3.

5. Ibid., p. 4.

6. The term presbyterian denotes a style of church polity generally favored by nonconformists in Elizabethan and Jacobean England. It is similar in many respects to the type of congregationalism that would later develop in Massachusetts Bay, but it is distinct from the highly structured Presbyterianism of the Scottish Kirk.

7. Increase Mather, *The Life of Richard Mather*, pp. 3-5; J. A. Picton, *Memorials of Liverpool, Historical and Topographical Including a History of the Dock Estate* (London, 1873), 2:554. During the reign of Elizabeth, Toxteth Park was referred to as a wasteland (Valentine D. Davis, *Some Account of the Ancient Chapel of Toxteth Park, Liverpool, from the Year of 1618 to 1883, and of its Ministers, Especially Richard Mather, the First Minister* [Liverpool, 1884] , p. 1).

8. This may have been Peter Harrison who also preached at Hindly near Wigan in Lancashire.

9. The account of Richard Mather's conversion described by his son shows a striking similarity to normal adolescent crises of identity described

in some detail by psychologist Erik H. Erikson in *Young Man Luther: A Study in Psychoanalysis and History* (New York, 1958), pp. 14-15, 41, 42; see also Erikson's *Identity: Youth and Crisis* (New York, 1968), pp. 53-54, 87, 119, 124-32; these symptoms with additional psychological ramifications are also described by Claude Lévi-Strauss, *Structural Anthropology*, Anchor ed. (New York, 1967), p. 161. See Increase Mather, *The Life of Richard Mather*, pp. 5-6; while his father's conversion is spoken of as an event worthy of much awe by Increase, a more cynical view of the great experience was expressed by Anthony à Wood, who noted laconically, Richard Mather "was called to teach ... at Toxteth Park near to Liverpool in the said county, an. 1612, where pretending to receive a new light within him, was converted to godliness an. 1614"; *Athaenae Oxonienses*, 3d ed. with additions and a continuation by Phillip Bliss (London, 1817), 3:832.

10. Lévi-Strauss, *Structural Anthropology*, pp. 167-69.

11. Cotton Mather, *Magnalia*, vol. 3; Lawrence Hall, "The Ancient Chapel at Toxteth Park and Toxteth School," *Historic Society of Lancashire and Cheshire* 87 (1936): 37.

12. Increase Mather, *The Life of Richard Mather*, pp. 6, 7.

13. Ibid., p. 7.

14. Ibid. Cotton Mather gives the date as November 13, 1618 (*Magnalia*, 3:124); there is no record of the exact date the chapel was built. It is only tradition that assigns Mather as the first minister. It is certain that Richard Poile (Poyle) preceded him, but the date of his departure is not known. One authority suggests he may have stayed on until Mather's ordination in 1619, but there is no evidence to substantiate this; Lawrence Hall, "Toxteth Park Chapel in the Seventeenth Century," *Transactions of the Unitarian Historical Society* 5 (November 1934): 356-59.

15. Increase Mather, *The Life of Richard Mather*, p. 7.

16. Picton, *Memorials*, 2:556. Because Toxteth Park Chapel was extraparochial, it had no register. Christenings, weddings, and funerals at the chapel were entered in the Walton-on-the-Hill register (*The Registers of the Parish Church of Walton-on-the-Hill in the County of Lancaster*, ed. Arthur S. Smith [Wigan, Eng., 1900]); Increase Mather, *The Life of Richard Mather*, pp. 8-9. The parish register contains the entry "Richard Mather of Walton parishe, Katrin Houlte of this Parishe" (*The Registers of the Parish of Bury in the County of Lancaster*, ed. W. J. Lowenberg [Rochdale, Eng., 1898], p. 356).

17. Increase Mather, *The Life of Richard Mather*, p. 8; Horace E. Mather, *The Lineage of Rev. Richard Mather* (Hartford, Conn., 1891), p. 33.

18. J. A. Picton, *Selections from the Municipal Archives and Records of Liverpool from the Thirteenth to the Seventeenth Century Inclusive* (Liverpool, 1883), 1:200.

19. George T. O. Bridgeman, "The History of the Church and Manor at Wigan in the County of Lancaster," 16, pt. 2, *Remains Historical and Literary Connected with the Palatine Counties of Lancashire and Chester* (Manchester, Eng., 1899), pp. 367-69.

20. Bishop Bridgeman's Register, EDA 3/1, Cheshire Record Office, Chester, pp. 385-89; John Bridgeman, who had replaced Thomas Morton as bishop of Chester, was consecrated at Lambeth in May 1619 (ibid., p. 196). See Bridgeman, *The Articles of Which the Church Wardens and Swornemen Throughout the Diocese of Chester Are to Take Notice* (London, 1643), 38 pages, unnumbered.

21. Bridgeman, *Articles.*

22. Simon Byby was also instrumental in getting John Cotton appointed to Saint Botolph's Church in Boston, England, despite some reservations on the part of officials who thought him too far from the prescribed doctrines of the established church (Thomas Hutchinson, *The Hutchinson Papers* [Albany, N.Y., 1865], 1:271). See also Increase Mather, *The Life of Richard Mather*, p. 10.

23. Court Book (Diocese of Chester), R.VI.A.23, vol. 2, Borthwick Institute, York, Eng., p. 316. Increase Mather gives the date for the second trial as 1634 (*The Life of Richard Mather*, p. 11); this is in error, for the visitation of Chester was conducted earlier (Court Book [Diocese of Chester], R.VI.A.23, vol. 2, p. 376).

24. Increase Mather, *The Life of Richard Mather*, p. 11.

25. For over fifty years the wearing of the surplice had been one of the tests of conformity. As early as 1590, warnings were issued to those who failed to observe the requirement ("Visitation of the Diocese of Chester by John, Archbishop of York, Held in the Collegiate and Parish Church of Manchester, 1590, with the Archbishop's Correspondence with the Clergy," *Remains Historical and Literary Connected with the Palatine Counties of Lancaster and Chester*, 96: 4-5). See also Increase Mather, *The Life of Richard Mather*, p. 11.

26. Cotton Mather, *Magnalia*, 3:125.

27. Increase Mather, *The Life of Richard Mather*, p. 20.

28. Letter of John Cotton to a Puritan Minister in England, December 3, 1634, original in the Hutchinson MSS, Massachusetts Historical Society, Boston, reprinted in Alexander Young, *Chronicles of the First Planters of the Colony of Massachusetts Bay, from 1632 to 1636* (Boston, 1846), pp. 438-44.

29. Cotton Mather, *Magnalia*, 3:19.

30. Isabel M. Calder, *Letters of John Davenport, Puritan Divine* (New Haven, Conn., 1937), p. 39.

31. Thomas Shepard, *The Autobiography of Thomas Shepard*, in *Publications of the Colonial Society of Massachusetts* (Boston, 1932), 27: 375-76.

32. John Wilson to John Cotton, February 3, 1628, *Winthrop Papers* (Boston, 1931), 2:57.

33. The letters from Cotton and Hooker were not Mather's first contact with the network for dissemination of nonconformist propaganda that had developed in England in the years since the reign of Elizabeth. Shortly before his difficulties with the hierarchy, he acquired at least two letters written by Cotton which he thought were important enough to make copies before passing them on. One dealt with the time of day when the sabbath began, the other was addressed to Samuel Skelton in New England and concerned his apparent separatism. The copies are among the Richard Mather MSS at the American Antiquarian Society, Worcester, Mass. By 1632 at least one other nonconformist tract had found its way to Mather's parish in Lancashire, and, as he had done with Cotton's letters, Mather made his own copy. The document, with a heading "Five Questions Answered," was a tirade against the wearing of vestments (Richard Mather MSS, Gratz Collection, nos. 8-23, Historical Society of Pennsylvania, Philadelphia).

34. Increase Mather, *The Life of Richard Mather*, pp. 13-14.

35. Ibid., pp. 14-18.

36. John Foxe, *The Acts and Monuments of John Foxe* (New York,

1965), 7:328, 497. Another staple in Mather's reading fare at this time was the catalog of horrors contained in John Brinsley's *The True Watch* (London, 1622).

37. Richard Mather, *An Heart-Melting Exhortation* (London, 1650), p. 66.

38. Foxe, *Acts and Monuments*, 7:194.

39. Increase Mather, *The Life of Richard Mather*, p. 17.

40. Mather's fourth son, Joseph, was born in 1634. The date of the child's death is not known, but it is thought he died while very young (Horace E. Mather, *The Lineage of Rev. Richard Mather*, p. 33).

41. Richard Mather, *Journal of Richard Mather*, 1635, vol. 3: *Collections of the Dorchester Antiquarian and Historical Society* (Boston, 1846), p. 5. The entry was dated April 16, 1635, but was obviously written after that date, for it described events which occurred later in the journey; Richard Mather, *Journal*, April 16, 1635.

42. "Governor Hinckley's Verse on the Death of His Second Consort," *New England Historical and Genealogical Register* 1 (January 1847):95.

43. Richard Mather, *Journal*, April 16, May 23, 25, 1635.

44. Ibid., August 15, 1635; John Winthrop, *Journal History of New England*, unnumbered volume in *Original Narratives of Early American History*, ed. James K. Hosmer (New York, 1908), 1:155-57.

45. Richard Mather, *Journal*, August 16, 1635.

46. The portion of Mather's *Journal* written after the arrival and landing at Boston has not survived.

CHAPTER   II

1. Young, *Chronicles*, p. 427.

2. Larzer Ziff, *The Career of John Cotton: Puritanism and the American Experience* (Princeton, N.J., 1962), p. 49.

3. Ibid.; Cotton Mather, *Magnalia*, 3:20-21.

4. Winthrop, *Journal*, 1:51-52, 95.

5. Richard Mather, "Some Objections against Imposition in Ordination," Richard Mather MSS, American Antiquarian Society, Worcester, Mass., p. 3.

6. *Records of the First Church in Boston, 1630-1868*, vol. 39: *Publications of the Colonial Society of Massachusetts* (Boston, 1961), p. 19. The two-and-one-half-month delay in welcoming Mather to fellowship does not imply a reluctance to admit him. It was usual at that time for weeks and even months to elapse before recent arrivals were formally joined to the church. The hesitancy is indicated in "Some Objections against Imposition in Ordination."

Although Mather was able to demonstrate his correct understanding of the ordination rite to the Boston church in 1635, there were other difficulties in the colony on the subject for a number of years. At the church in Concord, when new elders were ordained in 1637, the members resolved "such as had been ministers in England were lawful ministers by the call of the people there, notwithstanding their acceptance of the call of the bishops, . . . but being come hither, they accounted themselves no ministers, until they were called to another church, and that, upon election, they were ministers before they were solemnly ordained" (Winthrop, *Journal,*

1:212-13). In 1639 there was another disagreement over the meaning of ordination, necessitating a meeting of the colony's clergy, in part, to convince a Weymouth cleric of the correctness of the doctrine ("Conference of the Elders of Massachusetts with the Rev. Robert Lenthal, of Weymouth, Held at Dorchester, Feb. 10, 1639," *Congregational Quarterly* 19 [April 1877] :232-48).

7. Increase Mather, *The Life of Richard Mather*, pp. 23-24. The mention of a vacancy at Roxbury was probably an error on the part of Increase Mather. At this time, the town had two ministers, Thomas Weld and John Eliot.

8. Justin Winsor, ed., *The Memorial History of Boston, Including Suffolk County Massachusetts, 1630-1880* (Boston, 1882), 1:424; Winthrop, *Journal*, 1:50; *Records of the First Church at Dorchester in New England, 1636-1734* (Boston, 1891), p. iv; "Letter of Samuel Fuller to Governor William Bradford, June 28, 1630," *Collections of the Massachusetts Historical Society* (Boston, 1794), 1st ser. 3:74-85. For a more complete discussion of the reasons and events leading to the move to Connecticut, see Edmund S. Morgan, *Visible Saints: The History of a Puritan Idea* (Ithaca, N.Y., 1965), pp. 107-9; Perry Miller, *Errand into the Wilderness*, Torchbook ed. (New York, 1964), pp. 24-27, and "Preparation for Salvation in Seventeenth-Century New England," *Journal of the History of Ideas* 4 (June 1965):265-68.

9. "Letter of Israel Stoughton to Dr. John Stoughton," *Proceedings of the Massachusetts Historical Society* (Boston, 1924-1925), 58:453.

10. Winthrop, *Journal*, 1:132; *Records of the Dorchester Church*, pp. xiii-xviii; Williston Walker, *The Creeds and Platforms of Congregationalism*, Pilgrim ed. (Boston, 1960), pp. 151-52.

11. Winthrop, *Journal*, 1:173-74.

12. Walker, *Creeds and Platforms*, pp. xx, 153; Charles H. Pope, *The Pioneers of Massachusetts: A Descriptive List, Drawn from Records of the Colonies, Towns and Churches, and Other Contemporaneous Documents* (Baltimore, Md., 1965), p. 307; Richard Mather, "A Plea for the Churches of Christ in New England," Richard Mather MSS, Massachusetts Historical Society, Boston, sec. 3, p. 367; *Records of the Dorchester Church*, pp. xx-xxi.

13. *Records of the Governor and Company of the Massachusetts Bay in New England*, ed. Nathaniel B. Shurtleff (Boston, 1853), 1:168.

14. Thomas Shepard to Richard Mather, April 2, 1636, Cotton Mather MSS, Massachusetts Historical Society, Boston.

15. Winthrop, *Journal*, 1:173-74.

16. The description given is a composite account from Mather's own "Plea," sec. 3, p. 367; Edward Johnson, Wonder-Working Providence of Sion's Savior in New England, unnumbered volume in *Original Narratives of Early American History*, ed. J. Franklin Jameson (New York, 1910), pp. 215-16; and from Winthrop, *Journal*, 1:173-74, 199, 292.

17. Winthrop, *Journal*, pp. 177-78.

18. Ibid., p. 177.

19. Ibid., pp. 177-78; Richard Mather, uncataloged notation stored between pages of a letter of Thomas Shepard to Richard Mather, April 2, 1636.

20. Darrett B. Rutman, *American Puritanism: Faith and Practice* (Philadelphia, 1970), pp. 83-88.

21. Richard Mather to Thomas Shepard, uncataloged letter stored between pages of a letter of Thomas Shepard to Richard Mather, April 2, 1636.

22. Ibid.

23. Increase Mather, *The Life of Richard Mather*, p. 10; Richard Mather, uncataloged notation, April 2, 1636.

24. Increase Mather, *The Life of Richard Mather*, p. 24.

CHAPTER   III

1. Winthrop, *Journal*, 1:195 n; Emery Battis, *Saints and Sectaries: Anne Hutchinson and the Antinomian Controversy in the Massachusetts Bay Colony* (Chapel Hill, N.C., 1962), pp. 4, 15; Charles F. Adams, *Three Episodes of Massachusetts History* (Boston, 1893), 1:393; [John Winthrop], *A Short Story of the Rise, Reign, and Ruine of the Antinomians* (London, 1644), p. 31.

2. Adams, *Three Episodes*, 1:395.

3. *Records of the First Church in Boston*, 1:19.

4. [Winthrop], *A Short Story of the Antinomians*, preface; Battis, *Saints and Sectaries*, pp. 90-91, 101-8, 115, 137; Winthrop, *Journal*, 1:195 ff.

5. David D. Hall, ed., *The Antinomian Controversy, 1636-1638: A Documentary History* (Middletown, Conn., 1968), p. 382.

6. Winthrop, *Journal*, 1:208; [Winthrop], *A Short Story of the Antinomians*, preface; *Records of Massachusetts Bay*, 1:207, 211-12.

7. David D. Hall, *The Antinomian Controversy*, p. 349.

8. *Records of Massachusetts Bay*, 1:211-12.

9. David D. Hall, *The Antinomian Controversy*, pp. 382, 387; Adams, *Three Episodes*, 2:533-37; *Records of Massachusetts Bay*, 1:21.

10. *Records of Massachusetts Bay*, 1:217; "Conference of the Elders," pp. 232-33; Winthrop, *Journal*, 1:292-93.

11. "Conference of the Elders," pp. 233-34, 236-48. This was Mather's *An Apologie for Church Government* (London, 1643). It was written in 1638 and 1639, and manuscript copies circulated in Massachusetts Bay and in England for four years before publication. *Records of Massachusetts Bay*, 1:252; Winthrop, *Journal*, 1:293.

12. *Records of Massachusetts Bay*, 1:252, 254; Winthrop, *Journal*, 1:293.

13. Winthrop, *Journal*, 1:279.

14. There is no doubt that Richard Mather was the primary author of the two books in the volume even though the testimony of John Winthrop substantiates the title page in naming the "Elders of New England"—with whom Mather undoubtedly consulted—as the writers (Winthrop, *Journal*, 1:279, 293). Ample testimony to Mather's leading role in the authorship of the works is offered by John Cotton, Nathaniel Mather, Increase Mather, Thomas Weld, and Cotton Mather; see Cotton, "A Reply to Mr. Williams His Examinations, and Answer to the Letters Sent to Him by John Cotton," in *Publications of the Narragansett Club*, 1st ser. (Providence, R.I., 1867), 2:103; Cotton, *The Way of the Congregational Churches Cleared* (London, 1648), pt. 1, p. 70; Nathaniel Mather in the preface to Richard Mather's *A Disputation Concerning Church-Members and Their Children in Answer to Twenty-one Questions* (London, 1659); Increase Mather, *Order of the Gospel* (Boston, 1700), p. 73; Thomas Weld, *An Answer to W. R. His Narration of the Opinions and Practices of the Churches Lately Erected in New England* (London, 1644), p. 15. Writing later, Cotton Mather confirmed that his grandfather had written both works (*Magnalia*, 3:128).

15. Richard Mather, *An Apologie*.

16. Rutman, *American Puritanism*, pp. 115 ff. and passim; see also Erikson, *Youth*, p. 23, and *Young Man Luther*, esp. pp. 254 ff.

17. "Conference of the Elders," p. 240.

18. Ibid., pp. 232-35; Winthrop, *Journal*, 1:292-93; *Records of Massachusetts Bay*, 1:252.

19. "Conference of the Elders," p. 239.

20. Richard Mather, *An Apologie*, p. 3.

21. Ibid., pp. 32-33, 45-46.

22. Ibid., p. 44.

23. Ibid., p. 32.

24. Ibid., pp. 4-5.

25. Ibid., p. 19.

26. Richard Mather, *Church Government and Church Covenant Discussed in Answer to Two and Thirty Questions* (London, 1643). Like *An Apologie*, manuscript copies of this work circulated among clerics in Massachusetts Bay and in England for four years before publication.

27. The Westminster Assembly began its regular sessions on July 1, 1643, and continued to meet regularly for some six years. Although never formally adjourned, it held its last meeting in March 1652.

28. Winthrop, *Journal*, 2:71.

29. The first section of the book was printed by Richard Oulton and Gregory Dexter. The remaining two parts were the work of Thomas Paine and Matthew Simmons (Thomas J. Holmes, "Notes on Richard Mather's *Church Government*, London, 1643," *Proceedings of the American Antiquarian Society*, n.s. 33 [October 1924]: 239, 294). There was also a work by John Cotton circulating in England after 1642. It was published in London under the title *The True Constitution of a Visible Church*, but it was only a brief outline of church practice and by the time of its publication was quite dated; it had been written by Cotton in 1643 and circulated in manuscript under the title "Questions and Answers on Church Government."

30. The lengthy discussion of colonial church practice by Cotton was ultimately published in London in 1645 under the title *The Way of the Churches of Christ in New England*, thus it carries a later publication date than the 1644 *Keys to the Kingdom of Heaven* (London), though it was actually written several years before the latter book.

31. London, 1644.

32. Walker, "The Services of the Mathers in New England Religious Development," *Papers of the American Society of Church History* 5 (1893):65.

33. London, 1644.

34. All three books were published in London, Mather's in 1647, Rutherford's in 1644, and Hooker's in 1648.

35. W. R. [William Rathband], *A Brief Narration of Church Courses in New England* (London, 1644).

36. Weld, *An Answer to W. R.*

37. Richard Mather, *A Catechism, or The Grounds and Principles of the Christian Religion* (London, 1650). No copy of the second catechism survives. Sargent Bush, Jr., "Thomas Hooker and the Westminster Assembly," *William and Mary Quarterly* 29 (April 1972): 293-94.

38. Richard Mather, *An Heart-Melting Exhortation*, author's note at end of volume.

CHAPTER IV

1. *Records of the Dorchester Church*, p. 150.

2. Horace E. Mather, *The Lineage of Rev. Richard Mather*, p. 33; *Records of the Dorchester Church*, p. 131; quotation is from Cotton Mather, *Parentator* (Boston, 1724), p. 5.

3. Horace E. Mather, *The Lineage of Rev. Richard Mather*, p. 33.

4. *Harvard College Records*, pt. 1: *Publications of the Colonial Society of Massachusetts* (Boston, 1925), 15:82; John T. Winterich, *Early American Books and Printing* (Boston, 1935), p. 28; *The Bay Psalm Book*, with an introduction by Wilberforce Eames (New York, 1905), pp. vi, 5; Zoltan Haraszti, *The Enigma of the Bay Psalm Book* (Chicago, 1956), pp. 4-6.

5. *The Bay Psalm Book*, unnumbered page in preface; Haraszti, *The Enigma of the Bay Psalm Book*, pp. 8-9.

6. Winthrop, *Journal*, 1:viii. At services held to commemorate the ter-centenary of the *Bay Psalm Book*, Henry W. Foote noted that the psalms were sung in their 1640 form, and, although the seventeenth-century critics of the book complained that the versions of the psalms were exceedingly difficult to sing, the modern vocalists experienced no noticeable difficulty with either the words or the metrical constructions. Instead, they found the verses beautiful as well as singable (*An Account of the Bay Psalm Book*, vol. 7 in the *Papers of the Hymn Society of America*, ed. Carl F. Price [New York, 1940], p. 6).

7. Harold S. Jantz, "The First Century of New England Verse," *Proceedings of the American Antiquarian Society* 53 (October 1943):237.

8. *Records of Massachusetts Bay*, 2:62, 71.

9. The printing of election sermons did not become customary until approximately twenty years later; George P. Winship, *The Cambridge Press, 1638-1692* (Philadelphia, 1945), p. 48.

10. Rutman, *American Puritanism*, pp. 36-39.

11. William Perkins, *Works* (Cambridge, Eng., 1609), 2:736-37; Richard Mather, "The Summe of Seventie Lectures on the First Chapter of the Second Epistle of Peter," Richard Mather MSS, American Antiquarian Society, Worcester, Mass., passim; Thomas Lechford, *Plain Dealing or News from New-England* (London, 1642), pp. 16-17, 19; John Cotton, *The Way of the Churches of Christ in New England*, p. 67; *Records of Massachusetts Bay*, pp. 109-10; Winthrop, *Journal*, 1:324-26.

12. Winthrop, *Journal*, 1:325-27.

13. *Records of Massachusetts Bay*, 1:141-42.

14. W. Fraser Mitchell, *English Pulpit Oratory from Andrewes to Tillotson: A Study of Its Literary Aspects* (London, 1932), pp. 3, 5-7; Morison, *Intellectual Life*, p. 163; Winthrop S. Hudson, "Mystical Religion in the Puritan Commonwealth," *Journal of Religion* 28 (January 1948):51-54; James F. Maclear, "The Heart of New England Rent: The Mystical Element in Early Puritan History," *Mississippi Valley Historical Review* 42 (March 1956):651.

15. William Haller, *The Rise of Puritanism*, Torchbook ed. (New York, 1957), pp. 19, 50-51, 70; Patrick Collinson, *Elizabethan Puritanism* (London, 1967), pp. 39-40, 49, 184, 258; Max Weber, *The Sociology of Religion*, 4th ed. (Boston, 1963), p. 203.

16. David Korbin, "The Expansion of the Visible Church in New England: 1629-1650," *Church History* 36 (1967): 192-93; Rutman, *American Puritanism*, p. 15.

17. Ziff, *The Career of John Cotton*, pp. 29-31, 41-42.
18. Richard Mather, "The Summe of Seventie Lectures," pp. 13-14.
19. Ibid., p. 62.
20. Ibid., p. 26.
21. Ibid., p. 17.
22. Ibid., p. 377.
23. Ibid., pp. 44-45, 58, 42-43, 56-57.
24. Ibid., pp. 137-40, 146.
25. Ibid., p. 288.
26. Ibid., p. 56.
27. Ibid., p. 135.
28. Ibid., p. 56.

CHAPTER   V

1. George L. Haskins, *Law and Authority in Early Massachusetts* (New York, 1960), pp. 13-19, 63-65, 95. Several earlier commentators on seventeenth-century New England, Robert Baillie, Robert Child, and later William Hubbard, the historian, rejected Erastian notions entirely and, instead, tended to see the civil government dominated by the ministry; John Cotton, *The Way of the Congregational Churches Cleared*, pt. 1, p. 67; Winthrop, *Journal*, 2:306; William Hubbard, *A General History of New England* (Cambridge, Mass., 1815), p. 182. In more recent times, this same view was shared by James Truslow Adams, *The Founding of New England*, 2d ed. (Boston, 1949), and Vernon L. Parrington, *The Colonial Mind, 1620-1800* (New York, 1927). This view is hardly accurate. It was refuted by Aaron Seidman who denied earlier assertions of a union between secular and ecclesiastical powers, recognizing the theoretical and organizational separation between the two and discerning, in a limited way, a portion of the civil domination; "Church and State in the Early Years of the Massachusetts Bay Colony," *New England Quarterly* 18 (June 1945):211-33. On this subject see also Ziff, *The Career of John Cotton*, pp. 103-4. Later writers have extended and amplified Seidman's investigations, discerning that though the ministers sometimes influenced the civil government in those areas where their training best prepared them, at no time did they exercise domination over the magistrates; Edmund S. Morgan, *Roger Williams: The Church and the State* (New York, 1967), p. 79. For additional discussion of this point, see David D. Hall, *The Faithful Shepherd: A History of the New England Ministry in the Seventeenth Century* (Chapel Hill, N.C., 1972), pp. 121-55. Morgan asserts that Massachusetts Bay in the seventeenth century enjoyed a separation between civil and ecclesiastical powers that had been favored by Puritans in England but never put into practice (*Puritan Political Ideas, 1558-1794* [Indianapolis, Ind., 1965], p. xxxii), and he adds elsewhere that the colony instead of bonding church and state together "made a long step toward that separation which was to become the American way" (*Roger Williams*, p. 63). But he is forced to allow "The Puritan principle of separation of church and state did not absolve the state from its covenant-imposed responsibility for the church" (*Roger Williams*, p. 84) and its obligation to protect the true religion (*Puritan Political Ideas*, p. xxxii). Thus, though he does not admit the existence of an Erastian system in

New England, Morgan is forced to concede the presence of something he labels a "religious stewardship" in the colony (*Puritan Political Ideas*, p. xxvi).

2. James H. Cassedy, *Demography in Early America* (Cambridge, Mass., 1969), pp. 29-30; Haskins, *Law and Authority in Early Massachusetts*, p. 63; Morgan, *Roger Williams*, p. 67. The value of the meetings was further restricted by the suspicion of many colonists that the meetings would evolve into a coercive body; Robert Scholz, "The Reverend Elders: Faith, Fellowship, and Politics in the Ministerial Community of Massachusetts Bay, 1630-1710" (Ph.D. diss., University of Minnesota, 1966), pp. 3-4; *Records of Massachusetts Bay*, 1:142-43.

3. For a fuller discussion of these events, see Ziff, *The Career of John Cotton*, passim; Winthrop, *Journal*, 1:62.

4. *Records of Massachusetts Bay*, 1:160-61.

5. Ibid., p. 168.

6. Winthrop, *Journal*, 1:203.

7. Winthrop, *Journal*, 2:22-23; Cotton Mather, *Magnalia*, 3:78.

8. Winthrop, *Journal*, 2:22-23.

9. He died August 9, 1641 (Cotton Mather, *Magnalia*, 3:81).

10. Ibid., pp. 53-54; Winthrop, *Journal*, 1:326-27, 2:22-23; Massachusetts Archives (Ecclesiastical), State House, Boston, 10:26-30. Many other examples can be found of civil control of ecclesiastical matters: the magistrates' attempt to enforce sumptuary laws after the failure of the churches to do so (Winthrop, *Journal*, 1:331; *Records of Massachusetts Bay*, 1:274-75); the jailing and fining of a Boston constable after he questioned the magistrates' right to imprison a church member (Winthrop, *Journal*, 2:19-20, 46-48); the regular support of many ministers through taxes levied by the General Court; and the permission given in the *Body of Liberties* for the civil authorities to enforce the "Institutions of the Lord" (Morgan, *Roger Williams*, pp. 75-76, and *Puritan Political Ideas*, p. xxv).

11. Lechford, *Plain Dealing*, p. 14. Some idea of the extent to which the Bay Colony's clerical leaders had become dependent on civil authorities as a result of their inability to control ecclesiastical events can be garnered from a sermon preached in about 1641 by Thomas Shepard, the minister at Cambridge. Speaking partially to counter the doctrines of Rome and Arminius as well as the Antinomianism that only a few years earlier had caused such great difficulties for the colony, he said, "To exempt clergymen in matters of religion from the power of the civil sword is flat Popery; by means of which Antichrist hath risen, and hath continued in his pomp and power so long together. The indulgence of princes towards the Papal function in matters of religion hath undone Christendom. It is true, every error . . . when it is like a gangrene, of a spreading nature, then the magistrate in due time must cut it off speedily. . . . A Papist, an Arminian, may come in and leaven and damn many a soul" (Shepard, "Subjection to Christ in All His Ordinances and Appointments" in *Works of Thomas Shepard* [Boston, 1835], 3:342). Shepard buttressed his assertions, saying, "There is some supreme or higher power in the chief magistrates, princes, or chief court of justice. . . . subjection is required; to refuse to give it is to cast off the Lord's government. . . . It is true, [the magistrates] may abuse their power . . . but yet their power is one thing, and their abuse of it another" (ibid., p. 340).

12. Johnson, *Wonder-Working Providence*, pp. 98-99; Walker, *Creeds and Platforms*, p. 137; Joshua Coffin, *A Sketch of the History of Newbury*,

Newburyport and West Newbury from 1635-1845 (Boston, 1845), pp. 44-54; Cotton Mather, *Magnalia*, 3:143-48; Winthrop, *Journal*, 2:138-39. The term presbyterial is not used in the hard denominational sense, but covers a spectrum of believers whose conception of the correct form of church government ranged from merely wanting to expand the number eligible for baptism and to accord an increased measure of power to church presbyteries and synods to others who favored a fully integrated and systematized church order comparable to that in Scotland or that prescribed for England by the Westminster divines.

13. Walker, *Creeds and Platforms*, p. 138; quoted from Hanbury, *Memorials*, 2:343, where the source is given as *A Reply from Two of the Brethren to A.S. and Some Modest and Innocent Touches on the Letter from Zeland* (London, 1644), p. 7.

14. There was a single concession to the presbyterians on matters of intrachurch government. The synod, at one point, expressed the opinion, "It was generally desired That the *exercitium* of the churches' power might only be in the Eldership in each Particular Church" (Walker, *Creeds and Platforms*, p. 138).

15. Morgan, *Visible Saints*, pp. 129-38.

16. *Records of the Dorchester Church*, p. iv; "Letter of Samuel Fuller to Gov. William Bradford, June 28, 1630," 3:74-85; Winthrop, *Journal*, 1:132-34, 302, 303, 323-24, 2:3, 86-88, 97-98; *Winthrop Papers*, 4:81, 151; *Records of Massachusetts Bay*, 2:20, 90-96.

17. Winthrop, *Journal*, 1:133, 303, 2:86-88, 229-44. It is virtually impossible to find any statement in the extant record indicating the deputies had become antiministerial. The only indication of their motives is their voting pattern during these critical months, and here geography seems to be the most important single factor in determining the way each deputy cast his ballot. More than 70 percent of what has been described as an antiministerial vote came from Essex County, and there seem to be good reasons for this pattern which are unrelated to the deputies' assessments of the clergy; Robert E. Wall, Jr., *Massachusetts Bay: The Crucial Decade, 1640-1650* (New Haven, Conn., 1972), pp. 35-39, 70, 105, 144, 192-94. It is also unlikely the votes of the deputies were expressions of popular suspicion of the ministry. The refusal of only three churches, Hingham, Boston, and Salem, to attend the synod hardly indicates the ministers were suspected of planning the synod to begin enlarging the scope of baptism; David D. Hall, *The Faithful Shepherd*, p. 129. A more convincing explanation of the deputies' voting record is made by Wall, who interprets the disagreements between the assistants and the deputies not as a conflict between differing perceptions of what the colony should be but as a power struggle, with the deputies seeking to "reduce the prestige of the magistrates and thus enhance their own. They wanted power" (*Massachusetts Bay*, pp. 157, 222). The role of the elders in the dispute was so limited that while they did participate—largely in the capacity of advisers—the problems that divided deputies and assistants can be easily understood with only occasional references to their participation (ibid., chapt. 2).

18. The question of whether the attempts to gain redress locally were only ceremonial or tactical maneuvers and the real purpose of the petitioners was to take their case to England does not vitiate the fact that the petitioners knew the civil government was the source of power in the colony.

19. David D. Hall, *Faithful Shepherd*, pp. 150-51.

20. If any colonists actually feared congregationalism would be seriously compromised by those who moved to exploit the split between deputies and assistants, their worries may have been exaggerated in 1646 even though their perception of a potentially effective line of attack for dissidents was exceedingly keen. Two decades later, both Quakers and Baptists were to succeed in doing just that. The General Court's split on the issue of the death penalty for Quakers in 1661 and 1662 prevented additional executions and in the period from 1665 to 1668, disagreement between deputies and assistants was responsible for the Baptists gaining toleration; *Records of Massachusetts Bay*, 2:177-80.

21. Larzer Ziff, ed., *John Cotton on the Churches of New England* (Cambridge, Mass., 1968), p. 26.

22. John Cotton, *The Way of the Churches of Christ in New England*, p. 40. Although the book was not published until 1645, it was written several years earlier.

23. Ibid., p. 6.

24. Ibid., p. 19.

25. John Cotton, *Keys to the Kingdom of Heaven*, reprinted in Ziff, *John Cotton on the Churches of New England*, p. 154.

26. Ibid., pp. 156-57.

27. Richard Mather, *An Answer to Two and Thirty Questions*, pp. 82-83.

28. Winthrop, *Journal*, 2:274, 278-79.

29. Richard Mather, *An Answer to Two and Thirty Questions*, pp. 64-65.

30. Winthrop, *Journal*, 2:274; *Records of Massachusetts Bay*, 2:155-56.

31. The report of the first session of the synod is entitled *The Result of a Synod at Cambridge in New England, Anno. 1646* (n.p., 1654), p. 71. Extracts appear in Walker, *Creeds and Platforms*, pp. 189-93.

32. *The Result of a Synod*, p. 72.

33. Ibid., p. 19.

34. Ibid.; Cotton Mather, *Magnalia*, 5:21-22.

35. Winthrop, *Journal*, 2:326-27.

36. *Records of Massachusetts Bay*, 2:200.

37. The other five men were Nathaniel Rogers, John Norton, Edward Norris, Thomas Shepard, and Thomas Cobbet (ibid.).

38. Richard Mather, *An Answer to Two and Thirty Questions*, pp. 63-64; Walker, "The Services of the Mathers in New England Religious Development," p. 67 n; Holmes, "Notes on Richard Mather's *Church Government*," p. 296. For a discussion of Cotton's role, see Ziff, *The Career of John Cotton*, p. 225, and Everett H. Emerson, *John Cotton* (New York, 1965), pp. 78-79.

39. Richard Mather, "A Modell of Church Government," Richard Mather MSS, American Antiquarian Society, Worcester, Mass., secs. 9 and 10; *A Platform of Church Discipline* (Cambridge, Mass. Bay, 1649), Art. IX.

40. Richard Mather, "Modell of Church Government," pp. 63-64.

41. Ibid., p. 88.

42. Ibid., p. 89. Writing earlier, Cotton had attempted to delimit the extent of civil authority in church matters, but he was unwilling to make a sharp break with the past. He carefully prefaced his statements with remarks designed to soothe the sensibilities of any magistrates he might otherwise offend. He said, "Nevertheless, . . . we willing acknowledge a power in the civil magistrate to establish and reform religion, according to the word of God" (*Keys to the Kingdom of Heaven*, p. 154).

43. "Modell of Church Government," p. 89.

44. Ibid., pp. 89-90.

45. Ibid., preface.

46. *Platform of Church Discipline*, Art. XVII, sec. 1; "Modell of Church Government," p. 88.

47. "Modell of Church Government," p. 89.

48. Ibid., p. 90.

49. *Platform of Church Discipline*, Art. XVII, sec. 2.

50. *Records of Massachusetts Bay*, 3:177-78.

51. A set of fifteen objections to the platform entitled "Exceptions to Some Things in the Synod at Cambridge 1649" in an unidentified hand is among the Cotton Papers (Vol. 3, item 10, Prince Collection, Boston Public Library, Boston, Mass.); Richard Mather, "An Answer of the Elders to Certayne Doubts and Objections against Sundry Passages in the Platforme of Discipline," Richard Mather MSS, American Antiquarian Society, Worcester, Mass., passim; *Records of Massachusetts Bay*, 3:235-36, 240; Cotton Mather, *Magnalia*, 5:39; see also Richard Mather's letter to Cotton on this subject (Richard Mather MSS, American Antiquarian Society, Worcester, Mass.).

52. *Records of Massachusetts Bay*, 4, pt. 1, pp. 57-58, 3:240.

53. Ibid., 3:240.

54. For more discussion on this topic see Robert F. Scholz, "Clerical Consociation in Massachusetts Bay: Reassessing the New England Way and Its Origins," *William and Mary Quarterly* 29 (July 1972):391-414.

55. *Platform of Church Discipline*, Art. XVII. This power had eroded to some extent by 1644 when Cotton was able to write, "The kingdome of Christ is not of this world," and churches—particularly if the ruling magistrates were not Christians—could be gathered without civil consent. Even then, he was not willing to go all the way and reject the General Court entirely. He was still careful to qualify his remarks by pointing out that magistrates, "being also Brethren and members of Churches, are called of God to be Nursing Fathers unto the Church. . . . it cannot but encourage them . . . when . . . they are made acquainted with the persons and proceedings of such as gather into Church-fellowship, under the wing of their Government" (*The Way of the Churches of Christ in New England* [London, 1645], pp. 5-6).

56. *Platform of Church Discipline*, Art. XV, sec. 3.

57. Cotton, *Keys to the Kingdom of Heaven*, p. 154.

58. *Platform of Church Discipline*, Art. XIV, sec. 4.

59. Ibid., Art. XVI, sec. 3.

60. For further discussion of this point, see T. H. Breen, *The Character of the Good Ruler: Puritan Political Ideas, 1630-1730* (New Haven, Conn., 1970), pp. 81-82; Haskins, *Law and Authority in Early Massachusetts*, pp. 131-32, 136; William H. Whitmore, ed., *The Colonial Laws of Massachusetts Reprinted from the Edition of 1660* (Boston, 1889), pp. 6-8.

61. Examples of secular interference in ecclesiastical matters after 1650 can be found on a variety of questions: a minister accused of teaching false doctrine: Massachusetts Archives (Ecclesiastical), 10:74-81b, in *Records of Massachusetts Bay*, 4, pt. 1, pp. 42, 43, 70, 71, 113, 236; intrachurch difficulties: Massachusetts Archives (Ecclesiastical), 10:33-34, 35, in *Records of Massachusetts Bay*, 4, pt. 1, pp. 228, 309-10; payment of ministers: Massachusetts Archives (Ecclesiastical), 10:48, in *Records of Massachusetts Bay*, 4, pt. 1, pp. 227-28, 309-10; formation of new churches: Massachusetts

Archives (Ecclesiastical), 10:44, 55, in *Records of Massachusetts Bay*, 4, pt. 1, pp. 351, 378, 390, 393; the settling of elders in a church: Massachusetts Archives (Ecclesiastical), 10:31-32, 47, 55a, 82-83, 85-89, in *Records of Massachusetts Bay*, 4, pt. 1, pp. 113, 117; interchurch relations: Massachusetts Archives (Ecclesiastical), 10:36, 49-51. See also Thomas Hutchinson, *The History of the Colony of Massachusetts Bay*, 2d ed. (London, 1765), pp. 442-43 n; Joseph B. Felt, *The Ecclesiastical History of New England* (Boston, 1855), 2:53, 60.

The degree to which the magistrates had abandoned the clergy by 1667 was well illustrated by John Wilson who lamented that among the legion of sins that could be found in the Bay Colony, one of the most conspicuous was the indifference of magistrates to the problems of the churches. He said, "Another sin I take to be the making light of, not subjecting to the authority of synods without which, the churches cannot long subsist. And so for the magistrates being Gallio like, either not careing for these things, or else not using their power and authrity for the maintenance of the truth, gospel and ordinances of our Lord and Saviour Jesus Christ, and for bearing thorough witness against the contrary"; Isaac Backus, *A History of New-England with Particular Reference to the Denomination of Christians Called Baptists* (Boston, 1777), 1:387. Eight years later, Increase Mather expressed the same dissatisfaction with the civil authorities: "As to Publick concerns. . . . Reformation doth not goe forward. Magistrates [are] too slow in that matter"; *Proceedings of the Massachusetts Historical Society*, ser. 2, 13:357.

62. *Records of Massachusetts Bay*, 4, pt. 1, pp. 122, 151, 156-57, 194, 215, 313; see also David D. Hall, *The Faithful Shepherd*, p. 22.

63. Jonathan Mitchel, *Nehemiah on the Wall in Troublesome Times* (Cambridge, Mass. Bay, 1671), pp. 6-7, 16, 28, 31-32.

64. William Stoughton, *New Englands True Interest* (Cambridge, Mass. Bay, 1670), p. 13.

65. John Davenport, *A Sermon Preach'd at the Election of the Governor, at Boston in New England* (Cambridge, Mass. Bay, 1670), pp. 6, 12, 13.

66. *Records of Massachusetts Bay*, 4, pt. 2, p. 490.

67. Thomas Shepard, *Eye-Salve, or A Watchword from Our Lord Jesus Christ unto His Church* (Cambridge, Mass. Bay, 1673), p. 13.

68. Urian Oakes, *New England Pleaded With* (Cambridge, Mass. Bay, 1673), pp. 25-26, 54-55.

CHAPTER   VI

1. Increase Mather, *First Principles*, pp. 2-4.

2. Richard Mather, "Plea," sec. 3, p. 33.

3. Richard Mather, *An Answer to Two and Thirty Questions*, p. 22.

4. Morgan, *Visible Saints*, p. 129.

5. Winthrop, *Journal*, 2:67.

6. Entitled *A Treatise Concerning the Lawful Subject of Baptism* (n.p., 1643).

7. Richard Mather, "An Answer to Nine Reasons of John Spilsbury to Prove Infants Ought Not to Be Baptized," American Antiquarian Society, Worcester, Mass., pp. 1, 4-5, 11 ff., 66.

8. Increase Mather, *First Principles*, p. 5; John Cotton, in *The Way of the*

Churches of Christ in New England, recorded his opposition to broad baptism, but Increase Mather argued this was not really Cotton's opinion. Mather based his case on the allegation that the words in the book simply needed more explanation. He added, moreover, that the work had been printed from an imperfect copy and Cotton had been displeased with some portions of it (*First Principles*, pp. 6-7); Thomas Hooker, *A Survey of the Summe of Church Discipline*, p. 48.

9. Richard Mather, "Plea," sec. 3, pp. 232-33; sec. 4, pp. 47-48, 71, 90.

10. Ibid. Writing several years after his father's death, Increase Mather quoted material from the "Plea" to establish his father as a supporter of the Halfway Covenant as early as 1645. But he failed to cite other passages which showed Mather's indecision on the subject (*First Principles*, pp. 8-9).

11. *First Principles*, pp. 5, 8-9, 13, 22, 23-24, 38.

12. George M. Foster, "Introduction: What Is a Peasant," in *Peasant Society: A Reader*, ed. Jack M. Potter et al. (Boston, 1967), pp. 2, 6, 7, 10, 13; Robert Redfield, *Peasant Society and Culture* (Chicago, 1960), pp. 20, 40, 60-61; Gideon Sjoberg, "The Preindustrial City," in *Peasant Society*, pp. 15-24; Oscar Lewis, *Village Life in Northern India* (New York, 1958), p. 303.

13. Redfield, *Peasant Society and Culture*, pp. 41-42.

14. Ibid., pp. 43-44; McKim Marriott, "Little Communities in an Indigenous Civilization," in *Anthropology of Folk Religion*, ed. Charles Leslie (New York, 1960), pp. 177-78.

15. Eric Wolf, *Peasants* (Englewood Cliffs, N.J., 1966), pp. 100-101.

16. Ibid., pp. 101-6.

17. Michael Walzer, *Revolution of the Saints: A Study in Radical Politics* (New York, 1970), pp. 115-16.

18. Redfield, *Peasant Society and Culture*, p. 77; Wolf, *Peasants*, pp. 102-3; see also Max Weber, *The Sociology of Religion*, p. 9.

19. *Fourth Report of the Record Commissioners of the City of Boston 1880, Dorchester Town Records*, 2d ed. (Boston, 1883), p. 63, and passim; Richard Mather, "Will," pp. 248-55.

20. Richard Mather, *An Answer to Two Questions* (Boston, 1712), pp. vii-viii.

21. Richard Mather, "The Summe of Seventie Lectures," p. 24.

22. Richard Mather, *An Answer to Two Questions*, pp. 9-10.

23. Ibid., pp. 17-18.

24. See Robert F. Scholz, "Clerical Consociation in Massachusetts Bay," pp. 391-414.

25. Increase Mather, *First Principles*, p. 11; *Records of the Dorchester Church*, pp. 164-65.

26. *The Public Records of the Colony of Connecticut*, ed. J. Hammond Trumble (Hartford, Conn., 1850), 1:281.

27. *Records of Massachusetts Bay*, 3:419; 4, pt. 1, p. 280.

28. The four men were John Warham, Samuel Stone, Richard Blinman of New London, and John Russell of Wethersfield (*Records of Connecticut*, 1:281).

29. Richard Mather, *Answer to Twenty-one Questions*, p. 1. All quotations are from the London edition published in 1659. The 1657 manuscript is included in the Richard Mather MSS at the American Antiquarian Society, Worcester, Mass.

30. Ibid., pp. 2-3.

31. Ibid., pp. 20, 21.

32. Ibid., pp. 21-24.

33. *Records of the Dorchester Church*, p. 168.

34. Ibid., p. 22; "Letter of Dorchester Church to Roxbury Church, April 24, 1660," *Proceedings of the Massachusetts Historical Society*, 1st ser. 17 (1879-1880):143; Robert G. Pope, *The Half-Way Covenant: Church Membership in Puritan New England* (Princeton, N.J., 1969), p. 33; *Roxbury Land and Church Records: Sixth Report of the Record Commissioners* (Boston, 1881), p. 88.

35. *Records of the Dorchester Church*, pp. 34, 35, 55, 165, 168, and passim.

36. *Dorchester Town Records*, pp. 29-31.

37. Ibid., pp. 23, 29.

38. Ibid., pp. 29-31.

39. Of the men who received more land than Mather but less than Stoughton in the 1637 apportionment, John Glover, Thomas Makepeace, and a Mr. Whitman had departed from Dorchester long before the controversy over the Halfway Covenant. The fourth, Humphrey Atherton, died in 1661, leaving an extensive estate that was divided among his three sons-in-law, two of whom were not residents of Dorchester. The third son-in-law, Richard Mather's son Timothy, left no record of his attitude toward broadening eligibility for baptism.

40. Lemuel Shattuck, "The Minott Family," *New England Historical and Genealogical Register* 1 (April 1847): 171-72; *Records of the Dorchester Church*, passim; *Dorchester Town Records*, passim. Robert Spurs, the one man who favored modifications in the church's position on baptism but who lacked wealth and association with the local leadership, was indeed in unusual company on this issue, but his presence, perhaps, could be explained by other factors. Spurs cannot specifically be identified as an advocate of the Halfway Covenant. He merely requested a liberalization of the policy on baptism so that his adult daughters, one of whom was married, could receive the sacrament under his covenant. It was a request that skirted the central issue and had little bearing on the later resolution of the conflict. But Spurs might have been an ambitious fellow and saw baptism for all his children as a way for the family to gain social and economic preferment.

Spurs had not joined the church until 1665, at an age somewhat beyond the average for admission, and when he did, he lost no time in demanding the benefits of membership for his family. He was assertive and may have seen ecclesiastical liberalism as a way to associate with his social superiors. If this were the case, his wish was eventually fulfilled. In the years after his admission to the church, he developed the qualities requisite for upward mobility, acquired considerable property, and though once admonished for "giveing entertainement in his hous of loos and vaine persons" (*Records of the Dorchester Church*, p. 70), the church-seating arrangements for 1693 and 1698 indicate he had become a man of means. In both these years he was assigned a place either on or near the end of the deacon's bench (ibid., p. 243). Whatever may have moved Spurs to make his demands, however, his presence in 1665 among the wealthy proponents of the Halfway Covenant does not seriously affect the conclusion that those of wealth and power supported a change in church doctrine.

41. Richard Mather, *Answer to Twenty-one Questions*, pp. 3, 11.

42. *Records of the Dorchester Church*, pp. 22, 33-34.

43. Hannah Minot was the daughter of Israel Stoughton, one of Dorchester's leading citizens. James Minot was a son of George Minot, a founder of the church and a leading figure in the town (Shattuck, "The Minot Family," pp. 171-72); *Records of the Dorchester Church*, pp. 33-36.

44. Richard Mather, *Answer to Twenty-one Questions*, pp. 23-24.

45. *Records of the Dorchester Church*, pp. 33-36.

46. Ibid., pp. 39-40, and passim.

47. Increase Mather, "Letter to John Davenport," October 1662, reprinted in *Collections of the Massachusetts Historical Society*, ser. 4, 8:205; *Records of the Dorchester Church*, p. 39; Jonathan Mitchel, *An Answer to the Apologetical Preface Published in the Name and Behalf of the Brethren That Dissented in the Late Synod*, published as a preface to Richard Mather's tract supporting the synod under the single title *A Defense of the Answer and Arguments of the Synod Met at Boston in the Year 1662* (Cambridge, Mass. Bay, 1664); John Davenport, *Another Essay for the Investigation of the Truth* (Cambridge, Mass. Bay, 1663), preface.

48. *Records of Massachusetts Bay*, 4, pt. 2, p. 62.

49. *Records of the Dorchester Church*, p. 40.

50. Charles Chauncy, *Anti-Synodalia Scripta Americana* (London, 1662); John Allin, *Animadversions upon the Antisynodalia Americana* (Boston, 1644).

51. Robert G. Pope, *The Half-Way Covenant*, p. 73.

52. Increase Mather, *First Principles*, postscript, p. 7.

53. John Davenport, *Another Essay*, pp. 2, 64.

54. By 1670 the discord over the Halfway Covenant moved a committee of deputies from the General Court to conduct an investigation of the colony's ministers to discover why they could find no common ground for agreement. Such presumptuous acts could hardly have happened prior to 1662. In their report, the deputies attacked the clerics as "troublers in our Israell" and accused them, among other things, of infringing on church liberties. The following year, a group of ministers, in response to the accusation, presented a petition to the General Court asking for absolution from the charges. The court responded, saying, "The acts of this honoured Court, being the supreme authority, are not liable to question" (*Records of Massachusetts Bay*, 4, pt. 2, p. 493).

55. Cotton Mather, *Magnalia*, 3:47; Increase Mather, *The Life of Richard Mather*, pp. 25-26; *Records of the Dorchester Church*, p. 55.

56. Cotton Mather, *Magnalia*, 5:63.

57. Adams, *The Founding of New England*, p. 263; Perry Miller, *The New England Mind: From Colony to Province* (Cambridge, Mass., 1962), pp. 98, 102-5. See also Scholz, "Clerical Consociation in Massachusetts Bay," pp. 391-414.

58. Robert G. Pope, *The Half-Way Covenant*, pp. 20-23, 96, 113, 267-68.

EPILOGUE

1. *Collections of the Massachusetts Historical Society*, 4th ser. (Boston, 1858), 8:76-77.

2. The passage is not quite clear in the original. Winthrop wrote, "Three

of our elders, viz., Mr. Mather, Mr. Allen and Mr. Eliot, took with them an interpreter, and went to the place where Cutshamekin, the Indian sachem *blank*" (Winthrop, *Journal*, 2:276).

3. Cotton Mather, *Magnalia*, 3:197; Richard Mather, in John Eliot and Thomas Mayhew, Jr., *Tears of Repentance: Or a Further Narrative of the Progress of the Gospel amongst the Indians in New England* (London, 1653), preface.

4. *Tears of Repentance*, preface.

5. Ibid.

6. Murdock, *Increase Mather*, pp. 39, 44, 50-51; *Harvard College Records*, 3:3, 23-24, 25, 139.

7. *Harvard College Records*, 1:206-7, 3:283 n; Cotton Mather, *Magnalia*, 4:128.

8. Horace E. Mather, *The Lineage of Rev. Richard Mather*, p. 33; Increase Mather, *Life of Richard Mather*, p. 25; *Report of the Records Commission Containing Boston Births, Baptisms, Marriages, and Deaths, 1630-1696* (Boston, 1908), p. 56; Thomas Morton, *The New English Canaan* (Boston, 1883), p. 331; Chilton L. Powell, "Marriage in Early New England," *New England Quarterly* 1 (July 1928):323, 327; see also Cotton Mather, *Ratio Disciplinae Fratrum Nov-Anglorum* (Cambridge, Mass. Bay, 1726), pp. 115-16.

9. *Records of the Dorchester Church*, p. 21; *Harvard College Records*, 3:139; Cotton Mather, *Parentator*, pp. 15-16.

10. Richard Mather, *Farewell Exhortation to the Church and People of Dorchester* (Cambridge, Mass. Bay, 1657), p. 5.

11. Cotton Mather, *Magnalia*, 3:128.

12. Miller, *The New England Mind: From Colony to Province*, pp. 29-30.

13. Cotton Mather, *Parentator*, p. 23.

14. Murdock, *Increase Mather*, p. 61; *Records of the Dorchester Church*, p. 22.

15. Cotton Mather, *Parentator*, p. 54; Murdock, *Increase Mather*, p. 72.

16. William Stoughton was born in Dorchester in 1632. The son of Israel Stoughton, he graduated from Harvard in 1650 and traveled to England. He returned after finding the Restoration uncordial. Being a bachelor of some wealth, he contributed his services to religious and literary institutions. Though never ordained, he preached the election sermon in 1668. He entered politics and held many high positions. Deeply involved in the Salem witchcraft outbreak in 1692, he was one of the few who never repented or regretted his participation in the affair. He died in Dorchester in 1701. *Records of the Dorchester Church*, p. 40.

17. Morison, *Intellectual Life*, pp. 167-68; John Minot, "Notes on Sermons by Richard Mather, William Stoughton and Others, Preached during the Years of 1663-1664," MS in Alderman Library, University of Virginia, Charlottesville; *Records of the Dorchester Church*, p. 43.

18. *Records of the Dorchester Church*, pp. 5, 7; Winthrop, *Journal*, 2:26.

19. Committee of the Dorchester Antiquarian Society, *History of the Town of Dorchester Massachusetts* (Boston, 1859), pp. 107, 192, 202-12; *Dorchester Town Records*, pp. 126-27; Marion C. Donnelly, "New England Meeting Houses in the Seventeenth Century," *Old Time New England* (June 1957): 286.

20. *Dorchester Town Records*, p. 127.

21. *Records of the Dorchester Church*, p. 46.

22. Ibid., pp. 9, 46-47, 251-52, and passim.

23. Ibid., pp. 51-52.

24. *Dorchester Town Records*, p. 126; *Records of the Dorchester Church*, pp. 47-48, 49.

25. Cotton Mather, *Magnalia*, 3:38.

26. Calder, *Letters of John Davenport*, pp. 10-11; *Records of the First Church in Boston*, 1:xxxii-xxxiii. For a more complete discussion of the religious and political controversy, see Richard Simmons, "The Founding of the Third Church in Boston," *William and Mary Quarterly* 26 (April 1969):241-52.

27. Calder, *Letters of John Davenport*, p. 11; *Records of the Dorchester Church*, pp. 54-55; *Records of the First Church in Boston*, 1:liii, 62.

28. Calder, *Letters of John Davenport*, p. 11; *Records of the Dorchester Church*, p. 55; Cotton Mather, *Magnalia*, 3:129; Increase Mather, *The Life of Richard Mather*, p. 26.

29. Increase Mather, *The Life of Richard Mather*, pp. 25-29; Cotton Mather, *Magnalia*, 3:128, 129. The reference is to Thomas Goodwin's *Patience and Its Perfect Work under Sudden and Sore Tryals* (London, 1666).

30. Cotton Mather, *Magnalia*, 3:129.

31. *Records of the Dorchester Church*, pp. 9-10.

Bibliographical Essay

Every investigator of the Stuart Era has discovered that among the extensive list of titles—both of works that deal directly with the period and those that serve to increase understanding of the whole of the human species—there are always certain contributions that exert a profound and continuous influence on his own conception of the past. The works that have been most valuable in shaping my perceptions and in providing direction and guidance for this study are discussed or mentioned in the following essay.

It is customary in any work on early New England to acknowledge a debt to Perry Miller, for without his *Orthodoxy in Massachusetts, 1630-1650* (Cambridge, Mass., 1933), *The New England Mind: The Seventeenth Century* (Cambridge, Mass., 1954), *The New England Mind: From Colony to Province* (Cambridge, Mass., 1952), it is difficult to imagine what direction colonial American studies might have taken. Another to whom I owe a debt is A. L. Kroeber, whose pioneering works, though now very much dated, postulated many of the insights that launched the careers of two generations of anthropologists and sociologists. The mistitled but otherwise excellent book *The Heathens: Primitive Man and His Religions* (New York, 1956) by anthropologist William Howells provided a conceptual framework that was extremely useful for examining the religion of Massachusetts Bay in the seventeenth century; and this was also true of the work of still another anthropologist, albeit a part-time practitioner of the discipline, Homer W. Smith, whose *Man and His Gods* (New York, 1952) offered an approach to the study of religion that was, perhaps, overly cynical, but was still liberating to some extent. Claude Lévi-Strauss, an investigator into the nature of mankind, provided a measure of raw material in his *Structural Anthropology* (New York, 1967), but as yet his ideas have not been accorded their due in any area of the social sciences. Although I was not persuaded by the comprehensive conclusions Erik Erikson has drawn—in some instances from obviously insufficient data—his insights into adolescence and the continuing effect of early life experiences on later development, in *Young Man Luther* (New York, 1962) and *Identity: Youth and Crisis* (New York, 1968), often seemed applicable to the career of Richard Mather. *The Gathering Storm in the Churches* (New York, 1969) by Jeffrey K. Hadden, while concerned with the growing rift between Protestant clergymen and their parishioners in the past several decades, provided information on the relationship between pastor and flock that was especially valuable in trying to interpret events in seventeenth-century Dorchester. Darrett B. Rutman's *American Puritanism* (Philadelphia, 1970) has been severely criticized by reviewers, and much of the criticism is just, but his daring attempt to lay the foundation for a new interpretative synthesis deserves to be praised for providing inspiration if not enlightenment.

The works on Elizabethan and Stuart England that were helpful are too numerous to mention, but two of the most valuable were Patrick Collinson's *Elizabethan Puritan Movement* (London, 1967) and *The Rise of Puritanism* (New York, 1957) by William Haller. These works have become standard references over the years and they remain so despite the publication of Michael Walzer's *Revolution of the Saints* (Cambridge, Mass., 1965), an invaluable study that conveys an understanding of the revolutionary intensity of the Puritan movement. Peter Laslett did much to describe the nature of the preindustrial and preurban world of the seventeenth century; his *World We Have Lost* (New York, 1965) is a major step toward making the period more comprehensible.

The importance of *The Records of the Governor and Company of the Massachusetts Bay*, ed. Nathaniel B. Shurtleff (Boston, 1853), need hardly be mentioned, but the single most valuable source was John Winthrop's *History of New England*, ed. J. K. Hosmer (New York, 1908). Two documents that were of particular importance to a study of Richard Mather were the records of his church and town. Some vital information on the early years of the church's history was missing and the order of the entries often did not adhere to the chronological sequence, but these were minor matters. The *Records of the First Church at Dorchester in New England, 1636-1734*, ed. J. S. Barrows and William B. Trask (Boston, 1891), were largely intact. The same was generally true of the town records. The *Fourth Report of the Record Commissioners of the City of Boston, 1880:*

Dorchester Town Records (Boston, 1883) had shed some of its initial leaves, but the document was otherwise complete.

Information about seventeenth-century New England and New England religion came from a multitude of sources. Among the more valuable were Williston Walker's *Creeds and Platforms of Congregationalism* (Boston, 1960) [Originally published, 1893], which provided convenient, well-edited texts of a number of essential documents along with considerable background information, and Henry Martyn Dexter's *Congregationalism of the Last Three Hundred Years, as Seen in Its Literature* (New York, 1880), which contained a wealth of information on essential as well as peripheral practices of the congregational churches and an old but excellent bibliography. Cotton Mather's *Magnalia Christi Americana* (London, 1702) was helpful throughout, but the most indispensable account was the life of Richard Mather written by his son Increase. Although there have been at least six short sketches of the elder Mather's career in the three centuries since his death, all have drawn their information from *The Life and Death of That Reverend Man of God, Mr. Richard Mather* (Cambridge, Mass. Bay, 1670), and none of these later products added significantly in either fact or insight to the corpus of information on the Dorchester teacher's life. The spiritual biography by Increase was especially valuable not only because it contained vital information and pertinent observations on his father's character but, more important, it provided sufficient material for additional judgments to be made.

CHAPTER I

In addition to several descriptive accounts of England under James I and Charles I and histories of Puritanism already mentioned, Lawrence Stone's "Social Mobility in England, 1500-1700," *Past and Present* 33 (April 1966):17-35, and "The Educational Revolution in England, 1560-1640," *Past and Present* 28 (July 1964):41-80, provided interpretative background for reconstructing the milieu which nurtured Richard Mather. Portions of Erikson's *Young Man Luther* and *Identity* and Lévi-Strauss's *Structural Anthropology* gave it greater meaning. Valuable material on Mather's tiny corner of Lancashire was contained in J. A. Picton, *Memorials of Liverpool, Historical and Topographical* (London, 1873); Picton, *Selections from the Municipal Archives and Records of Liverpool from the Thirteenth to the Seventeenth Century Inclusive* (Liverpool, 1883); Lawrence Hall, "The Ancient Chapel at Toxteth Park and Toxteth School," *Historic Society of Lancashire and Cheshire* 87 (1936): 23-57, and "Toxteth Park Chapel in the Seventeenth Century," *Transactions of the Unitarian Historical Society* 5 (November 1934): 351-81; George T. O. Bridgeman, "The History of the Church and Manor at Wigan," *Remains Historical and Literary Connected with the Palatine Counties of Lancashire and Chester* (Manchester, 1889), vol. 16; and Valentine D. Davis, *Some Account of the Ancient Chapel at Toxteth Park . . . 1618-1883* (Liverpool, 1884).

Appropriate volumes published by the Lancashire Parish Register Society contained information on Richard Mather and his family. A number of articles in various volumes of the *New England Historical and Genealogical Register* also provided detail about the Mather family. But the only comprehensive genealogical work was *The Lineage of Rev. Richard Mather* (Hartford, Conn., 1890) by Horace E. Mather. Most of the factual material in the chapter came from Increase Mather's *Life of Richard Mather*, although extant portions of Richard's *Journal* (*Collections of the Dorchester Antiquarian and Historical Society* [Boston, 1850], vol. 3), contained information on the voyage from England to America.

CHAPTER   II

No history of Dorchester covers adequately the period from 1630 to 1636. *Annals of the Town of Dorchester* in the *Collections of the Dorchester Antiquarian and Historical Society* (Boston, 1846), vol. 2, by James Blake, and William Orcutt's *Good Old Dorchester* (Cambridge, Mass., 1893) make no attempt to reconstruct the first five years of settlement. Events must be pieced together from the introduction to the *Records of the Dorchester Church; Records of Massachusetts Bay;* Winthrop's *Journal; Dorchester Town Records; The Memorial History of Boston . . . 1630-1880,* ed. Justin Winsor (Boston, 1882); "Letter of Samuel Fuller to Governor William Bradford, June 28, 1630," *Collections of the Massachusetts Historical Society* (Boston, 1794); and "Letter of Israel Stoughton to Dr. John Stoughton," *Proceedings of the Massachusetts Historical Society* (Boston, 1924-1925), vol. 58. Edmund S. Morgan's *Visible Saints: The History of a Puritan Idea* (Ithaca, N.Y., 1965) was especially helpful in developing a sequence of events and ideas in the village during the early period.

Mather's failure to gain admission to the Boston church and the possibility that it was his views on ordination that prevented his acceptance was suggested by "Some Objections against Imposition in Ordination" (Richard Mather MSS, American Antiquarian Society, Worcester, Mass.). This was made to seem even more likely by the available knowledge of his circumstances in Massachusetts Bay immediately after his arrival and by problems later encountered in achieving an understanding of the function of the laying on of hands. The documents that reveal his perceptions on the difficulties of gathering a church and also indicate his willingness to cooperate with colonial authorities are the letters exchanged by Mather and Thomas Shepard in the days immediately following the unsuccessful attempt to receive approval for forming a church in Dorchester. These are included in the Cotton Mather MSS at the Massachusetts Historical Society, Boston.

CHAPTER III

The most valuable sources for Mather's response to English critics of Massachusetts Bay doctrine and polity were his own polemical works written between 1638 and 1646. An examination of the content and the context in which they were written did much to explain his personal involvement in the discussions. *An Apologie for Church Covenant* and *Church Government and Church Covenant Discussed in Answer to Two and Thirty Questions*, both written in 1638 or 1639 but not published until 1643 (London), were produced at the request of the local authorities to mitigate a specific problem but were later employed to help solve another. The later polemics, *A Modest and Brotherly Answer to Mr. Charles Herle* (London, 1644), *A Reply to Mr. Rutherford* (London, 1646), and "Plea for the Churches of Christ in New England" (Massachusetts Historical Society, Boston), all must be considered within the framework created by Mather's ambition before they can be evaluated as part of a polemical outpouring or a system of doctrine. The writings of the participants on the English side of the Atlantic were extremely helpful in gaining an insight into reformed religion in the mother country. Works such as Charles Herle's *The Independency on Scriptures of the Independency of Churches* (London, 1643),

Samuel Rutherford's *Due Right of Presbyteries* (London, 1644), William Rathband's *A Brief Narration of Church Courses in New England* (London, 1644), Robert Baillie's *A Dissuasive from the Errours of Our Time* (London, 1645), and Daniel Cawdrey's *Vindiciae Clavium* (London, 1645) were all useful, but even more valuable to any analysis of Mather's work were the major statements of faith composed by John Cotton, *Keys to the Kingdom of Heaven* (London, 1644), *The Way of the Churches of Christ in New England* (London, 1645), *The Way of the Congregational Churches Cleared* (London, 1648), and Thomas Hooker's *A Survey of the Summe of Church Discipline* (London, 1648).

CHAPTER IV

Articles by Winthrop S. Hudson, "Mystical Religion in the Puritan Commonwealth," *Journal of Religion* 28 (January 1948): 51-56, and James F. Maclear, "The Heart of New England Rent: The Mystical Element in Early Puritan History," *Mississippi Valley Historical Review* 42 (March 1956): 621-52, added a new element to my understanding of the devotion to the preached word in Dorchester, while William Perkins's *Works* (Cambridge, Eng., 1609), vol. 2, provided information on the pattern and method for writing and presenting a seventeenth-century sermon in the nonconformist "plaine" style.

Those few of Mather's sermons that have survived are almost all included in Mather, "The Summe of Seventie Lectures on the First Epistle of Peter" (Richard Mather MSS, American Antiquarian Society, Worcester, Mass.). They provided the basis for the discussion of Mather's pulpit performance. The most trenchant analysis of the message Massachusetts Bay clerics attempted to impart is still that offered by Perry Miller; however, at least a portion of the doctrine and polity he identified as characteristic of early New England was not preached effectively in Dorchester. "The Summe of Seventie Lectures" forms the basis for the examination of Mather's preaching made by Robert Middlekauff in *The Mathers: Three Generations of Puritan Intellectuals, 1596-1728* (New York, 1971). Middlekauff asked questions very different from my own, and the result is two presentations that diverge in thrust and direction. We examined the same material from differing points of view, and our observations are understandably different. Some methodological direction was provided by Milman Parry's "A Comparative Study of Diction as One of the Elements of Style in Early Greek Poetry" (M.A. thesis, University of California, 1922). Emory Elliott's *Power and the Pulpit in Puritan New England* (Princeton, N.J., 1975) came too late to be of use.

CHAPTER   V

The events leading up to the synod of 1646 are described in detail by Williston Walker in *Creeds and Platforms of Congregationalism*. His work also includes a complete text of the platform adopted by the synod in 1648 and approved by the General Court three years later. The *Records of Massachusetts Bay* were indispensable to the study of the synod; the Massachusetts Archives (Ecclesiastical), vol. 10, was also useful. Two recent works, David. D. Hall, *The Faithful Shepherd: A History of the New England Ministry in the Seventeenth Century* (Chapel Hill, N.C., 1972), and Robert E. Wall, Jr., *Massachusetts Bay: The Crucial Decade, 1640-1650* (New Haven, Conn., 1972), contributed to a clearer view of events in the Bay Colony during the second decade of settlement, although Hall does not fully explore the significance of the antisecular character of the synod of 1646 and the completed platform of church discipline. Wall's book was particularly valuable for its investigation of the split between deputies and assistants in the General Court.

John Cotton's ideology was central to the evolution of Bay Colony religion during the years between 1640 and 1650, and Larzer Ziff's *The Career of John Cotton* (Princeton, N.J., 1962) provides adequate background information on the Bostonian's participation. Two of Cotton's own works, *The Way of the Churches of Christ in New England* and the *Keys to the Kingdom of Heaven*, contain excellent descriptions of congregational doctrine and polity in the years immediately preceding the synod; they also contain descriptions of several conflicts already resolved but which had their effect on clerical thought in the colony.

The Result of a Synod at Cambridge in New England Anno. 1646 (n.p., 1654), abstracted in Walker (pp. 189-93), is an indispensable record of the first session of the synod. Richard Mather's "A Modell of Church Government" (Richard Mather MSS, American Antiquarian Society, Worcester, Mass.) helped to determine the nature and extent of Mather's participation not only in the events leading up to the synod but also in other ecclesiastical matters over the previous ten years. Comparison of the "Modell of Church Government" with the completed *Platform of Church Discipline* (Cambridge, Mass. Bay, 1649) revealed much about his attitudes and his temporary ideological divergence from some of his clerical colleagues.

CHAPTER   VI

The best attempt at tracing the evolution of doctrine relating to baptism and church membership was Edmund S. Morgan's *Visible Saints*, although of almost equal value in providing considerable detailed information about the subject, including an investigation of the events surrounding the final adoption of extended baptism in Dorchester, was Robert G. Pope's *The Half-Way Covenant: Church Membership in Puritan New England* (Princeton, N.J., 1969). Mather's own writings were central to providing an understanding of the maturation of his ideas. His *Answer to Two and Thirty Questions* was his earliest expression of an opinion on the subject; his firm stand of 1639 had begun to vacillate by the time he wrote the "Plea" in 1645 and 1646, and by 1648 he had become a convert to the view held by Cotton. From that point forward, he labored to recruit adherents, and the arguments he relied upon for abandoning the earlier and more constricting requirements for infant baptism were included in his work *A Disputation Concerning Church-Members and Their Children in Answer to Twenty-one Questions* (London, 1659). The *Records of the Dorchester Church* provided all available information on the confrontations among Mather's flock over the Halfway Covenant, but unfortunately the accounts in the church record are always brief, usually vague, and often give the impression, in a subjective manner, that the penman himself was very uncomfortable with the dispute.

Peter Laslett's *The World We Have Lost*, along with Gideon Sjoberg's "The Preindustrial City," *American Journal of Sociology* 60 (March 1955):438-45, were useful in delineating relationships that contained potential for ideological divergence between villager and townsman. Darrett Rutman's article "Governor Winthrop's Garden Crop: The Significance of Agriculture in the Early Commerce of Massachusetts Bay," *William and Mary Quarterly* 20 (July 1963):396-415, was also useful in this respect.

There remains much to be done with the problem of defining the term peasantry and refining the peasant archetype, but the foundation work of the project has already been carried out by Robert Redfield in *Peasant Society and Culture* (Chicago, 1960) and by Eric R. Wolf in his ably written *Peasants* (Englewood Cliffs, N.J., 1969). One of the most recent attempts to circumscribe the term peasant was made at Seminar 1 of the Symposium on East European Peasantries held at Boston University in April 1973. The report, entitled "What Is a Peasant?" by Irwin T. Sanders, Tom Cheetham, and Roger Whitaker, explored several methods of defining and characterizing peasants more accurately, but added little to the work done by Redfield and Wolf. There are myriads of monographs and articles that could be used to provide data for construction of a paradigmatic peasant village. I have examined only a small fraction of these, but of them, works by Oscar Lewis, *Village Life in Northern India* (New York, 1958), McKim Marriott's "Little Communities in an Indigenous Civilization," in *Village India: Studies in the Little Community*, ed. McKim Marriott (Chicago, 1955), and George M. Foster's *Tzintzuntzan: Mexican Peasants in a Changing World* (New York, 1967) made it abundantly clear that seventeenth-century Dorchester was not a unique settlement; this observation received further confirmation in *Development and Conflict in Thailand*, Data Paper No. 80, Southeast Asian Program, Department of Asian Studies, Cornell University (Ithaca, N.Y., 1970), by Joyce Nakahara and Ronald A. Witton.

On the interrelated subjects of schism and resistance to change, Robert Le Vine's "Anthropology and the Study of Conflict: An Introduction," *Journal of Conflict Resolution* 5 (March 1961):3-15, with its description of the differing schools of thought on social conflict—one group considering it a eufunctional phenomenon essential for the operation of society and another group arguing that it is a maladaptation to cultural change—helped to interpret the social context of the disagreement over baptism and membership in Mather's church. When combined with the views expressed by Muzafer and Carolyn Sherif in *Groups in Harmony and Tension* (New York, 1953), Le Vine's interpretation of conflict and the Sherifs' discussions of leaders and leadership groups in conflict situations did much to clarify the politics of conflict in Dorchester. The conservative or traditional qualities of peasant society and the possible underlying causes that create division on seemingly unrelated issues were treated by both Ward H. Goodenough in *Cooperation and Change* (New York, 1963) and Gideon Sjoberg in "Contradictory Functional Requirements and Social Systems," *Journal of Conflict*

Resolution 4 (June 1960):198-208. In this same area, an analysis of the relationship of heresy, schism, and Christian disunity by Christopher Dawson in "What about Heretics: An Analysis of the Causes of Schism," *Commonweal* 36 (September 1942):513-17, was enlightening as was Gus Tuberville's "A Religious Schism in the Methodist Church: A Sociological Analysis of the Pine Grove Case," *Rural Sociology* 14 (March 1949):29-38.

Index